Implementing Public Policy

George C. Edwards III

Texas A & M University

Congressional Quarterly Press

a division of
CONGRESSIONAL QUARTERLY INC.
1414 22nd Street N.W., Washington, D.C. 20037

Cover Design: Richard Pottern

Printed in the United States of America

Library of Congress Cataloging in Publication Data

Edwards, George C.
  Implementing public policy.

    Bibliography: p.
    Includes index.
      1. Policy sciences.   2. Public administration — Decision making.   I. Title.

H61.E32   351.007´2   80-23705
ISBN 0-87187-155-6

Epigraph from "The Hollow Men" in *Collected Poems 1908-1962* by T.S. Eliot, © 1936 by Harcourt, Brace, Jovanovich, Inc.; © 1963, 1964 by T.S. Eliot. Reprinted by permission of the publisher.

To my parents
Mary and George Edwards

Foreword

What is a good public policy? How may it best be implemented? The search for answers to these questions, however approximate, is as old as the human race. On the other hand, attempts to provide more rigorous and systematic answers in the form of *policy analysis* are less than three decades old. These recent efforts build on a wide range of social science contributions, from Max Weber's study of bureaucratic power to the organizational theories of Chester Barnard and Herbert Simon, Charles Lindblom's analysis of incremental decisionmaking, and other modern investigations of policymaking and organizational behavior too numerous to mention.

The difficulties of implementation at the highest levels of government have been aptly set forth by Richard Neustadt in his classic analysis of presidential power. He tells of how in the early summer of 1952 outgoing President Harry S. Truman contemplated the problems of incoming General Dwight D. Eisenhower, should he be elected president:

> "He'll sit here," Truman would remark (tapping his desk for emphasis), "and he'll say, 'Do this! Do that!' *And nothing will happen.* Poor Ike — it won't be a bit like the Army. He'll find it very frustrating."[1]

Truman was right. Eisenhower did find it frustrating, but so has every president before and since. And, of course, the attempt to establish appropriate policy and ensure that it is carried out is common to executives, public and private, at all levels of a bureaucratic hierarchy.

That is why *Implementing Public Policy*, the sixth book in Congressional Quarterly Press' public policy series, is both appropriate and timely. In his simple but compelling book, Professor George C. Edwards III of Texas A & M University examines four sets of categories — communication, resources, dispositions, and bureaucratic structure — all of which may contribute to or inhibit the implementation of public policy. Discussion of these four factors and their interrelationships provides the organizational framework of this book.

Professor Edwards defines policy implementation in Chapter 1 as "the stage of policymaking between the establishment of a policy — such as the passage of a legislative act, the issuing of an executive order, the handing down of a judicial decision, or the promulgation of a regulatory rule — and the consequences of the policy for the people whom it affects."[2]

Communication — ensuring that those who are to carry out a policy know what they are supposed to do — is crucial to effective policy implementation. In Chapter 2 Professor Edwards examines a number of corollary principles of good communication, including appropriate transmission mechanisms and useful techniques for improving clarity and ensuring consistency. Here, as in other chapters, numerous case studies are provided, many of them excerpted from a rapidly expanding policy analysis literature.

Chapter 3 treats resources, another critical element in policy implementation. Among the central resources discussed by the author are staff and skills; information; authority, including sanctions; and physical facilities and equipment. The importance of equipment as an essential resource was dramatically demonstrated by the malfunction of the helicopters in the April 1980 attempt to rescue the American hostages held in Iran.

What are the attitudes of those who must carry out a policy? Are they sympathetic, neutral, or hostile? Drawing upon examples from the executive branch and the federal court system, Professor Edwards points out the importance of "dispositions" in Chapter 4. Changing personnel in government is one way to eliminate unfavorable dispositions; another way is to alter the incentives to implementors.

Chapter 5 explores the pervasive impact of bureaucratic structures on policy implementation. Edwards focuses on two dominant characteristics: the use of routinized behaviors, or standard operating procedures; and fragmentation, or the dispersal of responsibility for policies among many organizational units. In a speech in 1978, Jimmy Carter described this bureaucratic malaise as well as any contemporary president:

> There are too many agencies, doing too many things, overlapping too often, coordinating too rarely, wasting too much money — and doing too little to solve real problems.[3]

In his concluding chapter, Professor Edwards attempts to show how these and other basic factors interact with each other and thus promote or inhibit the carrying out of public policies. He also considers what types of policies are most likely to face problems and what prospects exist for improvement.

George Edwards' recent research has focused on the presidency and the policy process. He is the author of *Presidential Influence in Congress*, coauthor of *The Policy Predicament*, and coeditor of *Perspec-*

tives on Public Policy-Making. His numerous articles treat such diverse topics as budgeting, presidential performance, public opinion, and executive-legislative relations.

We are indebted to Professor Edwards for his contribution to our understanding of the problems that are endemic whenever and wherever human beings in organizations try to carry out tasks.

Robert L. Peabody

NOTES

1. Richard Neustadt, *Presidential Power* (New York: John Wiley & Sons, 1960), p. 9.
2. George C. Edwards III, *Implementing Public Policy* (Washington, D.C.: Congressional Quarterly Press, 1980), p. 1.
3. Ibid., p. 134.

Between the idea
And the reality
Between the motion
And the act
Falls the Shadow.

T.S. Eliot
"The Hollow Men"

Preface

All around us government is under attack. From Capitol Hill to City Hall, rhetoric is both heated and negative regarding public policies. Among the reasons for this outpouring of criticism is the view that government is not working. Public officials are seen as bungling, inefficient, unable to deliver on services, and sometimes even unwilling to carry out the intentions of top decisionmakers. As students of government, we want to know whether such criticism is appropriate and, if so, why government functions so poorly.

Only a few years ago very little scholarly attention was devoted to the subject of implementing public policies. While nearly everyone would have agreed that implementation was important, most scholars focused on other topics in their research. Since that time the literature on implementation has burgeoned. As I read through this rich and diverse research, however, I concluded that a book-length effort was needed to bring some order and a wider perspective to existing studies. There were very few general treatments of implementation. I felt it was particularly important to integrate existing knowledge into a framework that emphasized explanation and the broader significance of the descriptive case studies in the implementation literature. It is from these thoughts that this book has emerged.

In *Implementing Public Policy* I identify four critical factors affecting policy implementation and explain why they arise and what consequences they have. Numerous case studies are used to illustrate these relationships. Although this book might be subtitled *Why Things Go Wrong* or *The Politics of Slippage*, because I emphasize obstacles to effective policy implementation, I do not intend it to be discouragingly cynical. The book is *about* government and not *against* it.

As with every book, there are several people deserving of thanks. Jean L. Woy was a persistent yet understanding editor and Barbara R. de Boinville a talented and pleasant manuscript editor. Edna Lumpkin continued her wizardry at typing from my handwritten pages. Daniel Mazmanian, Carl E. Van Horn, and Robert Hearn read the entire manuscript and made numerous useful suggestions. To each of these persons I give my gratitude.

Finally, there are several close friends to whom I wish to express my sincerest appreciation: Bob Harmel, Carmella Magill, Dan Parker, Ed Portis, Susie Portis, Cathy Swanteson, Emily Twitty, and Arnold Vedlitz. Without their support this book would not have been written.

George C. Edwards III

Contents

1

Understanding Implementation

Public policies are rarely self-executing. The Supreme Court may hand down a decision to desegregate schools, Congress may pass legislation to restrict immigration, or the president may order troops to rescue U.S. hostages in Tehran — but little progress toward accomplishing these goals may occur. Without effective implementation the decisions of policymakers will not be carried out successfully.

Since the people who originally determine public policies are usually not the same people who implement them, there is considerable room for misunderstanding and distortion of decisionmakers' intentions. Perhaps the only public policy that executes itself is the president's decision to recognize a foreign government. On December 15, 1978, President Jimmy Carter announced in a joint communiqué with Peking that the People's Republic of China and the United States would formally recognize each other. On January 1, 1980, diplomatic relations between the two nations resumed. If a president recognizes a foreign country, diplomatic relations with it are thereby established. Most policies, however, require an intricate set of positive actions on the part of many people to be implemented.

The study of policy implementation is crucial for the study of public administration and public policy. Policy implementation, as we have seen, is the stage of policymaking between the establishment of a policy — such as the passage of a legislative act, the issuing of an executive order, the handing down of a judicial decision, or the promulgation of a regulatory rule — and the consequences of the policy for the people whom it affects. If a policy is inappropriate, if it cannot alleviate the problem for which it was designed, it will probably be a failure no matter how well it is implemented. But even a brilliant policy poorly implemented may fail to achieve the goals of its designers.

The following light-hearted observation by the famous British social critic Malcolm Muggeridge illustrates the importance of administration:

> I have always been deeply interested in the administrative side of love, which I find more absorbing than its purely erotic aspects. What Lady Chatterley and her gamekeeper did in the woods is, to me, of only passing interest, compared with how they got there, what arrangements were made for shelter in the case of inclement weather, and for refreshments, how they accounted for their absence, whether either party could recover incidental expenses, and if so, how. This attitude is, after all, not so unreasonable. Most great generals have admitted that planning campaigns and winning victories in the field is relatively easy compared with arranging transport and supplies. An army, Napoleon said, in one of his most celebrated remarks, marches on its stomach. So do lovers. If the administrative arrangements are faulty, the campaign which follows cannot but be laborious, and even victory brings little satisfaction.[1]

Implementing a public policy may include a wide variety of actions: issuing and enforcing directives, disbursing funds, making loans, awarding grants, signing contracts, collecting data, disseminating information, analyzing problems, assigning and hiring personnel, creating organizational units, proposing alternatives, planning for the future, and negotiating with private citizens, businesses, interest groups, legislative committees, bureaucratic units, and even other countries.

The general revenue sharing program, which began after passage of the State and Local Assistance Act of 1972, illustrates the degree of complexity involved in public policy implementation. One purpose of revenue sharing was to simplify policymaking by reducing red tape at the federal level and by giving state and local governments broad discretion in the use of federal funds.

Although revenue sharing might appear to be a straightforward process of sending checks to state and local governments, it is not. The amount of money each of the nearly 40,000 governmental units eligible for funds receives must be calculated. An enormous amount of data to serve as the basis of these calculations must be collected. The checks must be issued, printed, and delivered, each step requiring the services of a separate federal governmental unit. The federal government must make sure that the revenue sharing funds are not used for discriminatory purposes or to pay state and local employees or contractors lower than prevailing wage rates. It also must ensure that the funds are used in a manner consistent with the Hatch Act prohibiting certain political activities of federal employees and the National Environmental Policy Act. Finally, the uses to which the funds are put must be audited, evaluated, and reported.[2]

In 1975 the "simple" policy of revenue sharing involved the Office of Revenue Sharing, the Bureau of Accounts, the U.S. Postal Service, the Bureau of Economic Analysis, the Bureau of the Census, the U.S. Government Printing Office, the Bureau of Indian Affairs, the Internal Revenue Service, the Environmental Protection Agency, the Civil Service Commission, the Department of Labor, the Department of Justice, the General Accounting Office, the Equal Employment Opportunity Commission, and the Civil Rights Commission.[3] If a policy like revenue sharing requires such a complex implementation effort, the implementation of more elaborate policies will certainly be even more complicated.

IMPLEMENTATION PROBLEMS

Since policy implementation is so complex, we should not expect it to be accomplished in a routine fashion. Even presidents cannot assume that their decisions and orders will be carried out. Indeed, their experiences in recent years would turn even the most optimistic observers into cynics.

In 1962 President John Kennedy ordered U.S. Army troops located in Memphis to the campus of the University of Mississippi at Oxford to control rioting that resulted from the attempts of a black, James Meredith, to enroll. As the hours passed after giving the order, the commander-in-chief saw no progress toward Oxford. Frustrated, he demanded of Secretary of the Army Cyrus Vance, "Where are the troops?" No one seemed to know. When he talked on the phone to the general who supposedly was leading the troops, the general indicated he was awaiting orders from the Pentagon.[4] This was hardly Kennedy's only frustration in policy implementation. According to his closest adviser, Ted Sorensen, experiences of this nature led Kennedy, for the most part, to give up issuing orders at all. Instead, he relied upon suggestions and persuasion.[5] Kennedy once told an aide not to abandon the minor project of remodeling Lafayette Park across the street from the White House. "Hell," the president exclaimed, "this may be the only thing I'll ever get done."[6]

President Lyndon Johnson fared no better, even within his own Executive Office. For years he tried to get the Bureau of the Budget to assign five competent people to drag out of the federal agencies advance information about impending decisions and actions, but it never happened.[7] At other times actions were taken contrary to his orders. For example, in 1968 at the end of President Johnson's term of office, Attorney General Ramsey Clark filed several large antitrust suits, Secretary of Interior Stewart Udall ordered vast lands absorbed into the federal system, and Secretary of Labor Willard Wirtz ordered manpower programs to become more federalized — all against the wishes of the president.[8]

President Richard Nixon had implementation troubles of his own. An air force general carried out his own bombing campaign in Southeast Asia while the president was trying to avoid confrontation in order to facilitate peace negotiations, and Justice Department officials insisted upon antitrust prosecutions that Nixon opposed. Nixon's White House chief of staff, H. R. Haldeman, later wrote that by 1971 the president "realized that he was virtually powerless to deal with the bureaucracy in every department of government. It was no contest."[9]

Nixon also had trouble getting positive orders carried out. In a study of President Nixon's orders, commands, requests, and directives to the executive branch in 1969 and 1970, political scientist Raymond Chambers found noncompliance with more than half of them.[10] Nixon urged and exhorted his cabinet and other high ranking members of his administration to replace Democratic appointees with Republicans. Yet not enough personnel changes occurred, and the president had to wait until the beginning of his second term to make the changes he wanted.[11] It was this kind of frustration that led Nixon to scribble "government doesn't work" at the bottom of a memo informing him that some pet project would not get off the ground.[12] And these same problems led Secretary of State Henry Kissinger to say, "The outsider believes a presidential order is consistently followed. Nonsense. I have to spend considerable time seeing that it is carried out and in the spirit the President intended."[13]

President Jimmy Carter has also been frustrated by the federal bureaucracy:

> Before I became president, I realized and I was warned that dealing with the federal bureaucracy would be one of the worst problems I would have to face. It has been even worse than I had anticipated.[14]

Not only have Carter's policies been stymied by the vast federal bureaucracy, but the cabinet members that he personally appointed did not always carry out his wishes or do the job he wanted. In an interview following his shakeup of the cabinet in July 1979, President Carter expressed the opinion that for too long he had allowed some members to work against him. One cabinet member refused to make changes in his staff that the president wanted, and he too had to be fired.[15]

The experiences of recent presidents in implementation are summarized by Richard Cheney, President Gerald Ford's White House chief of staff:

> There is a tendency before you get to the White House or when you're just observing it from the outside to say "Gee, that's a powerful position that person has." The fact of the matter is that while you're

here trying to do things, you are far more aware of the constraints than you are of the power. You spend most of your time trying to overcome obstacles getting what the President wants done.[16]

State and local officials as well as presidents experience difficulties implementing policies. Senator Dale Bumpers, D-Ark., when he was governor of the state, described the bureaucracy as "a 700 pound marshmallow. You can kick it, scream at it, and cuss it, but it is very reluctant to move."[17]

While the implementation of most policies is the responsibility of the executive branch of government, the judiciary is also involved. Americans take pride in having "a government of laws and not men," but the law as established by the courts is not always implemented. In the 1954 *Brown v. Board of Education* decision, the U.S. Supreme Court declared racial segregation in public schools unconstitutional and ordered lower federal courts to implement its ruling.[18] In many districts, however, children entering public school the following year graduated from high school without ever attending a racially integrated school.

Sometimes courts order other branches or political jurisdictions to implement policies. Federal judge Arthur Garrity ordered South Boston High School to desegregate in 1974, but the next year he placed the entire school in federal receivership (under the court's control) and ordered all its administrators transferred because "the desegregation plan was not by a long shot being implemented. . . ."[19] In 1962 and 1963 the Supreme Court declared unconstitutional daily prayers and Bible readings in public schools. Yet a study of five midwestern cities several years later found that nothing had been done by the local school boards to implement the decisions.[20]

This brief overview of the frequent failure of public policy implementation should alert us to the sizable gap that often exists between a policy decision and its implementation. As Jeffrey Pressman and Aaron Wildavsky, the authors of an interesting study entitled *Implementation*, conclude:

> Our normal expectation should be that new programs will fail to get off the ground and that, at best, they will take considerable time to get started. The cards in this world are stacked against things happening, as so much effort is required to make them move. The remarkable thing is that new programs work at all.[21]

LACK OF ATTENTION TO IMPLEMENTATION

Policy implementation has had a low priority among most of our elected officials. Members of Congress and state legislators, whose responsibility it is to oversee the bureaucracy, often lack the expertise in administration to do so effectively. Moreover, legislators are very busy. The range of demands on members of Congress is enormous and expands as the role of the federal government increases. State legislatures generally have short sessions in which all of the state's legislative business must be transacted, including passing the budget. The rest of the time, legislators are private citizens primarily concerned with their personal affairs. Elected members of city councils, school boards, and other local decisionmaking bodies are almost always involved in government on a part-time basis and rarely have sufficient personal staff to aid them. Many mayors also work part-time. All these officials regularly must defer to school superintendents, city managers, and other professional administrators in matters of policy implementation.[22]

Often even the president and governors lack experience in administration. Although these executives are full-time public officials, like part-time employees they are extremely busy. No one could give attention to all the matters for which they are responsible. Programs must be passed; controversies must be either defused or contained to obtain and maintain support for legislation; and the public must be courted, votes must be won. Often re-election takes priority, and policy implementation takes a back seat.

Foreign affairs are always a top priority of presidents because of the inherent importance of these issues, and the unique constitutional responsibilities of presidents for them. Presidents often feel they can accomplish more in the international arena than at home wrestling over domestic issues with an unresponsive Congress or a recalcitrant executive branch. Many presidents bring to office a strong interest in international relations. Ceremonial functions performed in the role of chief of state are traditions maintained by the president to broaden his public support. All of these activities typically receive priority over implementation.

In addition, there is little incentive for our elected officials to emphasize implementation of policies once they attain their offices. They will receive little credit if policies are managed well because it is very difficult to attribute effective implementation to them personally. Moreover, to most people most of the time the functioning of government is not very visible.

Both citizens and the press, when they pay attention to government at all, are most interested in controversial scandals, the passage of new policies, or ceremonial functions. Policies such as inflation or civil rights that have an immediate and direct effect on their lives attract their attention. Yet even here the press and public are mainly concerned with the impact of policies — not the process of their implementation. Although implementation directly influences the final results, this does not seem to be enough to entice the mass public and the press that caters to it to turn their attention to policy implementation.

Given the short-run view adopted by most elected policymakers due to the necessity of seeking re-election frequently, and the limitations on the tenures of many chief executives, they will be more likely to try to provide the public with immediate gratification through the passage of legislation or the giving of speeches than with efforts to manage the implementation of policies. Moreover, they will often give little consideration to problems of policy implementation when they formulate policies. For example, in passing the Clean Air Amendments of 1970 Congress responded to public demands for pollution control but gave little thought to the costs of implementation or the lack of technology available to accomplish the goals mandated in the law.[23]

In sum, elected officials — those whom we as citizens can hold directly responsible for the implementation of public policies — generally devote little attention to this crucial aspect of policymaking. It is doubly important, therefore, that we understand the potential problems in implementation. Policymakers must be sensitized to these problems, and the public must provide them an incentive to devote more of their time to them.

APPROACHES TO STUDYING POLICY IMPLEMENTATION

Most implementation studies have been of the case study variety, and we shall rely in this book on case studies for much of our information.[24] Case studies usually focus upon one policy or one aspect of a policy. They provide rich detail about policymaking and delve into nuances that may be lost in broader treatments. Nevertheless, the case study approach to studying policy implementation is inherently limited. By its very nature of focusing narrowly on one issue, a case study cannot serve as the basis for generalizations about a wide range of policies. Case studies of implementation have not systematically identified or analyzed the factors that are critical in the implementation of public policy.

Another approach to public policy implementation is to focus on significant influences on policymaking. The most notable of studies of this kind is Graham Allison's *Essence of Decision.*[25] Allison presents three models of policymaking: the rational actor, organizational process, and bureaucratic politics models. The second and third of these models focus on standard operating procedures (SOPs) and bureaucratic politics, respectively, and have done much to sensitize us to the importance of these factors in policymaking. Our approach, while it has clearly been influenced by this work, will be different. Rather than focus on the importance of factors in policymaking in general, we shall emphasize how they affect implementation in particular.

In an insightful study Eugene Bardach has utilized the master metaphor of "games" to study implementation.[26] Bardach argues that the game framework he has developed illuminates policymaking by directing attention to the players (those involved with implementation), their stakes, strategies and tactics, resources, rules of play and communications, and the degree of uncertainty surrounding outcomes. Most of what is highlighted by "games," however, can be subsumed by our approach and much can be added. The game metaphor is an interesting but incomplete approach to studying implementation.

Yet another avenue to studying policy implementation is represented by the work of Donald Van Meter and Carl Van Horn and, more recently, by Paul Sabatier and Daniel Mazmanian.[27] These authors identify a number of factors that directly or indirectly influence implementation, and their approach helps put us on the right track.

The study of policy implementation is different from what is generally termed "policy evaluation." Policy evaluation is a rapidly growing and valuable tool for policymakers. Essentially, it compares the goals of programs to their outcomes, measuring program impacts such as increases in education, employment, or juvenile deinstitutionalization and decreases in recidivism, drug addiction, or illness that may be attributable to policies with these goals.

While the policy evaluation approach can be helpful in policy analysis, it does not tell the whole story about the success or failure of public policies. We cannot reasonably evaluate policies *until* they have been implemented properly. In general, we should not expect a program to produce the desired results if it has not been operating according to design. Moreover, unless policymakers have information on implementation, they will not know what to do with the results of evaluation studies. *Why* did a program fail? It might be because the original policy design was poor, or it might be because the design was never implemented. Information on implementation is critical for decisionmaking regarding the future of the program.

This point is illustrated by the following example. A state legislature established a program to teach welfare recipients the rudiments of parenting and household management and charged the state welfare department with responsibility for conducting workshops, distributing brochures, showing films, and training caseworkers to show how people with low incomes could better raise their children and manage their budgets. One large city was selected as a test site for the program, and the program was evaluated by a highly respected independent research institute. The results of this evaluation showed no measurable change in parenting and household management skills among low income persons after 18 months. As a result of these findings and their attendant publicity, the state legislature terminated the program.

This decision may seem very scientific and responsible, at least until one asks *why* the program failed. Unfortunately, the evaluators did not ask this question. Consequently, neither they nor the state legislature could interpret the results of the program evaluation within a meaningful context. The state parenting and household management program failed for a simple reason: it was never implemented. As a result of the pressures of urban welfare politics, no brochures were ever printed, no films were ever shown, no workshops were ever held, and no caseworkers were ever trained! If the public and state legislators had known this, they might have reacted differently to the results of the evaluation study. Indeed, the evaluation would probably not have taken place; the evaluators would have sensibly waited until the program was implemented.[28]

The importance of reliable information on implementation cannot be underestimated. When policymakers lack information about implementation, they may not only terminate a potentially successful program, but they also may expand a program inappropriately. The board of one county had a number of its drug addiction treatment programs evaluated. What was evaluated were the rates of readdiction for treated patients — not the implementation of the program. All but one of the programs were found to have mediocre success rates, the exception being a program enjoying a 100 percent success rate. The county board tripled the funding for this successful program, but within a year it showed the same unimpressive results as the others.

By enlarging the initially successful program, the county board had eliminated the key factors that had made it successful: its small size and dedicated staff. These factors had made possible intensive personal contact with the patients. When the program was enlarged, the original staff became administrators and lost their personal contact with the patients. Without information on the actual operation of the successful program, the board did not understand the basis for its effectiveness. Hence, the decision to expand the program proved counterproductive.[29]

OUR APPROACH TO STUDYING IMPLEMENTATION

In our approach to the study of policy implementation, we begin in the abstract and ask: What are the preconditions for successful policy implementation? What are the primary obstacles to successful policy implementation? In the next four chapters we shall attempt to answer these important questions by considering four critical factors or variables in implementing public policy: communication, resources, dispositions or attitudes, and bureaucratic structure.

Because the four factors are operating simultaneously and inter-acting with each other to aid or hinder policy implementation, the ideal approach would be to reflect this complexity by discussing them all at once. Yet, given our goal of increasing our understanding of policy implementation, such an approach would be self-defeating. To understand we must simplify, and to simplify we must break down explanations of implementation into principal components. Neverthe-less, we need to remember that the implementation of every policy is a dynamic process, which involves the interaction of many variables.

Each chapter has two goals: to see how the factor under discussion affects implementation and to explain why the factor may arise as an obstacle to policy implementation. Where it is reasonable to do so, subcategories of the basic factors are presented. In every case the factor influencing implementation is considered in a variety of cir-cumstances. Through this approach we hope to gain a deeper under-standing of the complex relationships involved in public policy implementation.

Communication

For implementation to be effective, those whose responsibility it is to implement a decision must know what they are supposed to do. Orders to implement policies must be transmitted to the appropriate personnel, and they must be clear, accurate, and consistent. If the policies decisionmakers wish to see implemented are not clearly speci-fied, they may be misunderstood by those at whom they are directed. Obviously, confusion by implementors about what to do increases the chances that they will not implement a policy as those who passed or ordered it intended.

Inadequate communications also provide implementors with discre-tion as they attempt to turn general policies into specific actions. This discretion will not necessarily be exercised to further the aims of the original decisionmakers. Thus, implementation instructions that are not transmitted, that are distorted in transmission, or that are vague or inconsistent present serious obstacles to policy implementa-tion. Conversely, directives that are too precise may hinder implementa-tion by stifling creativity and adaptability. The causes and con-sequences of communication failures are analyzed in Chapter 2.

Resources

No matter how clear and consistent implementation orders are and no matter how accurately they are transmitted, if the personnel responsible for carrying out policies lack the resources to do an effective job, implementation will not be effective. Important resources include staff of the proper size and with the necessary expertise; relevant and adequate information on how to implement policies and on the compliance of others involved in implementation; the authority to ensure that policies are carried out as they are intended; and facilities (including buildings, equipment, land, and supplies) in which or with which to provide services. Insufficient resources will mean that laws will not be enforced, services will not be provided, and reasonable regulations will not be developed. Chapter 3 analyzes the role of resources in policy implementation.

Dispositions

The dispositions or attitudes of implementors is the third critical factor in our approach to the study of public policy implementation. If implementation is to proceed effectively, not only must implementors know what to do and have the capability to do it, but they must also desire to carry out a policy. Most implementors can exercise considerable discretion in the implementation of policies. One of the reasons for this is their independence from their nominal superiors who formulate the policies. Another reason is the complexity of the policies themselves. The way in which implementors exercise their discretion, however, depends in large part upon their dispositions toward the policies. Their attitudes, in turn, will be influenced by their views toward the policies per se and by how they see the policies affecting their organizational and personal interests.

Implementors are not always disposed to implement policies as those who originally made them would like. Consequently, decisionmakers are often faced with the task of trying to manipulate or work around implementors' dispositions or to reduce their discretion. In Chapter 4 we examine both the problems that dispositions of implementors pose for implementation and the efforts of their superiors to implement policies in spite of these dispositions.

Bureaucratic Structure

Even if sufficient resources to implement a policy exist and implementors know what to do and want to do it, implementation may still be thwarted because of deficiencies in bureaucratic structure. Organizational fragmentation may hinder the coordination necessary to implement successfully a complex policy requiring the cooperation of many people, and it may also waste scarce resources, inhibit change, create confusion, lead to policies working at cross-purposes, and result in important functions being overlooked.

As organizational units administer policies they develop standard operating procedures (SOPs) to handle the routine situations with which they regularly deal. Unfortunately, SOPs designed for ongoing policies are often inappropriate for new policies and may cause resistance to change, delay, waste, or unwanted actions. SOPs sometimes hinder rather than help policy implementation. Both organizational fragmentation and standard operating procedures are discussed in Chapter 5.

Problems and Prospects

Each of the factors outlined above not only directly affects implementation, but also indirectly influences each of the other factors. In Chapter 6 we consider the interactions between these factors and their impact on implementation. The types of policies most likely to face implementation problems are then examined. Policies that are new, complex, controversial, highly decentralized, crisis-related, and/or established by the judiciary are the most difficult to implement successfully.

Because of the many obstacles to implementation, officials need to monitor or follow up implementation efforts to see that their decisions have been acted upon in ways they desire. For a variety of reasons, however, little follow-up takes place, and the opportunity to identify and remedy implementation failures before it is too late is lost. The causes and consequences of lack of follow-up and the prospects for improvement of policy implementation are also examined in the last chapter.

Context of the Approach

Public policies are made and implemented on the national, state, and local levels. Moreover, policies formulated by higher level jurisdictions are often implemented by lower level units of government. The president or the Supreme Court may begin to implement a policy, but it is often with a local school principal or welfare caseworker that the implementation process ends. Examples from the national, state, and local levels form the context for our discussion.

Within each level both the executive and judicial branches are responsible for implementing policies. So are independent regulatory commissions. We shall focus broadly upon implementation and not limit ourselves to only one branch of government. This will not only provide a more accurate picture of implementation, but also lend support for broader generalizations about it.

Because we are primarily concerned with the question of how policy decisions are implemented and why they are implemented as they are, we will view implementation from the top down. If policy implementation were viewed from the bottom up — from the perspective of consumers of policies — value judgments about the policies themselves would be inevitable. We would naturally be led to emphasize the impact of policies, their fairness, the decisions of citizens to obey laws, etc. These topics are of central concern to students of public policy, but for our purposes we are less interested in whether policies are just, widely favored, or successful in solving social problems than with how they are implemented.

For example, an armed attack to capture Mexican oil fields may be a very foolish policy yet still be successfully implemented; the oil fields could be captured. While in principle we are concerned about the rationality of policy decisions, in this book we shall focus on implementing decisions, whatever their wisdom. Thus, we will examine policy implementation from the viewpoint of high-level decisionmakers who want to see their decisions become functioning policies true to their intent.

Advantages of the Approach

The first advantage of the approach outlined above is that it is *straightforward* — a frequently underrated attribute in the social sciences but one that will make understanding policy implementation easier. Communication, resources, dispositions, and the bureaucratic structure are thoroughly discussed without resorting to obscure jargon or esoteric analogies. Each factor is also easily related to common public policy situations. This is of considerable value to us as we examine the effects of each factor on policy implementation.

Another advantage of our approach is that it is *parsimonious.* There is an economy or simplicity in the logical formulation of our discussion. This is useful in theory building because it helps to simplify a complex subject and leads us to focus on the most central relationships in the subject under study in ways in which more elaborate schemes do not.

Focusing on a few critical factors rather than on a checklist also forces us to *explain* relationships, and explanation is ultimately what we want to gain from our study of implementation. It is not enough to rely upon a series of "points to ponder." Instead we must pay particular attention to justifying our selection of factors, and by doing so we must demonstrate their impact on policy implementation. In this way we work toward understanding why things happen as they do, and with this knowledge we should be able to improve implementation in the future.

This leads to a final advantage: our approach to studying implementation is *conducive to providing remedies* for implementation failures. While this analysis is not likely to solve the problem of poor implementation of public policies, it will take us at least one large step on the right path. Specifying the factors critical to implementation helps identify the features of implementation processes that must be manipulated to improve implementation. By increasing our understanding of implementation, we should be in a better position to fashion solutions to implementation problems and to design programs that will reduce the problems in the future.

Awareness of the critical factors in implementing public policy improves the likelihood of spotting ahead of time potential obstacles to successful implementation. We want to be in a position to predict possible trouble spots so we know what to look for, what we shall have to take special care about, and what we will have to manipulate before implementation begins. This is when the most can be done to increase the chances of successful implementation.

Furthermore, by focusing on prerequisites for the successful implementation of any policy, some of the problems inherent in the study of the implementation of a specific policy can be avoided. Rather than trying to measure the success of a particular policy, which is often difficult because of the nebulous goals of policies, we emphasize what logically must take place for any policy to be implemented successfully.

A final word is necessary. Our approach often emphasizes the negative side of policy implementation, i.e. implementation problems. This is inherent in a book trying to explain why things go wrong. At the same time, we recognize that not all implementation efforts fail. Social Security checks are distributed, roads are built, students are taught, and weapons are purchased. But whether students are being properly taught and whether weapons systems are being efficiently purchased is another question. While we do not want to leave the impression that policy implementation is universally a disaster, there are few policies lacking room for improvement.

, In sum, this book identifies systematic influences on policy implementation, examines the causes and consequences of these critical factors as they operate in actual implementation processes, and briefly analyzes the interactions between the factors, the types of policies most likely to face implementation problems, and the prospects for improvement of implementation. Implementation efforts on the national, state, and local levels and of all relevant branches of government and the private sector provide the context for our study.

NOTES

1. Malcolm Muggeridge, *Affairs of the Heart* (New York: Walker & Co., 1961), p. 61.
2. Richard P. Nathan, Allen D. Maxwell, Susannah E. Calkins and Associates, *Monitoring Revenue Sharing* (Washington, D.C.: Brookings Institution, 1975), pp. 20-23.
3. Ibid.
4. Lawrence F. O'Brien, *No Final Victories* (New York: Ballantine Books, 1974), p. 142.
5. Theodore C. Sorenson, *Watchmen in the Night* (Cambridge, Mass.: MIT Press, 1975), p. 30. See also Sorenson, *Kennedy* (New York: Harper & Row, 1965), p. 322.
6. John Herbers, "Nixon's Presidency: Centralized Control," *New York Times*, March 6, 1973, p. 20.
7. William Carey, "Presidential Staffing in the Sixties and Seventies," *Public Administration Review* 29 (September/October 1969): 453.
8. Harry McPherson, *A Political Education* (Boston: Little, Brown & Co., 1972), pp. 450-451; George Christian, *The President Steps Down: A Personal Memoir of the Transfer of Power* (New York: Macmillan Co., 1970), pp. 234-242. See also Doris Kearns, *Lyndon Johnson and the American Dream* (New York: Harper & Row, 1976), p. 242.
9. H. R. Haldeman, *The Ends of Power* (New York: Times Books, 1978), p. 149.
10. Raymond L. Chambers, "The Executive Power: A Preliminary Study of the Concept and of the Efficacy of Presidential Directives," *Presidential Studies Quarterly* 7 (Winter 1977): 21-37.
11. Richard M. Nixon, *RN: The Memoirs of Richard Nixon* (New York: Grosset & Dunlap, 1978), pp. 352, 355-356.
12. William Safire, *Before the Fall: An Inside View of the Pre-Watergate White House* (New York: Doubleday & Co., 1975), pp. 262. See also pp. 554-555 for another example of Nixon's frustration with bureaucrats.
13. Morton H. Halperin, *Bureaucratic Policies and Foreign Policy* (Washington, D.C.: Brookings Institution, 1974), p. 245.
14. G. Calvin Mackenzie, "Personnel Appointment Strategies in Post-War Presidential Administrations" (Paper delivered at the annual meeting of the Midwest Political Science Association, Chicago, Illinois, April 1980), introductory page.
15. "How Carter Sees It," *Newsweek*, July 30, 1979, p. 25.
16. Stephen J. Wayne, "Working in the White House: Psychological Dimensions of the Job" (Paper delivered at the annual meeting of the Southern Political Science Association, New Orleans, Louisiana, November 1977), p. 10.
17. "State-Local Report: Structural Reform of Bureaucracy Grows Rapidly," *National Journal*, April 5, 1975, p. 503.
18. *Brown* v. *Board of Education of Topeka* 347 U.S. 483 (1954).
19. "Southie Rides Again," *Newsweek*, December 22, 1975, p. 30.
20. Kenneth M. Dolbeare and Phillip E. Hammond, *The School Prayer Decisions* (Chicago: University of Chicago Press, 1971). See pp. 32-33 for a broader sampling of noncompliance.
21. Jeffrey L. Pressman and Aaron B. Wildavsky, *Implementation* (Berkeley: University of California Press, 1973), p. 109.

22. For example, see Harvey J. Tucker and Harmon Ziegler, *Professionals versus the Public: Attitudes, Communication and Response in Local School Districts* (New York: Longman, 1980).
23. Charles O. Jones, "Speculative Augmentation in Federal Air Pollution Policymaking," *Journal of Politics* 36 (May 1974): 438-464; Helen Ingram, "The Political Rationality of Federal Air Pollution Legislation," in *Approaches to Controlling Air Pollution,* ed. Ann F. Friedlaender (Cambridge, Mass.: MIT Press, 1978), pp. 12-56.
24. The most notable of these studies has been *Implementation* by Pressman and Wildavsky, but many other case studies will be cited throughout this book.
25. Graham Allison, *Essence of Decision* (Boston: Little, Brown & Co., 1971).
26. Eugene Bardach, *The Implementation Game: What Happens After a Bill Becomes a Law* (Cambridge, Mass.: MIT Press, 1977), pp. 55-56.
27. Donald S. Van Meter and Carl E. Van Horn, "The Policy Implementation Process: A Conceptual Framework," *Administration and Society* 6 (February 1975): 445-488; Paul Sabatier and Daniel Mazmanian, "The Implementation of Public Policy: A Framework of Analysis," *Policy Studies Journal* 8 (Special Issue No. 2, 1980): 538-560.
28. Michael Q. Patton, *Utilization-Focused Evaluation* (Beverly Hills, Calif.: Sage Publications, 1978), pp. 149-150.
29. Ibid., p. 154.

2

Communication

The first requirement for effective policy implementation is that those who are to implement a decision must know what they are supposed to do. Policy decisions and implementation orders must be transmitted to the appropriate personnel before they can be followed. Naturally, these communications need to be accurate, and they must be accurately perceived by implementors. Many obstacles lie in the path of the transmission of implementation communications, however, and these obstacles may hinder policy implementation, as we shall see below.

If policies are to be implemented properly, implementation directives must not only be received, but they must also be clear. If they are not, implementors will be confused about what they should do, and they will have discretion to impose their own views on the implementation of policies, views that may be different from those of their superiors. In the second section of this chapter, the problems created by lack of clarity in implementation instructions are examined and explanations of why this ambiguity occurs are presented.

Another aspect of the communication of implementation directives is their consistency. Contradictory decisions confuse and frustrate administrative staff and constrain their ability to implement policies effectively. In the final section of this chapter, we discuss the conditions under which inconsistent communications are likely to arise and the impact of such communications on policy implementation.

TRANSMISSION

Before people can implement a decision, they must be aware that the decision has been made and an order to implement it issued. This is not always as straightforward a process as it may seem. Ignorance or misunderstanding of decisions frequently occurs. One of the numerous obstacles to transmitting implementation instructions is the disagreement of implementors with them. Disagreement over policies can lead either to outright blockage or distortion of communications as implementors exercise their inevitable discretion in handling general decisions and orders. Similar problems of distortion may arise as information passes through multiple layers of the bureaucratic hierarchy. The use of indirect means of communication and the absence of established channels of communication may also distort implementation instructions. Finally, the reception of communications may be hindered by implementors' selective perception and disinclination to know about a policy's requirements. Sometimes implementors attempt to ignore the obvious and try to guess at the "true" meaning of communications. As we illustrate the impact of these obstacles on effective communication, we will also see their consequences for policy implementation.

Executive Branch

Although most executive branches have highly developed lines of communication throughout the bureaucracy, this does not guarantee that communications will be transmitted successfully. The Bay of Pigs fiasco illustrates this point.

On April 17, 1961, a force of 1,200 Cuban refugees — recruited, trained, and supplied by the U.S. Central Intelligence Agency (CIA) — landed 90 miles south of Havana with the announced goal of overthrowing the communist-oriented regime of Fidel Castro. Within three days the "invasion" had been crushed, inflicting a disastrous blow to American prestige, not to mention that of the new president, John F. Kennedy. The CIA never told the leader of the brigade sent to invade Cuba that the president had ordered the soldiers to go to the mountains and fight a guerrilla war if the invasion failed. The CIA disregarded the president's order, which it thought might weaken the brigade's resolve to fight or encourage the brigade to go to the mountains too quickly.[1]

Sometimes aides and other officials ignore executive directives with which they disagree primarily to avoid embarrassment for their chief. Such orders are generally given in anger and without proper consultation. Our best examples come from the White House. After President Johnson had made the decision not to run for a second term, he fired an assistant secretary of agriculture for his support of Robert Kennedy's candidacy for the presidency. That evening Joseph Califano, one of Johnson's aides, told the resigning official to forget the whole thing.[2] President Kennedy once called Newton Minow, the chairman of the Federal Communications Commission, and told him to "do something" about the Huntley-Brinkley NBC nightly news, which had carried a long speech attacking the president. Fortunately, Minow did nothing.[3]

President Nixon especially liked to let off steam by issuing outrageous orders. At one time he instructed Secretary of State William Rogers to "fire everybody in Laos." He often told aides to "go after" reporters and once ordered that all reporters be barred from Air Force One. He also directed that a 24-hour surveillance be kept on a dissenting senator and that all State Department employees be administered lie detector tests to stop leaks. These and similar outbursts were ignored by H. R. Haldeman and other aides close to Nixon. They knew the president would view things differently when he calmed down.[4]

Disregard of directives given in anger, unlike other barriers to effective communication, usually have benefited presidents. Their close associates have provided them safe outlets for their frustrations and protected them from their worst instincts. One might even argue that President Nixon would have been better served if Haldeman had not been so responsive to his desires for political intelligence during the 1972 presidential campaign. It was this demand that led to Watergate.

In most instances, implementors have considerable discretion in interpreting their superiors' decisions and orders. Orders from the top are rarely specific. Personnel at each rung in the bureaucratic ladder must use their judgment to expand and develop them. Obviously, this process invites distortion of communications, and the further down in the bureaucracy implementation directives go, the greater the potential for distortion. Moreover, as we shall see in Chapter 4, subordinates do not always interpret the communications of superiors in a way that advances the goals of the original decisionmakers. Bureaucrats often use their discretion to further their personal interests and those of their agencies.[5] Interest groups also take advantage of the discretion granted bureaucrats by pushing for their own demands at intermediate and low decisionmaking levels.

It is for these reasons that observers of the federal bureaucracy often recommend that presidents and other high officials make every attempt to commit their directives to writing (in detail where possible), use personalized communications where appropriate, and show persistence in attempting to convey accurately their orders to those who actually implement policies.[6]

President Dwight Eisenhower liked to have National Security Council decisions announced at the council's meetings so that those who were to implement them (at least those at the top of the hierarchy) got the word in his presence. Political scientist Fred Greenstein points out that Eisenhower's "great personal effectiveness in face-to-face settings spurred identification with his purpose."[7] To reduce transmission problems, former CIA Director William Colby recommends that the president meet regularly with the CIA chief so the latter can keep in tune with the president's concerns regarding intelligence.[8]

In general, the more decentralized the implementation of a public policy, the less likely that it will be transmitted to its ultimate implementors accurately. Decentralization usually means that a decision must be communicated through several levels of authority before it reaches those who will carry it out. The more steps a communication must traverse from its original source, the weaker the signal that is ultimately received will be.[9] A president can tell a secretary of state to go to another country and deliver a policy pronouncement to its prime minister, or the Supreme Court can order a state legislature to be reapportioned, with little concern that their messages will not be accurately transmitted. But they cannot have the same confidence about messages aimed at caseworkers in a city welfare office or police officers walking their beats. The distance between the original source of the communication and the implementors is too great.

Many laws are implemented by persons in the private sector. Laws requiring gas station owners to sell gas on certain days to only certain motor vehicles (such as those with odd-numbered license plates) are a good example. While simple and highly visible policies such as this one may be easily transmitted through the press or by mailings, most policies implemented by the private sector are more complex and less visible. Thus, the transmission of these policy directives is more problematical.

According to one study, many realtors know little about open housing laws that prohibit discrimination in the sale or rental of housing.[10] Similarly, thousands of loan officers in banks, stores, and automobile dealerships are uninformed concerning consumer credit laws. The vastness of the credit bureaucracy causes problems in disseminating information to the public. Borrowers as well as lenders need to be aware of the law so that they will know if they have been denied credit illegally and what their legal remedies are.[11] Since most Americans use credit, the number of people involved in the transmission of credit information numbers into the tens of millions. Because the number of people is so great and the information is relatively complex for the average person, we cannot assume that it is accurately transmitted to the typical consumer.

At times, executives and their staffs prefer *not* to transmit policy directives personally; they would rather get others to do their communications for them. President Johnson wanted Secretary of the Treasury Henry Fowler to apply "jawboning," or powerful persuasion, to try to lower interest rates. Because Fowler opposed such efforts, Johnson decided not to communicate his wishes to the secretary directly. Instead

he called House Banking Committee Chairman Wright Patman, a sup-
porter of "jawboning," and asked him to pressure Fowler.[12] Any time
a step is added to the chain of communication, the potential for distortion is increased. Those who speak for others will have their own
styles, their own views, and their own motivations. Not even presidents
can depend upon other people to transmit directives exactly as they
would desire.

In 1971 President Nixon employed a roundabout means of communication in an attempt to make the Federal Reserve Board more responsive to his wishes. He had aide Charles Colson leak to the press a
"shot across the bow" of Arthur Burns, the board's chairman. The
story was that the president's advisers were urging him to increase
the size of the board — a threat to Burns — and that Burns was
hypocritically asking for a raise while opposing raises for other federal
employees. The fact that neither of these points was true (the president
later had to deny them) undoubtedly influenced Nixon's choice of
transmission channels.[13]

The technique of communicating indirectly through the press is
a common one at all levels of government. Communicating through
leaks in the press, however, invites even more message distortion than
communicating through another individual. The press is under no obligation to aid the official providing the leak. It may alter the message
to serve its own purposes, or it may distort the communication in-
advertently. Moreover, because this mode of communication is so indirect, there is no guarantee that those at whom a message is aimed
will receive it at all. Nor can the sender ensure that the recipient
will understand the message's significance, even if it is received. Messages communicated through the press are usually nebulous to protect
the sender's identity. If senders did not wish to remain anonymous,
they would not use the press in the first place.

Some officials do not have personalities well suited to direct
communication. According to former White House chief of staff H. R.
Haldeman, Nixon attacked problems or persons from the side, often
through subordinates when the "victim" was not looking.[14] Nixon aide
William Safire adds that the president was reluctant to get on the
phone and issue an order himself because he wanted to avoid the
possibility of rejection.[15]

As we saw above, the channels of communication between the
public and private sectors are not well-developed, and this can create
real problems even for the president. Within weeks after Vietnam and
Cambodia fell completely under the control of communist forces in
the spring of 1975, the United States became embroiled in another
military incident in Southeast Asia. On May 12 Cambodian communist
troops captured the American merchant ship *Mayaguez* and its crew

of 39. President Gerald Ford responded with combined forces of navy, marine, and air force units to retake the ship and free its crew. Because of the newness of the Cambodian government, the primitive communication system in the war-torn country, and our status as an enemy, President Ford had no way to communicate rapidly and directly the United States' demands for the return of the ship and its crew. He had to put his message over the international press wire services in the hope that some Cambodian official somewhere would read it and communicate it to the Cambodian government.[16] In this case the effort to communicate through extremely indirect channels seems to have worked, but the chances of success in such instances are limited.

Courts

The judiciary is generally quite deficient in the area of regular channels of communication. In most instances, judges of higher level courts have no institutionalized means of communicating with lower courts. The U.S. Supreme Court sends its decisions only to the lower court from which the case originated. Although judges across the entire country are obligated to follow relevant Supreme Court decisions, the Court does not send them its decisions. It depends on judges to learn of them on their own.

While some judges keep abreast of current decisions, many do not.[17] Busy judges in an adversary system of justice may wait for attorneys to present new legal doctrines in the courtroom. Yet attorneys often do not perform this function, especially at the trial court level where most judicial activity takes place and where decisions of higher courts are generally implemented (when they are implemented within the court system). The attorneys who practice in these courts are frequently ignorant of higher court decisions.[18] Even if they are not, they may sometimes hesitate to argue too much "law" in routine cases for fear of alienating the judge.

After a time a higher court decision may be transmitted to lower courts via citations by yet other judges. But communication channels within the judiciary are so poor that lower court judges may not even know that their superiors have made a decision, much less its content. And the further from the source of a decision one looks, the more likely this will be true.[19]

Some judges at points between the highest and lowest courts may oppose a higher court's decision. The official reactions of state supreme courts to the U.S. Supreme Court's criminal rights decisions in the 1960s included sarcasm, criticism, challenges to the factual premises of the cases, statements of concern over the effects of the decisions, and statements urging the lower courts to apply the decisions narrowly.

Naturally, this mixture of negative responses did not aid accurate transmission of the Supreme Court's decisions. (Such comments, however, do enable elected state judges who disagree with a Supreme Court decision to follow the decision under protest.)[20]

While lower court judges are obligated to follow the decisions of higher courts, they must wait to do so until the relevant suits are brought to them. In most cases, those who ultimately implement court decisions are the police, school officials, and others whose behavior is directly affected by them. After the Supreme Court makes a decision, it does not send out copies of it to local police departments or school boards. Nor does it issue any additional guidelines for implementing its decisions. In effect, the Supreme Court and all lower courts rely upon officials in other branches of government and often at other levels of government to learn of their decisions and to implement them. The problem here, as it was for transmission of decisions within the judiciary, is that implementors may not understand completely what the judicial decisions are.

Supreme Court decisions, as well as those of other high courts, are printed in bound volumes at the end of a session and may be obtained earlier in advance sheets published by private companies. These are not always readily available to implementors, however, especially at lower levels of government and in rural areas.[21] Many lawyers do not subscribe to a service that provides Supreme Court decisions. Moreover, the language of the decisions is difficult for most nonlawyers to understand. Law reviews and specialized legal journals carry discussions of judicial decisions, but their audiences are primarily those with legal backgrounds; the police officers on the beat who are supposed to enforce court decisions are little helped by these discussions.

Others connected with the judicial system cannot be depended upon to transmit judicial decisions to those who must implement them. For example, many prosecutors do not consider part of their job informing the police of court decisions regarding police procedures. Moreover, they may be ignorant of the decisions themselves. Judges are equally lax in this regard, and trial court judges, those closest to the police, usually do not publish their decisions or explain the basis of them. State attorneys general give advisory opinions, but they are available only upon request and are not widely circulated. Few police officers attend the meetings state attorneys general sometimes hold or read the bulletins that they publish. Finally, only a few police departments have legal advisers or officers designated to transmit information from the courts to the police.[22] For these reasons, police administrators have had to rely primarily upon newspapers for information on judicial decisions, even when they involve officers in their own departments.[23]

The comments of trial court judges may also hinder the transmission of higher court decisions. At a Chicago police department staff meeting held several weeks after an important Supreme Court decision on police procedures, the chief judge of the criminal courts was asked what he recommended the police do about it. "Boys, that's a decision of law," he responded. "You let us lawyers worry about that sort of thing. You're overworked as it is." This statement probably encouraged division commanders at the meeting to ignore a subsequent memo on the case and to de-emphasize the decision in their own communications to subordinates.[24] Similarly, in Cincinnati certain judges were hostile to the Supreme Court's *Mapp v. Ohio* decision concerning the admissibility of evidence gained from illegal searches and seizures by state law enforcement officials. These judges tried to help the police avoid the decision's requirements — hardly an activity conducive to the effective communication of the Supreme Court's decision to its ultimate implementors, the police.[25]

As we have seen, the judicial system cannot always be depended upon to transmit court decisions to those who must implement them. Implementors of court decisions are left largely on their own to learn of the laws with which they must comply. One study of a Supreme Court school prayer decision concluded that there "was not a shred of evidence" that legal channels were of significance in the transmission of information.[26]

In such a situation sources outside the judicial system may be more important than formal legal sources in transmitting court decisions.[27] There are many publications for police, educators, and other implementors. Often these may prove useful, but they are rarely comprehensive or detailed in their coverage of court decisions. Professional organizations of school administrators, police chiefs, and district attorneys may provide information on court decisions. Private groups that have a special interest in seeing decisions implemented may make efforts to disseminate the decisions to the relevant officials. (The National Association for the Advancement of Colored People, for example, helped disseminate information on racial discrimination decisions.) For the most part, however, this hit-or-miss system of transmission is far from satisfactory and leaves considerable room for misinformation.[28]

Communications inside executive branch bureaucracies are also deficient in the coverage of judicial decisions. They are neither routinized nor systematic. The training in law that most officials receive is generally inadequate. In the case of the police, many of the intradepartmental communications that do occur are oriented toward "living with" or avoiding court decisions — not toward implementing them in good faith. Moreover, any materials that might be made available to the police (or any other implementors) require time to master, time that few public employees will allocate to learning the law without strong incentives. Usually these incentives have not existed.[29]

Press coverage of judicial decisions is of little utility in transmitting their content. Network television and most newspapers and magazines give very limited coverage to courts; when they do report a decision, it is usually distorted, oversimplified, or exaggerated — just what we would expect from reporters who are not experts on the law. Full opinions of appellate courts are rarely printed. Moreover, the basis or rationale for a decision is often omitted from press coverage.[30] This is a critical omission. The reasons for a decision can guide implementors in applying it to situations not covered in the immediate case and can increase public acceptance of it. When a decision is represented accurately and its rationale is given, the attentive public will usually learn that the decision was not arbitrary and its application has limits.

In recent years the Supreme Court has tried to aid reporters through giving them the full texts of decisions as they are being read from the bench, announcing decisions over several days instead of just Mondays, providing headnotes (summaries) of decisions, releasing the daily list of court orders in advance, and scheduling newsworthy cases so reporters can cover the oral arguments in court. These reforms are a positive step toward improving communication between the court and the public.[31] Nevertheless, press coverage of the Court's decisions remains inadequate as a source of guidance for those who must implement them.

Oddly, misrepresentation of decisions by the press can lead to more changes than a court ever ordered. Bus lines in 11 southern cities complied with a decision as it was represented (incorrectly) in reports declaring that the Supreme Court had ordered the desegregation of intrastate buses.[32]

Reception of Communications

As we noted earlier, the reception of messages by implementors is just as vital to implementation as relaying them. Selective perception, i.e., screening out information that is contrary to one's existing values and beliefs, can hinder public officials' understanding of the content of policies. Although the Supreme Court in 1962 prohibited religious exercises, even voluntary ones, in public schools, some local elites selectively perceived that the ruling referred only to mandatory prayers. Since they did not coerce anyone in their schools to participate in religious exercises, they disregarded the Court's decision. Most of them could not believe that the activities in their schools could be unconstitutional. Coupled with this selective perception was a disinclination to know about what "obviously doesn't affect us."[33]

In such situations officials may be unaware of court decisions that affect them. This is what one scholar found in his study of the communication of Supreme Court decisions on criminal rights. Prosecutors, defenders, judges, and police chiefs in small towns in Illinois and Massachusetts were often ignorant of the Court's decisions.[34] Another author found that even the most professional police departments he examined were unaware of information regarding their responsibilities for implementing decisions.[35] Two researchers discovered a similar lack of understanding of Supreme Court decisions on prayers in the public schools among teachers, principals, school board members, and, to a lesser extent, school superintendents in the midwestern cities they studied. They also found a state deputy attorney general for education affairs who was ignorant of crucial decisions.[36]

Bureaucrats, in their efforts to interpret directives, are often guided by innuendos about policy directions and personnel and by the refusal of superiors to talk to certain people. In an attempt to determine what their superiors "really" intended, they may discount what seem to be clear proclamations.[37] For example, the attitudes of central administrators toward innovations in education provide a signal to participants in these projects "as to how seriously to take project goals and how hard they should work to achieve them."[38]

CLARITY

If policies are to be implemented as those who enacted them intended, implementation directives must not only be received, but must also be clear. Often the instructions transmitted to implementors are vague and do not specify when or how a program is to be carried out. Lack of clarity provides implementors with leeway to give new meaning to policies, meaning that sometimes is contrary to the original intention of the law. This section begins with a discussion of the obstacles to effective implementation created by vague laws. We then discuss efforts to reduce implementors' discretion. The implementation difficulties created by ambiguous court decisions are also examined in this section. Ambiguity does not always hinder implementation, however. As we shall see, implementors need flexibility and can be hampered by overly specific instructions.

There are numerous reasons for lack of clarity in implementation directives. Among the factors we consider are the complexity of public policies, the desire not to irritate segments of the public, a lack of consensus on the goals of a policy, the problems in starting up a new policy, avoiding accountability for policies, and the nature of judicial decisionmaking.

Vague Laws

The phrase "maximum feasible participation" in the Economic Opportunity Act of 1964 was intended by those who drafted the act to mean that only citizens excluded from the political process were to receive benefits from the law. This original interpretation, however, was never clearly stated. The people running local community action programs interpreted the phrase to mean involving the poor in running the programs and in political activism, and they acted on the basis of this interpretation. The misunderstanding of "maximum feasible participation" was compounded by the fact that few persons in the administration or Congress knew what the architects of the policy intended the phrase to mean.[39]

Many federal programs provide grants to lower level jurisdictions, but the laws are frequently vague, contributing to a less-than-effective supervision of the expenditure of the funds. Title I of the Elementary and Secondary Education Act of 1965 established a program of grants to state education departments and through them to local school districts. The funds were intended to meet the "special needs of educationally deprived children" — not to supplant already existing resources reserved for the educationally deprived. The act, however, did not specify clearly who the "educationally deprived" were or what an acceptable program to meet their needs was. Many thought the law was intended to be a *general* aid bill under another name.

The U.S. Office of Education's initial guidelines on the expenditure of these funds by local school districts reflected this ambiguity. No wonder many local education agencies also viewed the funds as general aid and often spent them for materials or services that did not help educationally deprived children! It took several years for the Office of Education to tighten its regulations constraining local education agencies' allocation of Title I funds.[40] When it did this, the federal funds did go to aid disadvantaged children more than in other federally funded education programs.[41]

Title V of the Elementary and Secondary Education Act was designed to "strengthen" state departments of education and improve educational programs. But "strengthen" is an ambiguous term and the relationships between educational programs and improved performance is not well understood. Moreover, the law contained no objective criteria by which to judge projects and did not tell the state departments how they ought to change. Consequently, little change has taken place.[42]

The Department of Health, Education and Welfare (HEW) and one of its subdivisions, the U.S. Office of Education, also had problems implementing Title VI of the 1964 Civil Rights Act. (As of May 7, 1980, all of HEW's educational programs were transferred to the new cabinet-level Department of Education.) The 1964 Civil Rights Act, which prohibited the provision of federal funds to programs that discriminated against citizens on the basis of race, color, or national origin, did not have a clear legislative history to provide explicit direction for administrators. Neither did the White House give implementors much help. HEW's guidelines regarding funding for school districts were considered insufficient at the Office of Education, which developed its own directives. Moreover, HEW did little to develop information programs to help communities understand federal policies.

Often the dissemination of information that occurred was the result of activities by the U.S. Commission on Civil Rights or private groups — institutions without program implementation responsibilities. Understandably, school officials in the South were uncertain about the procedures by which their compliance with Title VI would be reviewed. They were not alone in their confusion. Even Office of Education staff members were unable to use their agency's guidelines to evaluate compliance efforts.[43] When HEW finally developed specific administrative standards for determining compliance with the law, progress on school desegregation accelerated. The more precise were desegregation guidelines, the more desegregation took place.[44]

In 1966 Congress passed the Demonstration Cities and Metropolitan Development Act. The purpose of the Model Cities program, as the act came to be known, was to help revitalize America's urban areas. The act called for innovation, coordination, and citizen participation, but these vague terms were not clearly defined. Officials at the Department of Housing and Urban Development (HUD) who had to implement the law were uncertain what their goals should be. Furthermore, Congress showed little interest in the specifics of future guidelines when it passed the policy, and it did not follow up on the program carefully once it was under way.

Like the legislative branch, the executive branch paid little attention to the process of developing guidelines for the Model Cities program. The White House was more interested in which cities were selected for participation and in trying to obtain the cooperation of other departments whose support the new policy required. Under these conditions, it is no wonder that the guidelines sent from HUD's central office to regional officials were vague and often increased rather than reduced confusion at the local level.[45]

Let us examine the requirement that there be citizen participation in Model Cities projects. As two authors concluded, "It was one thing for HUD to insist upon an 'organizational structure' for participation, but quite another to decide what kind of structure met the intent of the guidelines."[46] Did HUD expect cities to establish separate citizen boards? If so, what did "separate" mean? Was the citizen organization supposed to be subordinate or equal to the city government? If cities had a veto power over Community Development Agency (CDA) actions, did this include the comprehensive plan as a whole, individual projects, specific decisions within the projects, or all, some, or none of these?

Lower level officials faced similar problems in interpreting the national policy directive that citizen representatives be "acceptable" to residents of the model neighborhood. They were not told how to evaluate the "acceptability" of citizen leaders chosen by elections in which a turnout of more than 20 percent of the eligible voters was unusual. Nor did their instructions include information on what election techniques, such as mass meetings, literature, and television announcements, should be required to promote acceptability. They also faced, without higher level guidance, the question of what electoral units within a neighborhood were legitimate if various ethnic, racial, religious, and other interests were to feel represented adequately on the citizen boards.

The central office of HUD had endorsed the principle that citizens were to have staff and technical assistance made available to them, but the application of this guideline was not easy. It was not clear who might make legitimate claims on the staff's time or to whom the staff was directly accountable. How large should the staff be? What should its members be paid? Who should control the hiring of the staff? How should the staff be deployed? Should the citizen staff consult and share information with the CDA staff? Could the CDA head use the citizen staff? The unanswered questions were numerous. It is worth noting that Model Cities was relatively *precise* for an urban program.[47]

The provisions of the 1972 Water Pollution Control Act Amendments were very detailed, but the law still left room for considerable elaboration through administrative rulings and regulations. Federal officials in the Environmental Protection Agency (EPA) had substantial leeway in its implementation as they defined such phrases as "best practicable control technology currently available" and the "best available technology economically achievable" for controlling water pollution.[48]

A key aspect of the legislative intent of the act was set forth in Section 208, which contained detailed provisions regarding planning water pollution control. A subsection of Section 303 provided for a continuous planning process and required states to submit plans for this process. Congress was less interested in Section 303 than in Section 208, and the EPA was told to give Section 303 secondary priority. Nevertheless, the EPA made this subsection "the keystone of their entire water management and planning strategy." This originally obscure clause, according to one authority, became the primary tool for the implementation of the act. Moreover, EPA's interpretation of the clause expanded the authority the subsection originally delegated to the agency. Conversely, the implementation of Section 208 was delayed as long as possible by the EPA, despite Congress' great interest in its being rapidly and effectively implemented.[49]

The EPA's implementation of state program grants also resulted in a considerable change from the intent of Congress. It tried, in effect, to change one categorical grant program into four or five and thus give Washington maximum flexibility to reallocate funds where it felt the need was greatest. It did this by adding criteria that state programs must meet in order to receive grants, criteria that were not included in the act.[50]

This is not the only example of implementing agencies finding leeway in legislation designed to protect the environment. Following passage of the National Environmental Policy Act in 1969, the Army Corps of Engineers ordered its officials to prepare environmental impact statements for all its projects. The Soil Conservation Service (SCS) in the Department of Agriculture, interpreting the same law, mandated that environmental impact statements be prepared only for all *pending* projects. The Corps followed the law's intention to involve the public in a two-way communication on its projects. The SCS only instituted a one-way public information program and consulted with interested parties to a lesser degree. The Corps also took a much speedier and more aggressive role in demanding balanced environmental impact statements and providing detailed guidelines for their preparation. In short, the Army Corps of Engineers and the Soil Conservation Service interpreted the law differently. The Army Corps of Engineers saw the National Environmental Policy Act as a new mandate. The Corps' decisions and decisionmaking procedures reflected this mandate. The Soil Conservation Service, at least for four years, misinterpreted the same law as a reiteration of is existing policies and procedures. The SCS thus saw little need for change.[51]

While the two agencies interpreted the new law differently in the ways mentioned above, their leaders also shared certain interpretations — incorrect ones — and communicated these to their subordinates. Both centered their attention on environmental impact statements and disregarded, for the most part, other provisions of the law. Although those who wrote the law intended to emphasize policy goals, the agencies that implemented the act were preoccupied with its procedural requirements. The Corps and the Soil Conservation Service failed to develop guidelines concerning the achievement of such goals as stewardship for future generations, achieving the widest possible range of beneficial uses of the environment without degradation, maximizing the recycling of depletable resources, enhancing the quality of renewable resources, preserving diversity and the national heritage, and achieving balance between population and resource use.[52]

We should not be overly critical of these two agencies. The language of the act was vague, providing little direction on how to strike a balance between environmental goals and "other essential considerations of national policy." The act did not specify the "appropriate weight" to be given environmental impacts in reaching decisions. Similarly, the act did not specify the number or types of alternatives to the typical projects that were to be considered.[53]

Unanticipated Change. Lack of clarity in policy may not only inhibit intended change; it also may lead to substantial unanticipated change. From 1962 through 1972 the Social Security Act provided open-ended grants-in-aid to the states for social services. However, neither the law nor the Department of Health, Education and Welfare, which administered the program, clearly defined "services." This imprecision became the basis for an unintended rapid growth in the funds expended for the program as states asked for larger and larger grants. Moreover, the states used most of the money to pay for services they already provided. The act turned out to be fiscal relief for the states, contrary to the intentions of both Congress and the president.[54]

It is difficult to enforce administrative controls without legislative underpinnings. The vague language of the act did not allow or encourage HEW or its regional offices to take firm stands against state abuses. The vagueness of the act also made administrators more vulnerable to political pressure from state officials for more funds for more uses.[55] Thus, there are times when officials may desire *less* discretion as they implement policy in order to provide themselves some protection in battles with special interests.[56]

Vague goals may lead officials to lose sight of the purpose of their implementation activity. In the words of Elliot Richardson, who has held several high federal executive positions:

> All too often uncertainty about objectives leads to a trap that might be called management by activity. This is a euphoric state of mind which equates more with better, which suggests that, as doing good things produces good results, doing twice as many good things will quite obviously produce twice as many good results. In other words, if you don't know where you're going, run faster.[57]

True Intentions. The potential for implementors to misunderstand their orders is great when they try to follow the "true" intentions of their superiors. According to former CIA Director William Colby, some people in the CIA took high-level "expressions of official hostility

... as a suggestion, consent or even authority to mount operations aimed at assassinating Castro. . . . The ambiguity with which covert policy vis-à-vis Castro was stated in this period led to vigorous efforts to achieve what the policymakers were *thought* to have meant. [emphasis added]"[58]

During his tenure as CIA director, Richard Helms ordered the agency to turn its attention from the domestic antiwar movement to international terrorism, but this directive was misinterpreted by a few in the CIA to be a cover story for continued domestic action. As William Colby has written, "The habits and language of clandestinity can intoxicate even its own practitioners." For this reason, internal directives must be "crystal-clear and thorough, especially when the secrecy of the operation prohibits external oversight."[59]

Reducing Discretion

There are times, of course, when the guidelines legislatures provide to administrators are clear. A prime example of this is Social Security, a program in which eligibility requirements, size of benefit levels, and other considerations are precisely established. This provides a minimum of discretion to administrators. On the whole, their decisions are consistent and predictable. Satisfaction with the administration of Social Security is generally quite high.

The Voting Rights Act of 1965 reduced the discretion of local voting registrars by limiting the use of literacy tests or similar voter qualification devices. In some cases the administration of voting registration was physically taken over by federal officials so that local officials could not inhibit voter registration. Another example of limiting implementors' discretion occurred in early 1973 when the Nixon administration issued new rules that restricted the way funds could be expended to aid the poor through social services. Funds could be used only for persons with specifically defined conditions of need and then only under a system of detailed accounting of the services provided. This was an attempt by the Nixon administration to restrict the options available to social workers.[60]

In response to the independent actions of U.S. attorneys around the country, the Justice Department produced a *U.S. Attorneys Manual* requiring advance approval for certain actions and allocating certain cases to the department itself. Specific forms and reports were also required, and many policies were outlined. Moreover, the manual established special department strike forces on crime, thereby removing various types of cases from the jurisdictions of some U.S. attorneys.[61]

Innovations in procedures are not always successful in constraining implementors. The National Environmental Policy Act requires agencies to produce environmental impact statements on their programs

and to take environmental concerns into consideration in their implementation decisions. Yet, as we have seen earlier, there is evidence
that these statements have had limited impact on projects. In the
case of the Army Corps of Engineers, the requirement to consider
environmental concerns actually freed it somewhat from the tough
and quantifiable criteria applied to projects by the Office of Management and Budget and allowed it to support projects in which the
economic costs exceeded the benefits, but in which the environmental
benefits, according to the Corps' calculations, made up the difference.[62]

It is generally easier to reduce the discretion of officials with orders
to stop doing something than to start doing something. For example,
an absolute ban on providing funds for abortions for poor women is
more likely to be unambiguous and more likely to be noticed if it
is violated than an order to begin implementing a new policy. The
implementation of most policies, however, requires positive actions
— not prohibitions. Moreover, usually a series of positive actions
extending over a long period of time and involving the technical expertise of numerous persons throughout a bureaucratic hierarchy is necessary to implement a policy. The complexity of such policymaking
makes it very difficult to communicate and enforce rules that effectively
reduce the discretion available to most policy implementors.

Ambiguous Court Decisions

Court decisions are often vague. The typical Supreme Court decision, for example, ends with instructions to a lower court to reconsider
its original decision in light of the more general decision of the Court.
Sometimes the party that wins in the Supreme Court eventually loses
in the subsequent lower court decision.[63]

The substance of court decisions may also be vague. In 1972 the
Supreme Court declared in *Furman v. Georgia* that "the imposition
and carrying out of the death penalty in these cases [the cases before
the Court at that time] constitute cruel and unusual punishment in
violation of the Eighth and Fourteenth Amendments."[64] Unfortunately,
the Court did not explain the rationale behind its decision. Legislators
were not given much guidance in rewriting statutes so that they would
be constitutionally acceptable. Nevertheless, most of the states and
Congress rewrote their capital punishment laws in the hope of satisfying
the Court. More than half of these states, however, had their new
statutes declared unconstitutional by the Court in *Gregg v. Georgia*
and *Woodson v. North Carolina* in 1976.[65] They had guessed incorrectly
in their attempts to implement the Supreme Court's decision.

In the famous *Brown v. Board of Education* case in 1954, the
Supreme Court declared segregation in public schools to be unconsti-

tutional. The next year the Court heard arguments on how to implement its decision. It decided that integration should take place "with all deliberate speed."[66] This was hardly a clear statement to the lower courts who were to implement the *Brown* decision. Considering the lack of specificity in the language, it is not surprising that little in the way of integration in the deep South occurred for the next decade. Fourteen years after the implementation decision in *Brown*, the Supreme Court finally abandoned the "all deliberate speed" formula and ordered the immediate end to all remaining dual school systems in *Alexander v. Holmes County Board of Education.*[67]

One of the Warren Court's earliest and most controversial decisions on the rights of suspected criminals was the *Escobedo* case.[68] It dealt with confessions and was unclear regarding the extent to which the Court had altered the existing rules on the admissibility of confessions and on the Court's ultimate goals in that area. Therefore, state supreme courts responded to the decision in a generally conservative manner (variously limiting the decision, criticizing the Court, and asserting that the criterion of voluntariness — which the Court had rejected — was still a major, viable test for the admissibility of confessions). Then came the *Miranda* decision in 1966.[69] It was straightforward and clear enough to have its requirements transcribed on cards that police officers could carry and read verbatim to suspects. State supreme court reactions to this more far-reaching case were more liberal than to *Escobedo*, negative responses centering on peripheral issues and the decision's extension to other areas.[70] *Miranda*, it should be noted, was an unusually clear decision.

Ambiguous or qualifying phrases in a court's decision may also hinder its clear communication. Justice Tom Clark wrote the majority opinion in *Mapp v. Ohio*, a 1961 decision that set forth the constitutional rules for legal searches and seizures by state law enforcement officials. Clark authored such ambiguous phrases as, "There is no war between the Constitution and common sense."[71] This statement was sometimes used by lower court judges to justify narrow interpretations of the decision. Clark's statement that "state procedural requirements governing assertion and pursuance of direct and collateral constitutional challenges to criminal prosecutions must be respected" led to the frequent denial by state judges of poorly timed or poorly phrased motions by defendants' attorneys to exclude illegally obtained evidence.[72]

Value of Flexibility

Vague policy decisions hinder effective implementation, but directives that are too specific may also adversely affect implementation. Implementors sometimes need the freedom to adapt policies to suit the situation at hand. The Rand Change Agent Study, an extensive evaluation of innovations in education, including many dealing with classroom organization, underscored the importance of adaptation in the implementation process:

> Because classroom organization projects require teachers to work out their own styles and classroom techniques within a broad philosophical framework, innovations of this type cannot be fully specified or packaged in advance. Thus, the very nature of these projects requires that implementation be a *mutually adaptive process.* Specific project goals and methods must be made concrete by the users themselves as they acquire the skills appropriate to the innovation.[73]

All of the successfully implemented projects the Rand team studied, even fairly straightforward technical projects, underwent mutual adaptation to some extent. Specifics evolved over time as modifications were made in the project designs and in the personnel and institutional settings of the implementors. The Rand researchers suggest that adaptation rather than standardization is the most realistic and fruitful objective for policymakers.[74] Similarly, in a study of federal education programs in six states, the authors concluded that "federal administrative practices which use one set of regulations to cover a variety of state practices are doomed, and . . . more flexible approaches are needed."[75]

One scholar has described the effective development of the Polaris missile system as one of "disciplined flexibility." This technique of implementation in the field of weapons development is not unlike mutual adaptation in the classroom. The technique is disciplined because of the physical constraints of submarines and the determination to meet accelerated deployment schedules. Flexibility is needed to avoid premature commitment to any particular performance goals. Guidelines evolved as the project's implementors proceeded through each step of the missile development process.[76]

A myriad of specific regulations can overwhelm and confuse personnel in the field and may make them reluctant to act for fear of breaking the rules. Strict guidelines may also induce a type of goal displacement in which lower level officials become more concerned with meeting specific requirements than with achieving the basic goals of the program. By rigidly adhering to the letter of a regulation, they may become so bogged down in red tape that the purpose of the rule is forgotten or defeated. Conversely, implementors sometimes ignore rigid legislative decisions. The Economic Development Administration, for example, attempted to circumvent at the regional level its own restrictions on making loans and formulated new and unsystematic criteria in Washington *after* it saw the applications for loans.[77]

At this point the already highly complex process of policy implementation becomes even more confusing. The choice of whether to guide implementors as much as possible or to build flexibility and adaptation into implementation is a difficult one to make. The evidence is mixed. The Rand researchers concluded that implementation directives should not be too specific, but other scholars have found that the lack of clarity surrounding innovations in education is a principal cause of implementation problems.[78]

While vague decisions can leave implementors confused or allow them to exercise their discretion contrary to the intent of a policy, highly specific language can make it more difficult for officials in the field to adapt programs to the particular needs of states or localities. Decisionmakers must consider each implementation situation individually and be sensitive to the issues raised above.

Reasons for Lack of Clarity

Complexity of Policymaking. The lack of clarity in many implementation orders can be attributed to several factors. Perhaps the most important is the sheer complexity of policymaking. Neither executives nor legislators have the time or expertise to develop and apply all the requisite details for implementing policy. They have to leave most (and sometimes all) of the details to subordinates. Former HEW Secretary Joseph Califano writes that when he was President Johnson's chief domestic policy aide he was unable to meet, consult, or guide more than one-third of the noncabinet agency and commission heads. Johnson saw even fewer.[79]

Police administrators often do not provide detailed policy guidelines on important matters to police officers. When should an officer intervene in a serious family dispute? When should firearms be used? Very little helpful direction is given to officers who must answer these questions. Although the inappropriate use of firearms by the police has been a cause of substantial conflict between citizens and the police in recent years, many police departments lack professional expertise and issue only very general statements, such as the following, to guide the discretion of police officers: "Firearms shall be used only in extreme cases, and in a manner consistent with the provisions of the state penal law." A police department relying upon such a vague guideline, unlike large departments that have supplemented state penal codes with detailed rules regarding the use of firearms, will be unlikely to have much success in controlling the exercise of officers' discretion.[80]

The federal government, like a local police department, has difficulty issuing specific, helpful directives. Regarding the community action programs of the war on poverty in the mid-1960s, one authority has written, "The Government did not know what it was doing. It had a theory. Or, rather, a set of theories. Nothing more."[81] According to former Secretary Califano, "the basis of recommendations by an American cabinet officer . . . nearly resembles the intuitive judgment of a benevolent tribal chief in remote Africa."[82]

Implementation of Title I of the pathbreaking Elementary and Secondary Education Act of 1965 relied heavily upon "intuitive judgment." As one author has written, "No one really knew how to run a successful compensatory educational program."[83] Therefore, local school districts received little guidance on how to spend their funds. Likewise, Project Head Start was "undertaken with a hunch and a prayer" and local officials could proceed with their own ideas with little central guidance.[84]

Public Opposition. The desire to avoid alienating politically influential groups in the public may cause vague implementation directives. In "victimless crimes" — crimes in which there is no complainant, such as gambling, prostitution, and illegal drug use — the potential for policy discretion in arresting violators is greater than in other types of crimes. The police do not always enforce these laws strictly, and many people feel that police discretion is exercised arbitrarily, with some offenders punished and others left alone. Although the lack of both public support and police resources makes discretion in the enforcement of laws against victimless crimes inevitable, police executives are reluctant to issue directives to officers specifying the circumstances under which the laws will and will not be enforced.[85] Such rules could create obvious political problems for them. Thus, police on the beat are left on their own to make these important decisions about the use of the coercive power of government, and the implementation of these laws is widely criticized as unjust.[86]

Competing Goals and the Need for Consensus. Another cause of vagueness in implementation directives is the difficulty decisionmakers have in reaching a consensus on goals. As we discussed earlier, for a decade the federal government provided funds to states for social services without defining what "services" meant. The states used the money for many purposes never intended by the president and Congress, and the program expanded way beyond all the expectations of the federal government as a result. The vagueness of the law was due in part to conflict within HEW between the Bureau of Family Services and other agencies, especially the Children's Bureau and the Office of Vocational Rehabilitation, over what constituted "services." Rather than alienate an agency, HEW chose to leave the term vaguely defined. In addition, members of Congress had conflicting intentions. The notion of funding services (rather than direct grants to individuals) appealed to conservatives as a method of saving money and decreasing dependency while it appealed to liberals as a way to help the poor and serve good purposes.[87]

The lack of clear policy goals is very common in America and occurs in all types of policies at all levels of government — from effluent limitations to block grants for community development, from the West Side Highway in New York City to the war in Vietnam, and from federal support for higher education to evaluation requirements for elementary and secondary education programs.[88]

In the United States we share wide agreement on the goals of avoidance of war, equal opportunity, and efficiency in government, but this consensus often dissolves when specific policy alternatives are under consideration. Disagreement over precise goals is inevitable in a large and diverse country in which people have different views of what government ought to do (such as the extent of its regulation of the economy), of what government can accomplish (such as the degree to which laws can alter racist behavior), and even of whether there is a problem in society that calls for any action at all (such as the use of saccharin or fluorocarbons in aerosol sprays). Just think of the different goals that might be attributed to a policy to increase spending for education: improving character and moral values; changing the social structure by fostering mobility; freeing parents for work; developing greater student knowledge and skills; increasing staff and student productivity; equalizing opportunity for learning and livelihood; creating jobs for minority teachers; building healthier bodies through improved physical education facilities; producing a winning football team to boost school or civic pride; integrating public schools; and many more.[89]

Lyndon Johnson once said, "If the full implications of any bill were known before its enactment, it would never get passed."[90] Clearly, imprecise decisions make it easier for policymakers to develop and maintain winning decisional coalitions. Different people or groups can support the same policy for different reasons. Each may hold its own conception of the goal or goals the program is designed to achieve. Ambiguous goals also may make it less threatening for groups to be on the losing side of a policy conflict, and this may reduce the intensity of their opposition.

When it is difficult to agree on goals, policymakers often seek general improvements, having a better notion of what they want to escape than what they want to achieve. In the words of David Braybrooke and Charles Lindblom:

> Policy aims at suppressing vice even though virtue cannot be defined, let alone concretized as a goal; at attending to mental illness even though we are not sure what attitudes and behavior are most healthy; at curbing the expansion of the Soviet Union even though we do not know what positive foreign policy objectives to set against the Kremlin's; at reducing the governmental inefficiencies even though

we do not know what maximum level of competence we can reasonably expect; at eliminating inequities in the tax structure even though we do not agree on equity; at destroying slums even though we are uncertain about the kinds of homes and neighborhoods in which their occupants should live.[91]

As we have seen, the de-emphasis on goals serves useful purposes for policymakers interested in enacting policies into law. Another consequence of vague goals, however, is the lack of clarity in policies. Thus, while vague goals may make it easier to pass laws, they increase the chances of slippage in implementing them.

Unfamiliarity of New Programs. The problems of starting up a new program may produce confusion in implementation instructions. Often the passage of a new policy is followed by a period of administrative uncertainty in which there is a considerable time lag before any information on the program is disseminated. This period is followed by a second one in which rules are made, but are then changed quickly as high-level officials attempt to deal with the unforeseen problems of implementing the policy and of their own earlier directives. Such was the case as the U.S. Office of Education attempted to implement the many new education programs passed in the 1960s.[92]

Avoiding Accountability. A cynical yet realistic explanation for lack of clarity in federal statutes is that Congress does not want them to be detailed. Congress would rather let executive branch agencies provide the specifics, not because of the latter's expertise, but in order to let the agencies take the blame for the rules that turn out to be unworkable or unpopular.

Title IX of the Education Act Amendments of 1972 stated that "no person in the United States shall, on the basis of sex, be excluded from participation in, be denied the benefits of, or be subject to discrimination under any education program or activity receiving Federal financial assistance." Such broad language allowed Congress to sidestep many touchy questions and leave their resolution to the Department of Health, Education and Welfare. Moreover, individual members of Congress can gain credit with their constituents by intervening on their behalf regarding the application of regulations. In addition, if goals are not precise, Congress cannot be held accountable for the failure of its policies to achieve them.[93]

Nature of Court Decisions. Court decisions may be vague due to the necessity of compromising in a multimember appellate court to reach a majority opinion.[94] In the *Brown* decision, for example, compromise was essential in reaching a unanimous majority opinion which the justices felt was very important.[95] Or a court may be able to reach agreement on a decision in a case but not on the rationale for the decision. In both the 1972 and 1976 death penalty cases, policymakers left implementors few guidelines to follow.

Dissenting opinions or those concurring in the majority's decision — but for different reasons — may help to clarify just what has and has not been decided, but they may also lead to confusion. A dissent, for example, may indicate that the new principle supported by the majority has not won universal acceptance. Such an opinion is especially likely to be influential in cases that have been decided by close votes and which therefore may be seen by others as ripe for reversing if the personnel on the court changes.

Courts seldom try to anticipate problems implementors may have in understanding their decisions. They usually decide only the issues directly presented to them in the case at hand, and they generally construct their opinions as narrowly as possible. Ready to defer to the executive and legislative branches of government, the courts decide cases if possible on statutory rather than on constitutional grounds. Few decisions interpret broadly the sweeping phrases of the Constitution. The narrow decisions of the courts may fail to overturn or differentiate precedents that seem to contradict their decisions. Thus, while decisions may be clear on one level, guidance for their applications may be largely absent. For example, the *Mapp* decision:

> ... did not tell the state courts to whom or under what circumstances the Fourth Amendment was applicable to them. It shed no light on such closely related questions as what constitutes probable cause to arrest or to search without a warrant or to grant an application for a warrant; nor did it say what was a reasonable search incident to arrest or as part of executing a search warrant. ... By rejecting the option of imposing pre-existing federal rules on the states, but nonetheless insisting on one 'standard of reasonableness,' the Court was certainly promoting a period of ambiguity and uncertainty.[96]

Lacking any mechanism to initiate cases, the courts must wait for cases to come to them if they wish to clarify their decisions. Because the U.S. Supreme Court hears only a relatively few cases each year, it may take years for it to decide cases that fill in the gaps left by previous decisions. Despite the fact that some of its decisions have not achieved broad compliance and thus might benefit from re-enforcement and elaboration in follow-up cases, the Supreme Court has often exercised its almost total discretion over its docket and chosen not to hear such cases. It heard very few school desegregation cases after *Brown*, for example, although the decision was widely defied.

CONSISTENCY

Implementation orders must be consistent as well as clear if policy implementation is to be effective. Transmitting clear but contradictory instructions will hardly make it easier for operational personnel to expedite implementation. Nevertheless, implementors are at times burdened with inconsistent directives. In this section we illustrate this communication problem and show how it affects implementation. Then we examine explanations for inconsistent implementation instructions.

The Economic Development Administration was given instructions to help jobless persons in areas of high unemployment by attracting or expanding industries. At the same time it was not to subsidize with loans competitors for existing businesses. Partly due to this communication problem — at least in Oakland, the site of the Pressman-Wildavsky study — relatively few jobs were created.[97] Similarly, in 1962 defense officials were told to remove U.S. missiles from Turkey *and* to preserve and strengthen NATO. Their orders implied they were not to irritate Turkey. Turkey wanted the missiles to remain.[98] Thus, despite President Kennedy's several orders to have them removed, the missiles were still in place on the Soviet Union's border during the Cuban missile crisis. This was embarrassing for the president, who opposed the presence of Soviet missiles so close to the U.S. mainland.

Inconsistency in implementation orders may provide operating agencies with substantial discretion in the interpretation and implementation of policy, discretion which may not be exercised to carry out a policy's goals. Environmental policy during the Nixon administration is an example. The president made a rhetorical commitment to supporting the National Environmental Policy Act (NEPA), but in practice his policy priorities were not significantly tied to environmental impacts. Similarly, the Office of Management and Budget, the president's principal tool for controlling the federal bureaucracy, did not treat environmental policy goals as a major consideration in the evaluation of the activities of all federal agencies as NEPA intended. Federal officials received inconsistent signals concerning the importance of environmental policy and were left to resolve the question largely on their own.[99]

Lower level government jurisdictions may be confused by inconsistency at a higher level. Title IV of the Elementary and Secondary Education Act was supposed to consolidate several programs into one, more effectively managed program. Although Congress consolidated seven categorical aid programs under Title IV, it created seven new categorical programs and added a second unit to the Office of Education. This made it difficult for federal officials to administer Title IV in a consolidated fashion, and it provided inconsistent signals to the states. No wonder they did not view Title IV as a coherent program and made little effort to coordinate the relevant programs at their level.[100]

Sometimes the inconsistency and vagueness of orders increases as directives multiply throughout different branches and levels of government. The implementation of the Comprehensive Employment and Training Act (CETA) is a case in point. The members of Congress and their staffs who were most knowledgeable and concerned about CETA gave the Department of Labor conflicting guidelines. The department received inconsistent directives and consequently its own standards were more and more inconsistent as they were communicated to the regional offices and local project sponsors. The communications from the regional offices to the local offices were soon no clearer than those issued from the departmental headquarters in Washington.[101]

Many of the factors that produce unclear communications are also responsible for inconsistent directives. The complexity of public policies, the difficulties in starting up new programs, and the multiple objectives of many policies all contribute to inconsistency in policy communications. Another reason that decisions are often inconsistent is that they are influenced by interested parties on both sides of an issue.

A number of interest groups were formed specifically to represent local CETA programs and urge a passive federal role in local manpower projects. Exerting pressure on the Department of Labor in support of these ad hoc groups were local government interest groups, including the U.S. Conference of Mayors, the National League of Cities, the National Association of Counties, and the National Governors' Conference. In favor of a stronger role for the Department of Labor were liberals in Congress, the AFL-CIO, government employee unions, the National Urban League, the Opportunities Industrialization Centers, and other community-based organizations.[102] Any attempts to please all these groups could only lead to inconsistency, and such attempts are endemic in an open and decentralized government such as ours.

The desire of some policymakers to appear consistent when really making a policy change may produce inconsistent communications to implementors. This occurs, for example, when an appellate court issues an opinion or series of opinions that are seemingly contrary to precedent but, as is usually the case, do not specifically overrule previous decisions or clearly establish a new policy. In such situations lower courts are faced with the task of making their decisions on the basis of the established precedent or what appears to be the trend of recent decisions. When guidelines are inconsistent, a judge may have to guess the proper direction in which to move.

During the 1930s and 1940s the Supreme Court wanted to toughen its stand against the liberal patent policies of the U.S. Patent Office, and it wanted to convey this message to the Patent Office and lower courts. At the same time, it wanted to say it was following precedent.

Therefore, the Court tried to convey its change in policy through the tone of its decisions while technically maintaining doctrinal continuity with its previous decisions. The inconsistency inherent in such an approach, however, allowed the Patent Office and some lower courts to follow the thrust of the old decisions rather than the new ones.[103]

CONCLUSION

Having examined in detail the relationship between communications and implementation, what generalizations can we reach? First, the more accurately policy decisions and implementation orders are transmitted to those who must carry them out, the higher the probability of their being implemented. Transmission lapses are prime causes of implementation failures.

How can we explain communication blockage and distortion? If those involved in the various stages of the implementation process agree with a policy, they are more likely to transmit communications about it accurately. High-level policymakers must rely upon others to transmit and carry out their decisions and orders. If a policy is at odds with implementors' preferences, they may use their discretion to ignore or distort it. The exercise of this discretion, however, can save officials from foolish decisions made in anger and without proper contemplation.

Implementation instructions are more likely to be transmitted accurately if a relatively small and cohesive group of people is responsible for implementation. The more persons who must be reached with communications, the greater the chances of missing some of them; and the more layers of bureaucracy through which communications must travel, the higher the probability of distortion. Policies that must be implemented by the private sector are especially susceptible to these problems.

When communications about policy implementation are direct, they may be transmitted accurately. On the other hand, when officials desiring anonymity to serve political or personal ends use indirect means of communicating with implementors, such as third parties and press leaks, the probability of distortion is significantly increased.

The better developed the channels of communication for transmitting implementation instructions, the higher the probability of these instructions being transmitted correctly. But well-developed channels of communication do not always exist. The executive branch faces this problem, but the judiciary is especially prone to it. The independence of courts from each other and the lack of any substantial judicial bureaucracy forces judges to rely upon those outside the judiciary to communicate their decisions. Policies implemented by private individuals also have a greater chance of transmission failure because of the absence of communication channels from public officials to them.

Transmission problems arise from the receiving end of communications as well as the sending end. The more a policy activates in those who are to implement it selective perception and a disinclination to know about the policy and its implications, the higher the probability it will not be perceived accurately. These subtle cognitive processes interfere with transmission. So do bureaucratic politics, as subordinates try to guess the "real" intentions behind a communication.

Implementation instructions that do not specify the goals of a policy and how to achieve them are common. If communications (including judicial decisions) are not clear, implementors will have more discretion to exercise in interpreting policy requirements. This discretion will not necessarily be used to further the aims of those who originally decided upon the policy. In some cases implementors simply do not understand a policy's goals or operational requirements; in others they make a conscious effort to exploit the ambiguity in communications to further their own policies or agency or personal interests.

Lack of clarity may lead to substantial unanticipated policy change as ambiguities are exploited to serve special interests in both the public and private sectors. Unanticipated change can also be caused by "management by activity," as implementors work harder to produce results to compensate for uncertainty about their objectives. Ambiguity also provides an environment in which implementors can easily misinterpret the "true" intentions behind superiors' communications, sometimes at the expense of the general thrust of a policy. This may be especially likely to arise in intelligence services where obscure communications are common.

Sometimes efforts *are* made to remove discretion from implementors by stating explicit eligibility requirements for benefits, eliminating options, carefully outlining procedures, and requiring detailed accounting of actions. Although it is generally easier to be clear about stopping certain behavior, most implementation requires complex, positive actions. Moreover, explicit procedures may only open up new loopholes for implementors to exploit.

Vague directives result in communication problems, but very specific implementation communications may overwhelm implementors with detail, leading to goal displacement, rigidity, or circumvention of regulations. Decisionmakers face the difficult task of issuing implementation instructions that are neither too detailed nor too vague. Educational innovations or weapons systems development, policies that require implementors to adapt novel policies to unanticipated circumstances, are perhaps especially in need of leeway in their implementation.

There are several reasons for the lack of clarity in many implementation communications. Public policy is generally complex and demands substantial time and expertise on the part of those who issue directives to implement it. Since most top decisionmakers have neither, they typically make general decisions and leave it to subordinates to fill in the blanks.

Other factors constrain top officials from sending clear implementation communications. Sometimes they desire to avoid antagonizing groups in the public who would rally in opposition to specific regulations or guidelines with which they disagree. More generally, some officials, especially legislators, may wish to avoid accountability for their decisions. Thus, they may make vague policies, leaving it to officials in other branches to take the heat for applying the law.

Special problems arise in the implementation of far-reaching policies such as eliminating air pollution. At the beginning of such a program, no one may know how to accomplish it. Fewer guidelines are available than in more routine policies. For new programs in general, there is a high probability of unclear communications, as officials lead them through their growing pains. At other times a lack of professional knowledge or understanding of a policy area among top officials may limit the clarity of the directives they issue.

A fundamental cause of vague policy decisions is the lack of consensus that frequently exists about the goals of a policy. Policymakers often do not attempt to clarify goals. Specific goals make it difficult for them to build supportive coalitions from among diverse interests. Moreover, when decisions require the agreement of several persons of similar status or influence, as in legislatures and appellate courts, policies are more likely to be vague because of the frequent necessity for substantial compromise on specifics in order to arrive at a decision.

A problem especially likely to arise for the judiciary is the inability to initiate actions. Judicial decisions may remain unclear until others bring cases to the courts so judges can elaborate upon and clarify their previous decisions.

Related to but conceptually distinct from the clarity of communications is their consistency. When implementors receive inconsistent instructions, they will inevitably be unable to meet all the demands made upon them. They may be effectively immobilized, or they may choose between directives on the basis of what they prefer.

The explanations for inconsistent implementation communications are much the same as those for lack of clarity: the complexity of public policy, the problems of starting up new programs, and the multiple objectives of many policies. Inconsistency, like ambiguity, also results from a desire not to alienate interests, and the greater the number of competing interests that seek to influence a policy's implementation, the greater the chance of inconsistent implementation instructions. Finally, the more concerned decisionmakers are with overturning precedent, the higher the probability of their decisions appearing to be inconsistent as they attempt to change policy without seeming to do so.

NOTES

1. Haynes Johnson, *The Bay of Pigs* (New York: W. W. Norton & Co., 1964), pp. 68-69, 86, 224.
2. Joseph A. Califano, Jr., *A Presidential Nation* (New York: W. W. Norton & Co., 1975), pp. 44-45.
3. David Wise, *The Politics of Lying: Government Deception, Secrecy, and Power* (New York: Vintage Books, 1973), pp. 370-371.
4. William Safire, *Before the Fall: An Inside View of the Pre-Watergate White House* (New York: Doubleday & Co., 1975), pp. 112-113, 285-287, 353, 566-557; H. R. Haldeman, *The Ends of Power* (New York: Times Books, 1978), pp. 58-59, 111-112, 185-187; Raymond Price, *With Nixon* (New York: Viking Press, 1977), p. 29.
5. See, for example, George C. Edwards III and Ira Sharkansky, *The Policy Predicament: Making and Implementing Public Policy* (San Francisco: W. H. Freeman, 1978), chapter 5; Carl E. Van Horn, "Implementing CETA" (Paper delivered at the annual meeting of the Midwest Political Science Association, Chicago, Illinois, April-May 1976), p. 26.
6. Hugh Heclo, *A Government of Strangers* (Washington, D.C.: Brookings Institution, 1977), pp. 206-207; Robert R. Sullivan, "The Role of the Presidency in Shaping Lower Level Policy-Making Processes," *Polity* 3 (Winter 1970): 211-212; Victor A. Thompson, *Modern Organization* (New York: Alfred A. Knopf, 1961), pp. 138-139; and Frederic V. Malek, *Washington's Hidden Tragedy: The Failure to Make Government Work* (New York: Free Press, 1978), p. 98.
7. Fred I. Greenstein, "Presidential Activism Eisenhower Style: A Reassessment Based on Archival Evidence" (Paper delivered at the annual meeting of the Midwest Political Science Association, Chicago, Illinois, April 1979), p. 9.
8. William Colby, *Honorable Men: My Life in the CIA* (New York: Simon & Schuster, 1978), p. 374.
9. See, for example, Daniel Katz and Robert L. Kahn, *The Social Psychology of Organizations* (New York: John Wiley & Sons, 1966), pp. 236-238.
10. Alan H. Schechter, "Impacts of Open Housing Laws on Suburban Realtors," *Urban Affairs Quarterly* 8 (June 1973): 452.
11. Joel F. Handler, *Social Movements and the Legal System: A Theory of Law Reform and Social Change* (New York: Academic Press, 1978).
12. Califano, *A Presidential Nation,* p. 207.
13. Safire, *Before the Fall,* pp. 429-436.
14. Haldeman, *Ends of Power,* p. 56.

15. Safire, *Before the Fall*, pp. 619-620.
16. Ron Nessen, *It Sure Looks Different from the Inside* (New York: Playboy Press and Simon & Schuster, 1978), pp. 125-126.
17. See Michael Ban, "Local Courts vs. The Supreme Court: The Impact of *Mapp v. Ohio*" (Paper delivered at the annual meeting of the American Political Science Association, New Orleans, Louisiana, September 1973).
18. Stephen L. Wasby, *Small Town Police and the Supreme Court: Hearing the Word* (Lexington, Mass.: Lexington Books, 1976), p. 104; Thomas E. Barth, "Perception and Acceptance of Supreme Court Decisions at the State and Local Level," *Journal of Public Law* 17 (1968): 308-350.
19. Lawrence Baum, "Implementation of Judicial Decisions: An Organizational Analysis," *American Politics Quarterly* 4 (January 1976): 94-95.
20. Bradley C. Canon, "Organizational Contumacy in the Transmission of Judicial Policies: The *Mapp, Escobedo, Miranda,* and *Gault* Cases," *Villanova Law Review* 20 (November 1974): 50-79.
21. Wasby, *Small Town Police,* p. 35, footnote 43 (p. 239).
22. Ibid., pp. 37-39 and Chapter 5; Kenneth M. Dolbeare and Phillip E. Hammond, *The School Prayer Decisions* (Chicago: University of Chicago Press, 1971), p. 52.
23. President's Commission on Law Enforcement and the Administration of Justice, *Task Force Report: The Police* (Washington, D.C.: U.S. Government Printing Office, 1967), p. 33.
24. Wasby, *Small Town Police,* p. 50.
25. Ban, "Local Courts vs. The Supreme Court," p. 5.
26. Richard Johnson, *The Dynamics of Compliance* (Evanston, Ill.: Northwestern University Press, 1967), p. 95. See also Samuel Krislov, *The Supreme Court in the Political Process* (New York: Macmillan Co., 1965), p. 154.
27. See Neal A. Milner, *The Court and Local Law Enforcement: The Impact of Miranda* (Beverly Hills, Cal.: Sage Publications, 1971).
28. Johnson, *Dynamics of Compliance,* pp. 85, 87, 91; and Stephen L. Wasby, *The Impact of the United States Supreme Court: Some Perspectives* (Homewood, Ill.: Dorsey Press, 1970), pp. 90-92.
29. Milner, *The Court and Local Law Enforcement*; Wasby, *Small Town Police,* passim; Wayne R. LaFave, "Improving Police Performance through the Exclusionary Rule. Part II: Defining the Norms and Training the Police,"*Missouri Law Review* 30 (Fall 1965).
30. For research on press coverage of judicial decisions in the 1960s, see Chester A. Newland, "Press Coverage of the United States Supreme Court," *Western Political Quarterly* 17 (March 1964): 15-34; and David L. Grey, *The Supreme Court and the News Media* (Evanston, Ill.: Northwestern University Press, 1968).
31. Newton N. Minow, John T. Martin, and Lee M. Mitchell, *Presidential Television* (New York: Basic Books, 1973), pp. 94-96.
32. Stephen L. Wasby, "Public Law, Politics, and the Local Courts," *Journal of Public Law* 14 (Spring 1965): 105-130.
33. Dolbeare and Hammond, *School Prayer Decisions,* pp. 75, 90-92, 126.
34. Wasby, *Small Town Police.*
35. Milner, *Court and Local Law Enforcement.*
36. Dolbeare and Hammond, *School Prayer Decisions,* pp. 52, 75, 78, 79 and 83.
37. Heclo, *Government of Strangers,* pp. 206-207.
38. Milbrey W. McLaughlin, "Implementation as Mutual Adaptation: Change in Classroom Organization," in *Social Program Implementation,* eds. Wal-

ter Williams and Richard F. Elmore (New York: Academic Press, 1976), p. 170.

39. Daniel P. Moynihan, *Maximum Feasible Misunderstanding* (New York: Free Press, 1969), p. 87. See also John C. Donovan, *The Politics of Poverty*, 2d ed. (Indianapolis: The Bobbs-Merrill Co., 1973), p. 40; and James L. Sundquist, ed., *On Fighting Poverty* (New York: Basic Books, 1969), p. 29.

40. Floyd E. Stoner, "Federal Auditors as Regulators: The Case of Title I of ESEA," in *The Policy Cycle*, eds. Judith V. May and Aaron B. Wildavsky (Beverly Hills, Calif.: Sage Publications, 1978), pp. 202-204, 206, 208; Stoner, "Implementation of Federal Education Policy: Defining the Situation in Cities and Small Towns" (Paper delivered at the annual meeting of the Midwest Political Science Association, Chicago, Illinois, May 1975), pp. 8-9; Stephen K. Bailey and Edith K. Mosher, *ESEA: The Office of Education Administers a Law* (Syracuse, N.Y.: Syracuse University Press, 1968), p. 103; John F. Hughes and Anne O. Hughes, *Equal Education* (Bloomington, Ind.: Indiana University Press, 1972), pp. 33, 47, 50; and Milbrey W. McLaughlin, *Evaluation and Reform: The Elementary and Secondary Education Act of 1976/Title I* (Cambridge, Mass.: Ballinger Publishing Co., 1975), p. 18.

41. Joel S. Berke and Michael W. Kirst, "Intergovernmental Relations: Conclusions and Recommendations," in *Federal Aid to Education: Who Benefits? Who Governs?*, eds. Joel S. Berke and Michael W. Kirst (Lexington, Mass.: Lexington, 1972), p. 401. For other examples of USOE guidelines confusing state and local education agencies, see p. 378.

42. Jerome T. Murphy, *State Education Agencies and Discretionary Funds* (Lexington, Mass.: D.C. Heath & Co., 1971), pp. 8, 21-22, 25.

43. Beryl A. Radin, *Implementation, Change, and the Federal Bureaucracy* (New York: Teachers' College Press, 1977), pp. 92, 103-105, 108-109, 134, 160-161.

44. Harrell R. Rodgers, Jr. and Charles S. Bullock III, *Law and Social Change: Civil Rights Laws and Their Consequences* (New York: McGraw-Hill Book Co., 1972), p. 199. See also Charles S. Bullock III, "The Office for Civil Rights and Implementation of Desegregation Programs in Public Schools," *Policy Studies Journal* 8 (Special Issue No. 2, 1980): 606-607.

45. Lawrence D. Brown and Bernard J. Frieden, "Guidelines and Goals in the Model Cities Program," *Policy Sciences* 7 (December 1976): 459-461, 470, 487. See also Judson L. James, "Federalism and the Model Cities Experiment," *Publius* 2 (Spring 1972): 69-94.

46. Brown and Frieden, "Guidelines and Goals," pp. 470-471.

47. Ibid. See also Rufus P. Browning, Dale Rodgers Marshall, and David H. Tabb, "Implementation and Political Change: Sources of Local Variations in Federal Social Programs," *Policy Studies Journal* 8 (Special Issue No. 2, 1980): 616-632.

48. Harvey Lieber, *Federalism and Clean Waters: The 1972 Water Pollution Control Act* (Lexington, Mass.: Lexington Books, 1975), pp. 95, 195; Robert J. Rauch, "The Federal Water Pollution Control Act Amendments of 1972: Ambiguity as a Control Device," *Harvard Journal of Legislation* 10 (June 1973): 572-585.

49. Lieber, *Federalism and Clean Waters*, pp. 100-105.

50. Ibid., p. 110.

51. Richard N. L. Andrews, *Environmental Policy and Administrative Change* (Lexington, Mass.: Lexington Books, 1976), pp. 100-103, 131.

52. Ibid., pp. 133-134. Daniel Mazmanian has informed me in personal correspondence that the Corps developed guidelines requiring the *assessment* of a broad range of possible impacts of their projects.

53. Richard A. Liroff, *A National Policy for the Environment: NEPA and Its Aftermath* (Bloomington, Ind.: Indiana University Press, 1976), pp. 84-87. For other examples of ambiguous policies, see Robert L. Butterworth, "The Arms Control Impact Statement: A Programmatic Assessment," *Policy Studies Journal* 8 (Autumn 1979): 82-83; Van Horn, "Implementing CETA," p. 26; Charles O. Jones, *Clean Air* (Pittsburgh: University of Pittsburgh Press, 1975), pp. 69, 133-134; Theodore R. Marmor, *The Politics of Medicare* (Chicago: Aldine, 1970), pp. 85-86; and Jeffrey L. Pressman and Aaron B. Wildavsky, *Implementation* (Berkeley, Cal.: University of California Press, 1973), p. 74.

54. Martha Derthick, *Uncontrollable Spending for Social Services Grants* (Washington, D.C.: Brookings Institution, 1975).

55. Ibid., pp. 13, 107.

56. See Gary Orfield, *Congressional Power* (New York: Harcourt Brace Jovanovich, 1975), p. 168.

57. Frederick V. Malek, *Washington's Hidden Tragedy*, p. 148.

58. Colby, *Honorable Men*, pp. 213-214.

59. Ibid., pp. 316-317.

60. Richard P. Nathan, "The 'Administrative Presidency'," *Public Interest* (Summer 1976): 47-48.

61. James Eisenstein, *Counsel for the United States: U.S. Attorneys in the Political and Legal Systems* (Baltimore: Johns Hopkins University Press, 1978), pp. 88, 90.

62. Andrews, *Environmental Policy*, p. 144.

63. See Walter F. Murphy, "Lower Court Checks on Supreme Court Power," *American Political Science Review* 53 (December 1959): 1017-1031; Jack W. Peltason, *Fifty-Eight Lonely Men: Southern Federal Judges and Desegregation* (New York: Harcourt Brace Jovanovich, 1961); "Evasion of Supreme Court Mandates in Cases Remanded to State Courts Since 1941," *Harvard Law Review* 67 (1954): 1251-1259; and Kenneth H. Vines, "Federal District Judges and Race Relations Cases in the South," *Journal of Politics* 26 (May 1964): 337-357.

64. *Furman v. Georgia*, 408 U.S. 238 (1972).

65. *Gregg v. Georgia*, 428 U.S. 153 (1976); *Woodson v. North Carolina*, 428 U.S. 280 (1976).

66. *Brown v. Board of Education of Topeka*, 347 U.S. 483 (1954); 349 U.S. 294 (1955).

67. *Alexander v. Holmes County Board of Education*, 396 U.S. 19 (1969).

68. *Escobedo v. Illinois*, 378 U.S. 478 (1964).

69. *Miranda v. Arizona*, 384 U.S. 436 (1966).

70. Neil T. Romans, "The Role of State Supreme Courts in Judicial Policy Making: *Escobedo, Miranda*, and the Use of Judicial Impact Analysis," *Western Political Quarterly* 27 (March 1974): 38-59.

71. *Mapp v. Ohio*, 367 U.S. 643 (1961).

72. Bradley C. Canon, "Reactions of State Supreme Courts to a U.S. Supreme Court Civil Liberties Decision," *Law and Society Review* 7 (Fall 1973): 113.

73. McLaughlin, *Evaluation and Reform*, p. 168.

74. Ibid, pp. 169, 178-179.

75. Berke and Kirst, "Intergovernmental Relations," p. 401.

76. Harvey M. Sapolsky, *The Polaris System Development: Bureaucratic and Programmatic Success in Government* (Cambridge, Mass.: Harvard University Press, 1972), p. 250. For other examples, see Helen Ingram, "The Political Rationality of Federal Air Pollution Legislation," in *Approaches to Controlling Air Pollution*, ed. Ann F. Friedlaender (Cambridge, Mass.: MIT Press, 1978), p. 41.

77. Pressman and Wildavsky, *Implementation*, pp. 75-78.

78. Neal Gross, Joseph B. Giacquinta, and Marilyn Bernstein, *Implementing Organizational Innovations: A Sociological Analysis of Planned Educational Change in Schools* (New York: Basic Books, 1971), pp. 123-129; and John Pincus, "Incentives for Innovation in Public Schools," in *Social Program Implementation*, Williams and Elmore, eds., p. 56.

79. Califano, *A Presidential Nation*, p. 23.

80. Jameson W. Doig, "Police Policy and Police Behavior: Patterns of Divergence," *Policy Studies Journal* 7 (Special Issue, 1978): 438.

81. Moynihan, *Maximum Feasible Misunderstanding*, p. 170.

82. Daniel P. Moynihan, *The Politics of a Guaranteed Income* (New York: Vintage Books, 1973), p. 240. See also the comments of former Price Commissioner C. Jackson Grayson in Theodore C. Sorensen, *Watchmen in the Night* (Cambridge, Mass.: MIT Press, 1975), p. 32.

83. Alice M. Rivlin, *Systematic Thinking for Social Action* (Washington, D.C.: Brookings Institution, 1971), pp. 80.

84. Ibid., p. 84.

85. Doig, "Police Policy and Police Behavior," pp. 438-439.

86. See Burton M. Atkins and Mark Pogrebin, eds., *The Invisible Justice System: Discretion and the Law* (Cincinnati: Anderson Publishing Co., 1978), Part II.

87. Derthick, *Uncontrollable Spending*, pp. 9, 13.

88. Rauch, "The Federal Water Pollution Control Act Amendments of 1972"; Regina Herzlinger, "Costs, Benefits, and the West Side Highway," *Public Interest* (Spring 1979): 84; Herbert Y. Schandler, *The Unmaking of a President: Lyndon Johnson and Vietnam* (Princeton, N.J.: Princeton University Press, 1977); Norman C. Thomas, *Education in National Politics* (New York: David McKay, 1975), p. 52; McLaughlin, *Evaluation and Reform*, p. 18; "HUD Authorization: House Panel Challenges Harris Move to Boost Block Grant Aid to Poor," *Congressional Quarterly Weekly Report*, June 3, 1978, p. 1398.

89. For examples of the diverse foreign policy goals, see Morton H. Halperin, *Bureaucratic Politics and Foreign Policy* (Washington, D.C.: Brookings Institution, 1974), p. 78; and Robert L. Gallucci, *Neither Peace nor Honor* (Baltimore: Johns Hopkins University Press, 1975), pp. 47-54.

90. Doris Kearns, *Lyndon Johnson and the American Dream* (New York: Harper & Row, 1976), p. 137.

91. David Braybrooke and Charles E. Lindblom, *A Strategy of Decision: Policy Evaluation as a Social Process* (New York: Free Press, 1963), pp. 202-203.

92. Mike M. Milsten, *Impact and Response* (New York: Teachers' College Press, 1976), p. 107.

93. See Morris P. Fiorina, *Congress: Keystone of the Washington Establishment* (New Haven: Yale University Press, 1977).

94. See J. Woodford Howard, Jr., "On the Fluidity of Judicial Choice," *American Political Science Review* 62 (March 1968).

95. S. Sidney Ulmer, "Earl Warren and the Brown Decision," *Journal of Politics* 33 (August 1971); Earl Warren, *The Memoirs of Chief Justice Earl Warren* (Garden City, N.Y.: Doubleday, 1971), pp. 2, 281-286.
96. Canon, "Reactions of State Supreme Courts," pp. 112-113.
97. Pressman and Wildavsky, *Implementation,* chapter 4.
98. Halperin, *Bureaucratic Politics,* pp. 241-242. For other examples of inconsistent orders, see Brown and Frieden, "Guidelines and Goals in the Model Cities Program," pp. 460-461, 469; and James, "Federalism and the Model Cities Experiment," pp. 69-94.
99. Andrews, *Environmental Policy,* pp. 42, 45.
100. Lorraine M. McDonnell, "Implementation of Federal Education Policy: the Role of the States" (Paper delivered at the annual meeting of the American Political Science Association, Washington, D.C., August-September 1979), pp. 12-13.
101. Van Horn, "Implementing CETA," pp. 22-26.
102. Ibid., p. 22. See also Milsten, *Impact and Response,* p. 107.
103. Martin Shapiro, *The Supreme Court and Administrative Agencies* (New York: Free Press, 1968), pp. 198-199.

3

Resources

Implementation orders may be accurately transmitted, clear, and consistent, but if implementors lack the resources necessary to carry out policies, implementation is likely to be ineffective. A state official with responsibility for air pollution control once remarked:

> The implementation plan was a good idea. Setting these ambient air quality standards was a good idea and setting program objectives to meet them was a good idea. . . . But what happens as we go along depends on what sort of resources we get. . . .[1]

In February 1980 the industrial licensing supervisor for the Texas Department of Health's radiation control unit resigned. He quit because his department lacked the manpower, equipment, funding, and legislative authority needed to protect Texans against nuclear hazards. Texas has hundreds of radioactive material licensees and only nine inspectors to police them. According to the supervisor, "The ratio of X-ray users to inspectors is many times worse."[2] Inspectors were spending most of their time responding to incidents of radiation exposure or contamination instead of pre-empting problems. Inadequate staff was not only hindering attempts to protect the public's health, but costing license applicants thousands of dollars as they waited to have their applications processed. Some of these applications were related to the oil exploration and energy production business, delaying the acquisition of energy supplies at a time of national scarcity.

As this example indicates, resources can be a critical factor in implementing public policy. Important resources include staff of sufficient size and with the proper skills to carry out their assignments and the information, authority, and facilities necessary to translate proposals on paper into functioning public services. In this chapter we examine how insufficient resources present obstacles to policy implementation. We also explain why these shortages occur.

STAFF

Probably the most essential resource in implementing policy is staff. In an era in which "big government" is under attack from all directions, it may seem surprising to learn that a principal source of implementation failure is inadequate staff. Although about five million military and civilian personnel work for the federal government and nearly thirteen million more work for state and local governments, there are still too few people with the requisite skills to do an effective job implementing many policies. (It is interesting to note that over the past 30 years, the number of state and local personnel has increased considerably more than the number of federal employees, as Figure 3.1 illustrates.) We must evaluate the bureaucracy, not only in terms of absolute numbers, but also in terms of its capabilities to perform desired tasks. In this section we illustrate the frequent inadequacy of staff, both in numbers and expertise, and examine its causes and consequences for implementation.

Figure 3.1

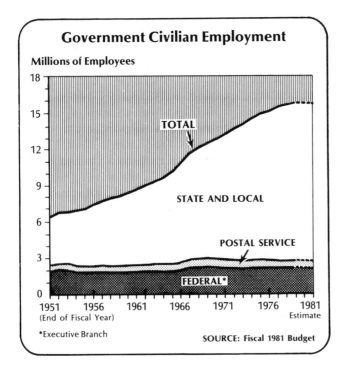

Government Civilian Employment

Millions of Employees

TOTAL

STATE AND LOCAL

POSTAL SERVICE

FEDERAL*

1951 1956 1961 1966 1971 1976 1981
(End of Fiscal Year)   Estimate

*Executive Branch

SOURCE: Fiscal 1981 Budget

Size

Education Policies. At one time the U.S. Office of Education (now the Department of Education) had responsibility for enforcing complex federal guidelines in about 20,000 school districts and hundreds of thousands of individual schools. Yet the Office of Education was able to assign only a handful of people to monitoring the use of federal funds in local school districts, and few of these officials were stationed at the field level. In 1968 the Department of Health, Education and Welfare tried to supervise school desegregation throughout the country with a staff of only 48 enforcement officers. The General Accounting Office, the investigatory arm of Congress, is able to examine only a few school districts each year. Effective monitoring of federal education programs is an enormous task, and the staff available to do the job is strikingly inadequate.[3]

Because of lack of staff and because of traditional federal government deference to the states, federal programs rely heavily upon state agencies for their implementation. This, however, does not solve the problem of lack of staff at the federal level; it merely transfers the problem to the states. Many federal education programs are channeled through state education agencies. Yet these agencies generally also suffer from insufficient staff and must rely upon local school districts (which they are supposed to be overseeing) to both carry out federal policies as they were intended and to report back on their success in doing so. The state education agencies are often too short-handed to coordinate the implementation of federal policies by school districts in their states, to monitor districts' compliance with federal regulations, or to evaluate carefully school districts' applications for federal funds.[4]

Massachusetts had a staff of four to oversee federal funds for compensatory education. These same officials had to handle programs for the children of migratory workers and children in state institutions for neglected and delinquent children, the NDEA Student Loan Cancellation program, the Bilingual Education Act, the Follow Through program, and technical assistance to the Head Start program. Clearly, not much effort could go into supervising the implementation of any of these programs.[5]

Similarly, Michigan had a staff of 10 to consider the requests for funds of 462 school districts. With this workload, making on-site visits to schools or providing services was literally impossible. Thus, the state department of education had to rely upon forms provided by local school districts for its indicators of compliance with the law.[6]

Despite the staff shortages of state departments of education, there are generally no alternatives for implementing federal or state education programs. State boards of education have a shortage of expert, independent staff and have little impact on the administration of grants. Governors usually have limited ability to oversee education programs. State department of education heads are often elected independently of the governor, and the governor's office is usually poorly staffed. Moreover, many governors have little interest or political incentive to involve themselves in education programs.[7]

Environmental Protection Policies. The task of cleaning and protecting the environment is staggering. There are more than 62,000 primary sources of water pollution in the United States, plus countless thousands of other sources in the form of sewers, irrigation return flows, and agricultural run-offs; more than 150 million polluting motor vehicles on the highways; about 2,000 potentially dangerous chemical plants and dump sites; between 2,000 and 40,000 sources of industrial air pollution, excluding small furnaces, in each of the 50 states; and more than 50,000 pesticides in use around the country.[8] These figures indicate the size of the bureaucracy necessary to enforce regulations, a size which the combined strength of the national, state, and local governments does not come close to meeting.

As we saw in our examination of education policy, federal programs frequently are implemented by the states. Environmental protection is no exception. We will consider the adequacy of resources at both the state and federal levels of government as we evaluate the implementation of environmental protection policies.

Staff resources for environmental protection are very limited. It is difficult to determine pollution levels and to verify the information on pollution that industries provide. Highly skilled personnel are essential. State environmental protection agencies have had from 15 to 200 inspectors to monitor the thousands of sources of pollution described above. To inspect each source annually, each inspector would have to inspect three to thirty sources each day. This schedule cannot be met, and annual inspections are insufficient to monitor pollution anyway. State agencies are forced to rely on potential sources of pollution for data on their operations. This can lead to serious inaccuracies. Similar sources can vary significantly in their emissions as a function of design details and operating practices.[9]

Regarding motor vehicle pollution, a recent General Accounting Office study found that state enforcement of automobile antipollution policy was spotty. Eight of ten cars on the road did not meet clean air standards because they were in disrepair or their emission control devices had been deactivated.[10]

The staff resources of the federal government are equally inadequate. Several years after the passage of the National Environmental

Policy Act (NEPA), the Council on Environmental Quality had only 50 professionals to oversee and coordinate the environmental activities of the entire federal government. This meant that the agency could allocate only one or two persons to each sector of the federal government, and many of the staff were not knowledgeable about either the environment or the federal government. These staff members were too few to give careful review to the detailed environmental impact statements prepared by federal agencies or to monitor their preparation.[11]

Other federal agencies face similar problems of limited and inadequate staff to implement environmental policies. The EPA was unable to meet the schedule set by Congress to classify pesticides. To monitor the testing and certification of hundreds of different models produced by domestic and foreign automobile companies, EPA at one point had assigned only 17 employees.[12] And out of the approximately 2,000 dangerous chemical plants and dump sites in the country, EPA has been able to check each year only about 135.[13]

One common cause of staff shortages in the government is the addition of responsibilities without a corresponding addition of personnel. The Soil Conservation Service received no increase in staff following the passage of NEPA, although the act required the service to prepare elaborate environmental impact statements about each of its projects. And the Army Corps of Engineers was also given this new responsibility without a corresponding increase in staff.[14] The construction of the Trans-Alaskan pipeline was of great concern to environmentalists, but there was inadequate staff to oversee it in order to protect Alaska's fragile environment. The General Accounting Office estimated that two-thirds of the pipeline construction activity was not seen by federal monitors, and the state of Alaska had no independent monitoring team.[15]

Energy Policies. The field of energy policy also presents interesting examples of inadequate staffing. After the near-disaster at the Three Mile Island nuclear power plant in 1979, it was discovered that only 26 of the 72 operating nuclear reactors in the country were covered by permanent federal safety inspectors.[16] Similarly, there are too few federal safety inspectors — only about 750 — to monitor adequately the compliance of more than 5,000 coal mines with safety regulations.[17]

Energy pricing and conservation are important concerns today, but the staff assigned to monitor compliance with these policies is too small to do the job. For example, there are approximately 175,000 service stations in the U.S., but the Department of Energy has only about 50 auditors to monitor their prices.[18] Likewise, at one time the Federal Energy Office was able to assign only one auditor to monitor Exxon's compliance with price regulations.[19] An even greater task will be monitoring thermostat settings in nonresidential buildings for compliance with federal regulations. New federal restrictions on thermostat settings went into effect July 16, 1979. Operators of nonresidential buildings across the country must set their thermostats no lower than 78 degrees in the summer and no higher than 65 degrees in the winter. The federal government has no staff to monitor an estimated five million buildings, including offices, factories, restaurants, and stores. The Energy Department would like the states to shoulder this burden, but the states have no staff to implement this policy either.[20]

Other Policies. Similar problems of limited staff and enormous workloads occur in the area of consumer protection. At one time the Food and Drug Administration had only 1,000 inspectors to monitor 50,000 U.S. food processing plants and 2,500 drug companies.[21] When flesh-eating piranhas were distributed to some home fish tanks, citizens of Florida learned that their state's Fish, Game, and Fresh Water Commission had only five people inspecting 30 million tropical fish each year![22]

As a result of a petition filed by consumer groups, the Federal Trade Commission (FTC) required all major companies to provide the agency with documented substantiation of their advertising claims. It subsequently received massive amounts of technical data, but neither the agency nor the consumer groups had the resources to use it. The volume of data was too massive even to determine whether or not all companies complied with the law. For all the agency knew, the information supplied by the companies could have been false or inadequate, or it may not have been supplied at all. After two years the FTC de-emphasized its regulation.[23]

Staff is inadequate in the area of safety regulation also. The Occupational Safety and Health Administration (OSHA) has responsibility for setting and/or enforcing health and safety standards in over a million work places, yet its staff is large enough to inspect the typical work place only once every several decades. Obviously, monitoring performance standards such as noise levels is out of the question.[24] The National Highway Traffic Safety Administration has had only 10 employees engaged in defect review of motor vehicles and no in-house research capability, leaving it largely dependent upon automakers' data on safety and defects. Moreover, the agency must work in cooperation with the Federal Highway Administration, which is dominated by highway interests and does not give a high priority to improving traffic safety.[25]

The enforcement of civil rights laws has suffered from lack of staff. The size of the Office of Civil Rights in the Department of Health, Education and Welfare (now the Department of Health and

Human Services), has not kept pace with the agency's increased responsibilities for protecting women, blacks, Hispanics, Indians, orientals, and the handicapped against discrimination. It has a large backlog of unresolved complaints and insufficient staff to make on-site inspections and to monitor education programs in school districts that have had or are suspected of having problems of discrimination.[26]

The enforcement efforts of governments have been largely reactive, that is, agencies wait for complaints before taking action to enforce civil rights laws. Even so, staff size has been inadequate. In 1976 the Equal Employment Opportunity Commission (EEOC) received 97,674 complaints, resolved 82,537, and had a backlog of 122,000 cases.[27] For the immense task of enforcing its fair housing laws, the federal government spent only 1/15 as much as it spent on the EEOC![28] In 1978 the Justice Department had 17 attorneys and 15 paralegals to monitor compliance with the Voting Rights Act in some 1,115 jurisdictions.[29] It is not difficult to visualize just how enormous staffs would have to be to implement civil rights legislation effectively.

There seems to be no end to the list. The Agricultural Marketing Service had to increase its staff of federal grain inspectors in the face of massive grain scandals at U.S. ports in the mid-1970s. The Immigration and Naturalization Service labors under the burden of attempting to prevent illegal immigration along 6,000 miles of U.S. open land border with only a few hundred officials on duty at any one time. With this situation, we should not be surprised that there are millions of illegal aliens in the country. Similarly, the head of the Houston area U.S. Customs Air Patrol Division recently stated that he lacked the staff to catch more than 1 percent of the planes involved in smuggling.[30]

As we saw in Chapters 1 and 2, the courts play a significant role in policymaking at all levels of government. Generally they give orders to others to implement policies. After that point courts are in a very weak position because they lack resources to oversee the implementation of their decisions. There are simply no personnel to carry out implementation responsibilities in the judicial branch. Court bureaucracies consist almost entirely of the judges themselves, personal aides, and a few administrators, warrant-servers, clerks, and secretaries who help to manage the movement of cases through the courts. There are usually few, if any, staffers to oversee the actions of other branches of government. As we have noted earlier, judges must wait for others to bring cases to them in order to monitor or alter their decisions.

Policy implementation in the private as well as public sector is hampered by inadequate staff. A scarcity of civil rights lawyers and funds for them in many cities led to a failure to file cases in court to update weak school desegregation plans.[31] Provisions in federal law allow coal miners' safety representatives to demand inspections of the mines, tour mines with federal safety inspectors, seek modification of safety standards, and obtain hearings on mine safety. There are more than 4,000 nonunion mines and only 11 safety representatives at these mines. Even union mines make little use of these provisions.[32]

General Problems. Inadequate staffing is a central problem in implementation. This generalization applies to carrying out policies directly and to overseeing the efforts of others, in both the public and the private sectors, who implement policies. If one were to add up all the government employees who implement public policies (police, social workers, hospital employees, meat inspectors, prison guards, judges, regulatory commissioners, game wardens, teachers, military officers, and many, many others) and then add to this number all the private individuals and institutions who implement public policies (industries that are not supposed to pollute, banks and credit card and finance companies that are not supposed to discriminate in credit decisions), one would begin to get an idea of the magnitude of the staff necessary to ensure that those who are supposed to implement policies actually do so. When one adds to this total the number of people needed to implement policies adequately, the total figure becomes astronomical.

Governments do not even come close to meeting these needs. The fear of creating a totalitarian bureaucratic monster and the pressures to allocate personnel to more direct services, such as garbage collection or the provision of agricultural expertise, keep staffs that monitor implementation small. While the scarcity of payroll funds coupled with the irresistible urges of policymakers to provide public services (at least in form) ensure that staffs will generally be inadequate to implement programs.

Sometimes policymakers are well aware of these limitations when they enact policies. For example, everyone knows that law enforcement agencies cannot enforce motor vehicle driving laws strictly. In effect, policymakers decide that the additional benefits from rigorous implementation are not worth the additional cost of hiring the necessary staff. At other times, however, no realistic estimate of the staff required to implement a program is made. Slippage in policy implementation is thereby virtually assured, and we should be hesitant to blame the bureaucracy for problems beyond its control.

While staff size can be critical for almost every policy, it is more so for some than others. Some policies cover everyone equally, such as national security policy; other policies are aimed at a specific clientele. Some policies serve people; other policies are intended to restrain them. It is much easier to implement a policy such as Social Security that distributes benefits recipients desire than a policy such as crime control that imposes unwelcome constraints on individuals. More personnel are required to enforce limitations on people than to write checks to them.

Skills

It is not enough for there to be an adequate number of implementors to carry out a policy. Implementors must possess the skills necessary for the job at hand. The lack of properly trained personnel has hindered the implementation of policies ranging from innovations in local schools to antidiscrimination in employment.[33] In the area of environmental protection, the staff of the Environmental Protection Agency lacked not only the time, but also the expertise to develop standards by which to judge the environmental impact statements prepared by federal agencies. The major staff turnover in late 1973 and early 1974 cost the agency much of whatever expertise it had developed.[34] In general, states lack qualified personnel to inspect potential sources of pollution and evaluate information on them. Massachusetts, for example, had only eight engineers to inspect and evaluate some 10,000 industrial sources of air pollution.[35]

A poorly trained staff can create hazards. In 1978, 7 of the 10 operator applicants at a Michigan nuclear power plant failed the radiation safety component of their licensing examinations, but were licensed anyway. Moreover, the operators never trained under simulated accident conditions.[36] The Kemeny Commission, which studied the nuclear accident at Three Mile Island, reported that the public utility manning the nuclear power plant lacked "sufficient knowledge, expertise, and personnel to operate the plant or maintain it adequately." [37]

Most of the field staff hired to implement the Comprehensive Employment and Training Act had no manpower training experience, and many staffers had never worked with local governments before. Thus, they were not able to provide much technical assistance to those running local training programs.[38]

When federal programs are implemented in whole or in part by state agencies, staff skills are also a problem. Although federal law requires that only successful programs are to be funded, state education agencies generally have lacked personnel with the skills necessary to evaluate the success of federal programs to aid educationally deprived children. Professionally trained personnel are not attracted to these agencies because of low salaries, and there is a high turnover rate among those who are employed because of the tenuous nature of the funding base (frequently from the federal government) for their positions. Similarly, teacher orientation for new programs has often been superficial.[39]

One problem at the federal level among career executives is the shortage of people with management skills. Often those with professional backgrounds are promoted until they become administrators, and thus no longer use their professional skills. Yet they often do not have the management expertise required for their new positions. There is little training in management for top career officials, whether they arrived at their positions from professional or administrative backgrounds. Their superiors — political appointees with short tenures in office — lack incentive to invest in the long-term development of skills, and the career executives themselves have not pressed for management training. One authority suggests that we need to make managerial competence a criterion for promotion, which in turn would provide the incentive to obtain these skills.[40]

Lack of management skills is an even greater problem at the state and local levels. Fewer resources are committed to professional training, and it is more difficult to recruit and keep competent administrators because of the generally lower salaries and lesser prestige and job security of executive positions.

Staffing problems are especially acute in new programs. When a program is established, officials must assemble a staff — sometimes from scratch — to implement it. Rarely is a ready-made staff waiting in the wings.[41] Because legislative bodies are usually more willing to initiate programs than they are to fund them, administrators often do not receive adequate funds to hire the number and type of personnel required to implement the policy. Inadequate staffing is a big problem for new programs because of the limited time to build a staff and the modest appropriations that policies frequently receive in their initial stages of implementation.

Money is not always the answer. Even with substantial funds it is not easy to find properly skilled personnel. This is especially true when a government agency is carrying out or regulating highly technical activities. Sometimes the necessary personnel are very difficult to hire because of the higher incomes and greater flexibility they can enjoy by working in the private sector. The military's problems in attracting physicians is a prime example. At other times, the needed staff may simply not exist, and a government agency must invest in developing expertise.

The federal government's efforts to regulate energy prices and allocations in the 1970s illustrate both problems. No one really knew how to accomplish these tasks, and few people outside the energy companies had the background to understand the industry. Thus, employees of the Federal Energy Office relied upon "on the job training."

INFORMATION

Information is a second essential resource in policy implementation. This information comes in two forms. The first is information regarding how to carry out a policy. Implementors need to know what to do when they are given directives to act. The second form of essential information is data on the compliance of others with governmental rules and regulations. Implementors must know whether other persons involved in implementing policies are complying with the law. In this section we examine the extent to which these resources exist, why this is so, and the consequences for implementation.

Knowing What To Do

As Chapter 2 pointed out, implementation directives are sometimes vague because high-level decisionmakers do not know what to require of implementors. This insufficient knowledge is a resource that hinders implementation directly as well as indirectly through the nature of communications.

Program information is particularly critical for new policies or those involving technical questions, such as air pollution abatement or the development of a new weapons system, because implementors are asked to meet goals neither they nor anyone else knows how to accomplish. Routine functions, such as dispersing funds, building roads, training troops, hiring typists, or purchasing goods, are relatively straightforward in their operation, and a wealth of information exists on how to carry out these functions. But the implementors of a new policy such as controlling hospital costs or developing a jet fighter do not share these advantages.

It is one thing for Congress to mandate the cleaning of the nation's air. It is something quite different for public agencies and private companies to figure out how to do it. For example, in early 1980 the head of the Environmental Protection Agency (EPA) told Congress his agency could not develop regional air quality standards to ease the acid rain problem along the East Coast. It lacked the knowledge and technical ability to set the standards. Even if the agency tried, he said, it would take 7 to 10 years.[42]

Before an agency such as EPA orders a costly change in an industry or its products (such as automobiles), the agency should be able to predict the effects of the change on the economic health of the industry in question. Such information, however, is frequently lacking. A study of air pollution policy development in the Pittsburgh area (including federal, state, and county efforts) concluded that there was little systematic inquiry into effects. What was known was not communicated, not enough resources were allocated to research, and debate by decisionmakers was generally uninformed.[43]

State air pollution agencies have had few resources at their disposal. This has resulted in simplistic plans for cleaning the air that often ignore the important factors of economic efficiency, uncertainty, and economic growth. State air pollution agencies have lacked models for linking air pollution emissions to ambient concentrations of pollutants. They also have lacked meteorological data, computer expertise, and information on the costs to each polluting source of decreasing emissions by varying amounts. The pollution regulations written by some states are unenforceable. The states wanted to control pollutants, but they did not know how to specify the manner or level of control they wanted. What they did instead was to order polluting sources to employ "suitable measures" or "reasonable precautions."[44]

The lack of knowledge of how to implement some policies has several direct consequences. As we have seen, some responsibilities will simply not be met, or they will not be met on time. Inefficiency is also likely to characterize the implementation of such policies. Some efforts will prove to be mistakes, and implementors will have to try again. Regulations may be inappropriate, causing other government units or organizations in the private sector to purchase equipment, fill out forms, or stop certain activities unnecessarily. As the process of implementation continues over time, implementors will learn more about what needs to be done and what can be done to implement a policy.

Monitoring Compliance

Implementation of policies often requires information on the compliance of organizations or individuals with the law. Compliance data, however, is usually difficult to obtain, in part because of the lack of staff which we discussed in the previous section of this chapter. When EPA Administrator Russell Train presented a progress report on the control of air pollution in 1975, he could only estimate compliance with his agency's standards. There was a lag of more than a year in gathering the required data.[45]

When the U.S. Office of Education began to enforce the 1964 Civil Rights Act as it related to education grants to states and localities, it did not even know, according to at least one author, how many school districts there were in the country. Top officials in the Department of Health, Education and Welfare had little knowledge of what was happening on the local level, and they had few means of finding out. Although private groups were of some help in monitoring compliance in 200 southern school districts (a tiny fraction of the total), most civil rights groups were largely ignorant of what was happening in the field and therefore could not augment the limited information base in Washington. Ultimately, the Office of Education had to rely on forms from school districts certifying that they had or were about to desegregate.[46]

Relying on information from those who are supposed to be doing the complying raises questions about effective implementation. Nevertheless, this is the situation with a great many policies, ranging from regulating oil prices to restricting the uses of grants from the Law Enforcement Assistance Administration (LEAA) to local police departments. Officials in the Department of Health and Human Services are currently very concerned about the rapidly rising costs of medical care, but they have no independent source of information on the supply, uses, and costs of hospital care. They must rely upon data from the American Hospital Association, a private group representing the interests of hospitals. As a result, consistent standards for reviewing expenditure plans are virtually nonexistent.[47] As we saw earlier, the Department of the Interior and the state of Alaska had inadequate staff to monitor the building of the Trans-Alaskan pipeline. Although the builders of the pipeline, the Alyeska Pipeline Service Company, violated environmental laws, public agencies had to depend upon the company for information on its own compliance with the laws. This data was not objective and did not uncover deceptions such as the falsified records of faulty welds.[48]

Enforcement problems are aggravated when official rules restrict the authority of agencies to collect information on implementation. LEAA has always been required by Congress to monitor usage of its grants by state and local law enforcement agencies. In the Crime Control Act of 1976, these oversight requirements were made extremely specific. Nevertheless, at least until 1978, LEAA was prevented from requiring states to submit the relevant information by Office of Management and Budget regulations that establish the data a federal agency may request from other governmental jurisdictions. Thus, LEAA has had to rely on the voluntary cooperation of the states, cooperation that has not always been forthcoming.[49]

State-level agencies, which often function as middlemen between federal and local agencies, cannot be depended upon to provide Washington with information on compliance at the local level. One study, for example, found that state education agencies relied heavily upon reports from school districts regarding their own compliance with federal laws.[50] State employees rarely went into the field to see for themselves.

Although Congress has given the states significant responsibility for implementing antipollution laws, the states have had difficulty exercising this new authority. It is technically difficult and very expensive to monitor air pollution emissions, and the states lack the resources to do this. While stack tests are of some help in measuring air pollution, performance of air cleaning equipment may quickly deteriorate with changes in maintenance, fuel, and operating practices. It is impossible to monitor many "fugitive emissions" and leakages from storage tanks. Usually state inspectors do no tests at all. They just visit a plant and look for obvious signs of pollution, such as odors and unusual smoke colors. Many violations of air pollution laws can go undetected by inspectors, and the fact that pollution control equipment is in place and apparently operating may provide them with inconclusive and unreliable information.[51]

The implementation of many policies depends heavily upon individuals in the private sector. Unfortunately, private citizens do not often initiate action or provide information on noncompliance. For example, those who are most likely to suffer discrimination in housing, employment, credit, and education are also poorly educated and thus least likely to know about antidiscrimination laws and the remedies available to them. They are also, because of their poverty, least likely to have the resources to pursue their claims and often do not receive the necessary outside help. Moreover, because they usually must continue to deal with their adversaries, such as employers, landlords, and banks, they may fear retaliation against their efforts to secure their rights.[52]

Consumers frequently lack the knowledge to obtain refunds to which they are entitled, and millions of taxpayers are ignorant of sections of the tax code that could save them money. (In addition, the costs of invoking sections of the law may exceed the benefits to be received.) Coal miners have not been well-informed by the Mine Safety and Health Administration of the working conditions to which they are entitled.[53] This naturally reduces their efforts to have health and safety laws enforced.

Lack of information also impedes compliance with court decisions. If lower courts are to enforce the Supreme Court's prayer in public school decisions, for example, local citizens must be familiar with the decisions and be willing to take violations of them to court. This often does not happen. Public policies are frequently not implemented because the public does not know what to do or how to monitor compliance.

AUTHORITY

Another resource important in implementation is authority. Authority varies from program to program and comes in many different forms: the right to issue subpoenas; take cases to court; issue orders to other officials; withdraw funds from a program; provide funds, staff, and technical assistance to lower level government jurisdictions; issue checks to citizens; purchase goods and services; or levy taxes. Policies that require government oversight or regulation of others in the public or private sectors are those for which authority is most likely to be inadequate. Usually there is sufficient authority to *give* aid to individuals or lower level governments. It is in *constraining* them that government is weakest. In this section we examine the limitations of authority which often face implementors and the consequences of this for policy implementation. We also suggest some explanations for the lack of authority that often exists.

Exercising Authority

Sometimes agencies simply lack authority, even on paper, to implement a policy properly. For example, the Department of Housing and Urban Development cannot initiate administrative actions to enforce the Fair Housing Act, and the Department of Justice cannot initiate suits on behalf of individuals claiming discrimination in the sale or rental of housing.[54] Part of the 1946 Hill-Burton Act required medical facilities receiving federal construction funds to make services available to all persons residing in their area and to provide a "reasonable volume" of free care for the indigent, an obligation that continues forever. Nevertheless, there has been no enforcement of this part of the act because the original law and the title of the health planning act that replaced it provided no sanctions against violators.[55]

When formal authority does exist, it is frequently mistaken by observers for effective authority. But authority on paper is one thing; authority effectively exercised is quite another. We can begin to understand why this is so by examining one of the most potentially damaging sanctions of higher level jurisdictions: the authority to withdraw funds from a program.

Withdrawal of Funds. Cutting off funds is a drastic action. It may be embarrassing to all those involved and antagonize the implementors of a program whose active support is necessary for effective implementation.[56] Cutting off federal funds from projects also alienates the members of Congress from the areas losing the money. One example is the Social Security Administration and hospital certification. The political costs of designating a hospital as unqualified to receive funds for caring for Medicare patients are great. The commissioner once told his subordinates not to terminate funds unless they got the approval of the congressman from the district. Denying funds to rural hospitals was an especially touchy subject since there was often only one hospital serving a community. When several rural Texas hospitals were not certified, a Texas representative proposed an amendment, which passed, allowing a requirement to be waived temporarily.[57] Requiring states or cities to repay misspent funds can also have severe political consequences. Most officials do not even try to exercise this authority.[58]

Representatives of a state or local power structure may also intervene to counter the authority of higher jurisdictions. In our decentralized political system, state and local interests are often quite powerful. California was supposed to comply with a federal law regarding the provision of minimum welfare grants by July 1, 1969. But it did not comply, and at the beginning of 1971 the Department of Health, Education and Welfare (HEW) ordered the termination of federal welfare funds to California. In response to this action Governor Ronald Reagan called Vice President Spiro Agnew and HEW Secretary Elliot Richardson to try to reverse the decision. The next day HEW withdrew its termination order. Finally, after two years of delay, California raised its welfare grants on July 1, 1971.[59]

When the Office of Education ordered that funds appropriated under the Elementary and Secondary Education Act be withheld from Chicago because it had failed to integrate its schools sufficiently, Mayor Richard Daley called President Lyndon Johnson, and the decision was reversed. The Office of Education lacked the political resources to exercise its authority to terminate funds. When implementors in a decentralized system do not receive the support of their superiors, they are vulnerable to pressure from local interests.[60]

To avoid political controversy, many administrators choose not to withdraw funds. One author found that between 1965 and 1970 funds were substantially and permanently cut off from only four — out of more than 20,000 — school districts for noncompliance with the 1964 Civil Rights Act although hundreds of school districts had not desegregated.[61] In an unusual case in 1973 a federal court of appeals had to order HEW to enforce the act.

The effectiveness of withdrawing misallocated funds is limited by alternative sources of funding. Most large school districts have at least 15 sources (some have many more), and they can move funds around to give themselves flexibility. By substituting "outside" grants for purposes for which a district already allocates funds, a district can release its own revenues for other programs. In effect, the outside, targeted funds become discretionary funds, and their withdrawal will not upset "regular" programs.[62]

Withdrawing funds, albeit a potentially severe sanction in the hands of implementors, is not always possible, as we have seen. It should be noted that it is only relevant for policies that award grants to lower level governments or private organizations. Governments usually do not withhold funds if one of their own components is not implementing a program effectively. They rarely take funds away from themselves.

Not only elected representatives of a locality intervene to have decisions overturned. Others besides public officials may act to counter the exercise of authority. In the first year after Congress' passage of the Elementary and Secondary Education Act, the Massachusetts Department of Education did not spend all the money authorized for it by the federal government. It denied many applications from local school districts for failing to meet the law's standards. This approach did not continue, however, because of criticism in the press and the subsequent public uproar.[63]

Officials may be reluctant to exercise authority for a number of other reasons. Terminating a project or withdrawing federal or state funds may hurt most those whom the policy is designed to aid. School-children, the elderly, or the poor are often the real victims of cutbacks. If a company loses federal contracts because of racial or sexual discrimination, it may be forced to lay off workers. Those with the least seniority may be the minorities the policy is trying to help. Similarly, cutting off federal funds for the educationally disadvantaged because of misallocation is most likely to hurt students from poor families. As Harold Howe, a former U.S. Commissioner of Education, has said, "Whenever we had to take money from somebody we suffered a defeat."[64]

Title IX of the 1964 Civil Rights Act prohibits discrimination on the basis of sex in education. Until 1979, however, courts had interpreted the law to mean that only the government and not private individuals could bring suits against universities. In that year the Supreme Court overruled this interpretation, and the U.S. government sided with those challenging the old interpretation. It did this because it did not have the resources to process all the complaints it received from individuals (as we might anticipate from our discussion of staff earlier in this chapter), and cutting off all federal funds was too drastic a sanction, punishing innocent students. Moreover, the government had to demonstrate the existence of a great deal of discrimination in order to withhold funds. Thus, the government argued that it would be more effective to allow a student to seek individual redress in court.

Strict implementation of the law may also injure innocent persons who are not the objects of government benefits. At one point in the debate over whether to suspend the 1975 federal air quality standards, Ford Motor Company claimed a suspension denial would force it to close its factories to avoid monetary penalties. This would lead, Ford argued, to a $17 billion decrease in the GNP and an increase of 800,000 persons in the nation's unemployed workforce.[65] In 1979 Chrysler Corp. asked the federal government for a $1 billion cash advance and a two-year postponement in complying with federal exhaust-emission and fuel-efficiency standards. The loss of thousands of jobs and at least a partial collapse of the money market were forecast by corporate officials if it did not receive the requested aid. Such dire warnings have won automobile manufacturers repeated suspensions in the enforcement of air quality standards from the federal government.

Naturally, consequences such as these make officials think twice about aggressive implementation efforts. This reluctance reduces the credibility of their threats to cut off funds, exercise other sanctions, or strictly enforce the law. Such threats also lose utility when jurisdictions, such as die-hard segregationist school districts, prefer to forego federal funds in order to avoid complying with federal law. One study of Georgia school districts, for example, found that the poorest areas were most willing to give up federal funds in order to maintain segregation.[66]

The desire for self-preservation keeps many agencies from withdrawing funds. Agencies like the Law Enforcement Assistance Administration, the Federal Highway Administration, and the Education Department are primarily involved in channeling grants to other levels of government. To survive they must give away money. If they fail to do so, they may look bad to Congress and superior executive officials. This may hurt them in their future quests for budgets and authority, resources of great significance for most bureaucrats.[67] Thus, they may sacrifice the social objectives of a program to the "maintenance" objectives of their bureaucratic unit.[68]

Other Authority. Some sources of authority may be more unusual but not necessarily more useful than others. As we saw in the previous chapter, the National Environmental Policy Act (NEPA) required agencies engaged in certain programs to prepare environmental impact statements. These statements on the environmental consequences of projects were supposed to inhibit environmentally harmful projects, through educating the agencies themselves and arousing private interests to challenge administrative decisions. Changes in policy, however, did not necessarily occur. The emphasis of NEPA was on procedural instruments, but agencies can change their procedures without achieving their goals.[69]

Statutes designed to increase public controversy over agency decisions on projects with significant environmental impacts have been moderately effective in furthering environmental goals. Delaying a project can pressure an agency to alter its design to avoid significant costs that would be incurred by inaction. When political controversy over a policy is backed by a credible threat of litigation, changes may occur. These conditions are not common, however, and project designs cannot always be altered. In addition, because controversy and judicial review come after a project decision has been made, they do not ensure that environmental goals are always systematically considered in the decisionmaking process. Controversy and judicial review are costly in terms of money, time, effort, and emotional commitment. Only in the most flagrant cases are they useful in mobilizing public support in opposition to projects potentially harmful to the environment. Even in these cases they are successful only in mobilizing the opposition of politically sophisticated groups with the financial resources to hire the legal and technical representation necessary to challenge an agency decision. Many policies with important environmental consequences, such as subsidies for super-tanker construction and expenditures for military research and development, have important consequences for the environment but touch people's lives less directly and therefore receive less critical attention from members of the public interested in environmental protection. Controversy and judicial review have also had limited impact on the coalitions of interests whose values influence administrative decisions or on agencies' internal policies and decisionmaking criteria for choosing projects.[70]

The sanctions available to courts are limited and sparingly used. It is rare for a judge to issue a contempt of court citation, the judiciary's most potent weapon, against a governor, legislature, or administrative official. If police officers violate a defendant's rights, the courts usually do not punish them, but merely exclude the evidence illegally obtained. Since officers' superiors in the police department may be quite sympathetic to their methods of obtaining evidence, they will probably be evaluated on the basis of the number of arrests they make rather than on the convictions resulting from these arrests. Thus, court sanctions will restrain police behavior here only to the extent that police officers mind losing convictions.[71]

Judges are generally quite reluctant to make substantive decisions on issues delegated to administrative discretion. Usually they will intervene only if administrative decisions are arbitrary and capricious. In other words, the courts normally review administrative decisions only in terms of procedure, not fairness. If agency decisionmaking procedures are found wanting, then the case is sent back to the agency for a rehearing. Ordinarily, administrative actions are not so outrageous or so clearly in violation of the law that judges will order a permanent or even a temporary injunction. If administrators appear to be trying to enforce the law — or if they say they will do so — then the courts normally will defer to a coequal branch of government. The courts, for example, would not make construction and environmental decisions concerning the Trans-Alaskan pipeline. Such matters were delegated to agency discretion. According to some observers, the courts just checked to see whether there was sensible administrative enforcement of the law on paper.[72]

Even if a court overturns local zoning laws that exclude certain groups from living in a community, for example, cities and towns can write new ones. While the courts may void such laws, they rarely will write new ones and police all zoning decisions. Courts lack the resources to build houses for the poor, and they usually will not become de facto planning boards for local communities.[73]

Many judges are reluctant to assume extensive administrative duties and often will not do so unless they believe agencies systematically violate the law. The courts' administrative duties have increased in recent years. In Alabama a federal district judge assumed responsibility for overseeing the state's mental hospitals and prisons. In Boston different federal judges took control of the city's public schools and the Housing Authority. These actions were necessary because the relevant agencies had refused to comply with court orders to desegregate or correct inadequate and unsafe conditions. Such actions are still rare, but they do indicate that judges will not necessarily endure endless noncompliance with their orders.

Implementation becomes more complicated when two or more levels of government are involved. This, however, is inevitable in a federal system. Another division of authority that may hinder implementation occurs when two or more agencies in the same jurisdiction must cooperate to exercise authority. One agency may allocate funds but require the cooperation of another agency to withhold them from a program.[74] If action by the courts is necessary, this complicates matters even further. The efforts of state environmental protection agencies to gain compliance with antipollution laws can take years and substantial resources. The agencies may not receive the necessary cooperation of the state's attorney general and of state and local judges. Penalties are almost never issued on a first violation; this provides little incentive to polluters to comply with the law, especially with the shortage of inspectors we noted earlier.[75]

For authority to be used effectively, the cooperation of legislatures may also be needed. Vigorous enforcement of air pollution laws has angered some state legislatures, causing them to decrease funding for the relevant state agency or to pressure the agency to transfer inspectors.[76] The Community Development Block Grant program in the Department of Housing and Urban Development provides funds to cities and counties, but some lack the necessary authority (which must be given by the state) to operate the program in their jurisdictions.[77]

Although government officials often lack effective authority over other public officials, this lack of control is small compared to their lack of authority over private individuals, groups, and businesses — upon whom the successful implementation of policies often depends. Therefore, they must make their policies attractive to the private sector. The Federal Housing Administration (FHA) was established to guarantee home mortgages and thereby aid prospective homebuyers in gaining mortgages with smaller down payments and longer repayment periods. Because the FHA requires the cooperation of bankers to make the loans, it tailored its loan guarantees to meet their needs. Until 1967 it required that a person's income and prospective home be "economically sound." This helped the banks avoid risks, but it did little for those in greatest need of aid in purchasing homes: very few loans were made to the poor.[78] The Occupational Safety and Health Administration has to rely heavily on voluntary compliance with the regulations by private businesses. Therefore, the fines it levies for noncompliance have generally been quite small.[79]

The Mine Safety and Health Administration in the Department of Interior has responsibility for enforcing federal mine safety regulations. Its orders to mine operators may be appealed to the Board of Mine Operations Appeals and then to the courts. The Department of Interior, however, has had the reputation of being "captured" by coal companies. The Board of Mine Operations Appeals has narrowly interpreted federal power, and the department has been unaggressive in appealing cases lost to the courts. Safety inspectors have at times been subject to verbal abuse, threats of bodily harm, gunfire, and tire-slashing; they have even been run off the property at some mines. Nevertheless, the laws against this behavior have seldom been enforced.[80]

Utility of Sanctions. The limitations on the effective exercise of authority are numerous. Nevertheless, sanctions can play an important role in policy implementation. Local officials may be willing to comply with an order of a higher jurisdiction but fear committing political suicide because of the opposition of their constituents. In these instances, the threat of sanctions can provide them essential political cover. One study of Georgia school districts found that certain school superintendents quietly advised federal officials of their willingness to comply with desegregation orders if the school board were threatened with dire consequences for noncompliance. Some school districts wanted to be sued so they could appear to be giving in to a court order rather than to the unpopular Department of Health, Education and Welfare. Coercion, or the appearance of coercion, was important to successful implementation, especially where opposition to desegregation was the greatest.[81] Similarly, Illinois state officials felt that a direct display of federal "clout" was necessary to gain the compliance of the superintendent of the Chicago public school system with the federal mandates to spend certain funds on disadvantaged children and to desegregate the schools.[82]

Of course, sanctions may also have a direct role in improving policy implementation. After the U.S. Office of Education, in response to abuses in Mississippi, cut off funds and demanded restitution of funds already received, the state of Texas did more to see that federal funds were used correctly.[83] The Atomic Energy Commission began to pay attention to implementing the National Environmental Policy Act only after it saw that it could be sued successfully for not doing so.

Service Orientation

Lacking effective authority, officials realize that they require cooperation from other implementors if they are to implement programs successfully.[85] Therefore, they often take a service rather than a regulatory orientation toward officials of lower level jurisdictions, who actually implement many programs. In other words, officials of higher level jurisdictions approach implementation from the standpoint of asking officials of lower level jurisdictions for assistance rather than from the standpoint of imposing the will of a higher level jurisdiction upon them. The hope is that through such an approach lower level officials will give them at least some of what they want.

When Medicare became law, the Social Security Administration (SSA) had to make choices about hospital quality (for eligibility to receive Medicare funds), utilization review (to prevent unnecessary care), and methods of hospital payments. Its choices indicate that the SSA did not utilize fully its authority to regulate Medicare payments. Certification of hospitals was not used as an enforcement tool, but as a tool of "education." The Social Security Administration was reluctant to use its authority to cut off Medicare funds to hospitals. The SSA never specified what constituted a long stay (requiring reviews) and never exercised its power to limit Medicare coverage to 20 days for hospitals which failed to make timely reviews of long stays. State health agencies as well as the SSA were reluctant implementors; they, too, evaluated hospitals by their procedures on paper rather than on their performance.[86]

This policy of consultation rather than enforcement meant that hospitals were certified that failed to meet Medicare's standards, deficiencies in medical care continued, and utilization review was often ignored. Time limits for improvements were not set, and inadequate hospitals, in many cases, had only to promise to do better in order to gain SSA's continued certification.[87]

The Social Security Administration was lenient with hospitals caring for Medicare patients because it needed to gain the cooperation of the hospitals. Since few hospitals are owned by the federal government, cooperation was essential for Medicare to work. Moreover, anticipating an increased demand for medical care due to the new availability of funds, the SSA did not want to enforce standards of quality that might limit the number of hospital beds available to patients covered by Medicare. Thus, a high priority was not to antagonize hospitals and to get the new program running smoothly.[88]

This is not the only example of lax enforcement by federal government officials. A study of public housing programs in Chicago found that the Department of Housing and Urban Development (HUD) was not enforcing the antidiscrimination provisions contained in statutes or in court orders. Instead, it set as its basic standard of compliance a resolution by the Chicago Housing Authority (CHA) stating it was obeying the law! Even more curious were HUD's activities regarding specific violations. It forced CHA to adopt a rule to assign public housing on a first-come-first-served basis, but it allowed CHA to operate contrary to the rule. Similarly, HUD made CHA remove a rule giving neighborhood residents priority in assigning housing, but allowed the authority to continue to operate as if the rule still existed. Thus, the federal agency exacted compliance with formal details of federal law, but allowed the local agency to have its way in major policy matters.[89]

The Office of Education regularly accepted from local school districts fabricated certifications of compliance with the 1964 Civil Rights Act.[90] In implementing the Emergency School Aid Act of 1972, which provided funds to school districts that were desegregating or had high concentrations of minority students, the Office of Education allowed school districts to use federal aid for general education purposes, for activities unrelated to desegregation, for schools not affected by desegregation, or for ineligible or already completed desegregation plans.[91]

Suspected violations of rules for spending federal funds for disadvantaged students were generally negotiated informally. The offending school districts usually promised not to breach the regulations in the future. Thus, for several years federal audits were not taken very seriously.[92] It was also common for states and localities to fill out the required federal forms and then ignore program requirements in their implementation efforts.[93]

When guidelines for federal aid to disadvantaged students were being written, the U.S. Office of Education took care to obtain the concurrence and support of state and local education officials. Federal officials focused on program evaluation requirements, and they sought to reassure educators that evaluations would not be used in a punitive fashion and that the continuation of local projects was not contingent upon progress reports (contrary to the expectations of some of the program's supporters in Congress). Eight years later the quality of evaluations of federal programs was quite poor, with little objective data to support claims of success and with unrepresentative, impressionistic, incomplete, or false evidence. Knowing that the state-local evaluations were poor and that federal funds were being misspent, federal education officials generally did not even read them. Thus, the law was not properly implemented, and the laissez faire administrative climate of its enforcement permitted this noncompliance to continue.[94]

State education agencies have traditionally been quite passive toward local school districts. They may cajole, suggest, urge, or even exhort certain actions, but they almost never require local education agencies to make changes in their educational practices. State education agency personnel see their proper role as providing technical assistance to local school districts — not enforcing the requirements of higher jurisdictions or setting program priorities.[95]

Because Medicaid's Early and Periodic Screening, Diagnosis and Treatment (EPSDT) program for children was picked up by so few states, Congress authorized cuts in funds for Aid for Dependent Children programs in states that were dragging their feet. While substantial penalties were assessed for failing to implement fully EPSDT, they have never actually been collected.[96]

The Water Resource Council has not exercised its discretionary authority in the allocation of funds and has spread them equally instead. Many states that have lagged in formal planning or have failed to participate in regional planning or to improve the integration and coordination of their water resource planning have not been penalized. The Water Resource Council has settled for paper performance rather than actual performance.[97]

Most regional officials and federal representatives adopted a policy of not interfering with the programmatic decisions of local prime sponsors of Comprehensive Employment and Training Act (CETA) projects, clearly violating federal regulations. They offered little guidance, giving the local sponsors great discretion. Because federal officials did not enforce the goal of serving the disadvantaged, local sponsors used their freedom and "skimmed" the most talented persons from the pool of potential trainees.[98]

The service orientation adopted by federal and some state officials toward officials of lower level jurisdictions is a product of many factors in addition to the need to maintain goodwill. Many federal and state officials have built up good personal relationships with officials of lower level jurisdictions over the years. Understandably, they are reluctant to jeopardize these relationships in an attempt to force their colleagues to conform to federal law. Officials of various levels of government may also share a professional ethos regarding their work, an ethos which includes deference to fellow professionals. Finally, officials in higher jurisdictions may have been recruited from the ranks of those in lower levels of government and therefore may not have much enthusiasm for regulating their former colleagues.[99]

FACILITIES

Physical facilities may also be critical resources in implementation. An implementor may have sufficient staff, may understand what he is supposed to do, may have authority to exercise his task, but without the necessary buildings, equipment, supplies, and even green space implementation won't succeed.

Schools often lack instructional materials,[100] prisons are often overcrowded, park space in urban areas is often scarce, and military equipment ranging from rifles to missiles is often said to be in short supply. The consequences of such a lack of facilities may be dramatic. Overcrowded prisons, for example, are generally viewed as a breeding ground for criminal behavior, not places where it is effectively discouraged. Schools lacking sufficient books and universities with substandard laboratories are unlikely to produce skilled graduates. Cities without parks force their children into the streets, and underequipped military forces are able to provide less than optimal national security.

Even the lack of seemingly mundane facilities can have significant consequences. The Merit Systems Protection Board (MSPS) was established by the Civil Service Reform Act of 1978 to handle federal employees' complaints and protect the whistleblowers in government who expose wrongdoing. By mid-1979, however, the three-member board was swamped with 4,600 backlogged cases, and almost everyone seemed to agree that the board was underfunded. Not only was the board short-handed; its facilities were also inadequate. According to board chairperson Ruth Prokop, the General Services Administration (the government's housekeeping organization) had not even appeared to drill holes in an office floor for a number of much needed telephones. Moreover, there was a lack of file cabinets. "We have files in cardboard supermarket boxes, under desks, stacked in corners, and stuffed in desk drawers," Mrs. Prokop said. "Hundreds of workhours are lost each month trying to answer the simple question: 'Where is the file on John Doe?' " There was also not enough money to establish field offices outside the metropolitan Washington, D.C., area despite the fact that most of the board's cases come from the field. These individuals' complaints were left to slide.[101]

There is also often a shortage of sophisticated equipment. Computers are essential to the implementation of modern defense policy; they issue paychecks, assign personnel, navigate ships, and track missiles. Nevertheless, a recent study of the military's computers found that the Defense Department is saddled with thousands of obsolete machines that leave the military services ill-prepared for a modern war. At one army base in the Midwest, the entire logistics system was operated on a $300 mini-computer purchased from a local Radio Shack. The base logistics officer had simply given up on the aging government machinery.[102]

How do implementors get the facilities and equipment they need? This question is not easily answered. A financially burdened public is generally not eager to increase taxes to pay for new facilities. Moreover, people often resist the placement of public facilities in their neighborhoods. If officials want to establish a minimum security prison, residents in the area are likely to protest. They fear prisoners may escape or that a prison would lower their property values. Public housing projects are often opposed for the same reasons. Nuclear reactors may be opposed, not only by those living closest to their proposed sites, but also by citizens throughout an entire state.

In the case of the obsolete military computers, government procurement rules presented obstacles to the purchase of new equipment. According to one official, any major computer purchase can be blocked by the General Services Administration, the General Accounting Office, the House Government Operations Committee, the Office of Management and Budget, and various offices within the military bureaucracy. "The result is that the local commander will decide to make do with what he's got rather than put his neck on the line for a system that can't be installed anyway for five or six years. The officer knows he will have been transferred by then anyway and won't have to worry about it." [103]

CONCLUSION

Resources are critical to effective policy implementation. Without them, policies that exist on paper are not the same policies that are carried out in practice. Slippage occurs.

Perhaps one of our more surprising findings is that staffs are often too small to implement effectively the policies for which they have been assigned responsibility. Since this shortage of personnel exists at every level of government, delegating the implementation of a policy to a lower level of government rarely alleviates the problem. The courts are especially limited in terms of staff, having only a very small bureaucracy to aid judges in their duties. Where implementation involves private individuals, personnel shortages also appear.

One consequence of personnel shortages is ineffectiveness in directly carrying out policies. An even greater problem is the severe limitations that often exist in monitoring the implementation activities of others or in regulating behavior. Whether it is private individuals or organizations or other levels of government being regulated, there is often a lack of staff to do the job. The courts are especially vulnerable here, with their miniscule bureaucracies.

If staff shortages are so common, why do they persist? The answers can be found in traditional American concerns about "big government." We have been hesitant to expand the bureaucracy out of fear of the exercise of power by public officials. We have also resisted spending tax revenues on government personnel when it could be spent on private individuals. This attitude is coupled with the irresistible urges of legislators to pass new programs. Staff shortages inevitably result. Many people feel that the benefits resulting from increasing staff size are not worth the increased costs of a large bureaucracy. The staff that does exist is usually allocated to providing services — a politically popular task — rather than to policing the actions of others, which always involves controversy.

Insufficient staff is especially critical to implementation when the policy involved is one which imposes on people unwelcome constraints, whether they be the requirements of grant policies, regulatory policies, or criminal law. Since such policies generally involve highly decentralized activities, a large staff is necessary if this behavior is to be monitored.

Skill as well as numbers is an important characteristic of staff for implementation. All too often public officials are lacking in the expertise, both substantive and managerial, needed to implement policies effectively. Delegating responsibility for the implementation of a policy to a lower level government jurisdiction usually only exacerbates rather than alleviates the problem.

Obviously, the more technical the policy involved and the more expertise required on the part of implementors, the more a shortage of skilled personnel will hinder policy implementation. The lack of skilled staff is especially a problem in new programs that require expertise, but for which there are few available personnel with experience.

Experienced and skilled personnel are often snatched up by the private sector, which can usually offer higher compensation. At other times personnel with the required skills do not exist.

A second critical resource in policy implementation is information. Implementors need to know how to carry out policies they are directed to implement. If policies are innovative and highly technical, finding someone who knows how to implement them is especially difficult. Often implementors have to learn on the job as they go along. Experience teaches them how to achieve a policy's goals. The consequences of many actions can only be guessed at because of lack of knowledge of the relationships between implementation behavior and policy outcomes. In general, policy sciences are not highly developed, and therefore we lack sophisticated models of how to move from the goals of a policy (as they exist in a newly passed piece of legislation, for example) to achieving those goals.

Monitoring the compliance of others with policy requirements also demands information. Yet implementors frequently lack the necessary data on the actions of the officials of other governmental units or jurisdictions or of private citizens and organizations. Often they rely upon those who are being monitored for information on their own compliance with the law — a situation unlikely to produce accurate data!

As a result of this lack of information, some policies are never implemented. Others are implemented on a trial and error basis as an understanding of how to implement a policy evolves slowly through the process of implementation and the responses of those involved on all sides. As for monitoring compliance with the law, there is every reason to believe that many, perhaps most, violations go undetected. While the most blatant instances of noncompliance may be uncovered, the more typical, less visible cases often remain hidden.

A lack of sufficient staff is a primary problem in acquiring the data necessary to enforce the requirements of policies. Sometimes government rules further restrict the acquisition of relevant information. Private individuals are in a poor position to monitor policy implementation in the private sector because of their lack of knowledge about complex public policies and the costs in time, money, and possible economic retaliation involved in discovering and reporting violations of regulations.

Authority is another resource important to policy implementation. Authority exists in many forms, from giving aid to constraining behavior. It is in regulating others where sufficient authority is most often lacking. Sometimes it does not exist, even on paper. At other times implementators have formal authority, but are constrained in their exercise of it. The embarrassment of having to rely upon coercion, the intervention of members of Congress or powerful local officials, criticism from the press, and simple self-preservation through positive actions such as awarding grants (to show the legislature a bureaucratic unit has a reason to exist) all limit the exercise of existing authority.

Authority may be inappropriate for tasks to which it is allocated. Governments may be able to manipulate funds from higher level jurisdictions to avoid sanctions for misuse of funds. Authority may also be too strong and therefore not credible, such as threatening to terminate a project as a result of a minor violation. Or implementors may be reluctant to exercise authority because this may hurt most those the policy is designed to help. Innocent third parties may bear a disproportionate share of the burden of the government's actions. Some persons, organizations, or jurisdictions may be willing to accept even stiff sanctions to avoid complying with a policy's requirements. Creating public controversy and seeking judicial review are tactics relevant to the implementation of only a few policies and rely heavily upon persons in the private sector to exploit them.

Courts are especially weak in terms of authority. They have few sanctions with which to encourage implementation, and they rarely exercise those they possess. Judges are generally reluctant to make substantive decisions on matters delegated to administrative discretion or to assume extensive administrative duties. Moreover, legislative bodies can easily overturn court decisions based on statutory interpretation.

When authority needs to be exercised over another level of government or between two or more branches of government, delays and complications are likely to result. Authority over individuals and institutions in the private sector, who often are responsible for policy implementation, is usually quite limited both in form and in fact.

When sanctions are exercised or the threat of sanctions is credible, they may be effective in improving implementation. Sometimes the threat of sanctions may provide essential political cover for officials of lower level jurisdictions to comply with the law, allowing them to make it clear to their constituents that they are doing so only under coercive pressures. At other times the real possibility of facing the costs of noncompliance, such as the loss of federal funding, may move officials to implement policies properly.

Lack of effective authority leads officials to adopt a service rather than a regulatory orientation toward those who are involved in regulation. One of the motivations behind such an approach is the obvious one of obtaining the cooperation of others through the creation of goodwill. A professional ethos of deference to fellow professionals, friendships developed over the years, and the recruitment of some officials of higher level jurisdictions from lower level governments serve to buttress this service orientation.

A lack of essential buildings, equipment, supplies, or land can hinder policy implementation as much as can inadequacies in the other resources we have examined. That there is frequently a shortage of facilities is clear. Budgetary limitations, intricate procurement regulations, and citizen opposition limit the acquisition of adequate facilities. This in turn limits the quality of the services that implementors can provide to the public.

NOTES

1. Charles O. Jones, *Clean Air: The Politics and Policies of Pollution Control* (Pittsburgh: University of Pittsburgh Press, 1975), p. 238.
2. "Radiation Unit Can't Do Job Ex-Official Says," *Houston Post,* March 1, 1980, p. 16A.
3. Jerome T. Murphy, "The Education Bureaucracies Implement Novel Policy: The Politics of Title I of ESEA, 1965-1972," in *Policy and Politics in America,* ed. Allan P. Sindler (Boston, Mass.: Little, Brown & Co., 1973), p. 173; Stephen K. Bailey and Edith K. Mosher, *ESEA: The Office of Education Administers a Law* (Syracuse, N.Y.: Syracuse University Press, 1968), pp. 154-155; Mike M. Milsten, *Impact and Response* (New York: Teachers College Press, 1976), p. 107; Beryl A. Radin, *Implementation, Change, and the Federal Bureaucracy* (New York: Teachers College Press, 1977), pp. 22, 59; Joel S. Berke and Michael W. Kirst, "Intergovernmental Relations: Conclusions and Recommendations," in *Federal Aid to Education: Who Benefits? Who Governs?,* eds. Joel S. Berke and Michael W. Kirst, (Lexington, Mass.: Lexington Books, 1972), pp. 386, 396; John F. Hughes and Anne O. Hughes, *Equal Education* (Bloomington, Ind.: Indiana University Press, 1972), p. 54; Floyd E. Stoner, "Federal Auditors as Regulators: The Case of Title I of ESEA," in *The Policy Cycle,* eds. Judith V. May and Aaron B. Wildavsky (Beverly Hills, Calif.: Sage Publications, 1978), pp. 206, 209; Harrell R. Rodgers, Jr. and Charles S. Bullock III, *Law and Social Change: Civil Rights Laws and Their Consequences* (New York: McGraw-Hill Books Co., 1972) p. 201.
4. Milsten, *Impact and Response* pp. 39-40; Berke and Kirst, "Intergovernmental Relations," p. 389; Michael W. Kirst, "The Politics of Federal Aid to Education in California," in *Federal Aid to Education,* eds. Berke and Kirst, p. 97; Lawrence Iannaccone, "The Politics of Federal Aid to Education in Massachusetts," in *Federal Aid to Education,* eds. Berke and Kirst, pp. 209, 211, 217-218.
5. Iannaccone, "The Politics of Federal Aid to Education in Massachusetts," pp. 197, 210.
6. Jay D. Scribner, "The Politics of Federal Aid to Education in Michigan," in *Federal Aid to Education,* eds. Berke and Kirst, p. 176.
7. Berke and Kirst, "Intergovernmental Relations," p. 388; Michael W. Kirst, "Federal Aid to Public Education: Who Governs?," in *Federal Aid to Education,* eds. Berke and Kirst, p. 69.

8. Charles L. Schultze, *The Public Use of the Private Interest* (Washington, D.C.: Brookings Institution, 1977); "More Love Canals?" *Newsweek,* May 14, 1979, p. 41; Marc J. Roberts and Susan O'Farrell, "The Political Economy of Implementation: The Clean Air Act and Stationary Sources," in *Approaches to Controlling Air Pollution,* ed. Ann F. Friedlaender (Cambridge, Mass.: MIT Press, 1978), p. 165; Helen M. Ingram and Dean E. Mann, "Environmental Policy: From Innovation to Implementation," in *Nationalizing Government: Public Policies in America,* eds. Theodore J. Lowi and Alan Stone (Beverly Hills, Calif.: Sage Publications, 1978), p. 144.

9. Roberts and O'Farrell, "The Political Economy of Implementation," pp. 162, 165. See also pp. 156-157.

10. "States Pondering Clean Air Plans as Filing Deadline Nears," *Congressional Quarterly Weekly Report,* March 17, 1979, p. 463.

11. Richard N. L. Andrews, *Environmental Policy and Administrative Change* (Lexington, Mass.: Lexington Books, 1976), pp. 38-40.

12. "Pesticide Program Criticized," *Congressional Quarterly Weekly Report,* January 8, 1977, p. 45; Jones, *Clean Air,* pp. 136, 268.

13. "More Love Canals?," p. 41.

14. Andrews, *Environmental Policy,* p. 113; Daniel A. Mazmanian and Jeanne Nienaber, *Can Organizations Change?: Environmental Protection, Citizen Participation, and the Corps of Engineers* (Washington, D.C.: Brookings Institution, 1979), pp. 38, 46; Richard A. Liroff, *A National Policy for the Environment: NEPA and Its Aftermath* (Bloomington, Ind.: University of Indiana Press, 1976), p. 117.

15. Joel F. Handler, *Social Movements and the Legal System: A Theory of Reform and Change* (New York: Academic Press, 1978), pp. 51-52.

16. "Congress to Take a New, Hard Look at Nuclear Power," *Congressional Quarterly Weekly Report,* April 7, 1979, p. 622.

17. Handler, *Social Movements and the Legal System,* p. 180.

18. "The Energy G-Men," *Newsweek,* April 30, 1979, p. 30.

19. "Energy Report: FEA, Oil Firm Seeks End to Secret, Highstakes Case," *National Journal,* December 13, 1975, p. 1707.

20. "Carter Orders Cooling Limit of 78 Degrees this Summer," *Congressional Quarterly Weekly Report,* July 14, 1979, p. 1397.

21. "Bitter Pills for the FDA," *Newsweek,* July 18, 1977, p. 93.

22. "Pet Store Owners Try to Recall Piranha," *Wisconsin State Journal,* July 17, 1976, Sec. 1, p. 3.

23. Handler, *Social Movements and the Legal System,* p. 84.

24. Albert N. Nichols and Richard Zeckhauser, "Government Comes to the Workplace: An Assessment of OSHA," *Public Interest* (Fall 1977): 53. For yet another example, see Martha Derthick, *Uncontrollable Spending for Social Services* (Washington, D.C.: Brookings Institution, 1975), pp. 40-41.

25. Handler, *Social Movements and the Legal System,* p. 94.

26. Charles S. Bullock III and Joseph Stewart, Jr., "When You Can't Do Everything at Once: Policy Implementation Under Conditions of Growing Responsibilities" (Paper delivered at the annual meeting of the American Political Science Association, New York, August-September 1978), pp. 12, 13, 21.

27. Handler, *Social Movements and the Legal System,* pp. 141-142.

28. "Study Cites Discrimination," *The Eagle,* April 12, 1979, p. 12A.

29. "Justice Unit Needs Help to Enforce Voting Rights," *New Orleans Times-Picayune*, June 18, 1978, sec. 1, p. 38.
30. "Customs Losing Air Battle," *The Eagle*, May 18, 1980, p. 5A.
31. Charles S. Bullock III and Harrell R. Rodgers, Jr., *Coercion to Compliance* (Lexington, Mass.: Lexington Books, 1976), p. 22.
32. Handler, *Social Movements and the Legal System*, pp. 180-181.
33. Neal Gross, Joseph B. Giacquinta, and Marilyn Bernstein, *Implementing Organizational Innovations* (New York: Basic Books, 1971), pp. 129-135; John Pincus, "Inventives for Innovations in Public Schools," in *Social Program Implementation*, eds. Walter Williams and Richard Elmore (New York: Academic Press, 1976), p. 56; Handler, *Social Movements and the Legal System*, pp. 141-142.
34. Andrews, *Environmental Policy*, pp. 39-40.
35. See, for example, Roberts and O'Farrell, "The Political Economy of Implementation," pp. 162, 165.
36. "Fallout Cover-up," *Newsweek*, April 30, 1979, p. 32.
37. "Kemeny Commission Cites Nuclear Risks, Sees Need for Fundamental Changes," *Congressional Quarterly Weekly Report*, November 24, 1979, p. 2667.
38. Carl E. Van Horn, "Implementing CETA" (Paper delivered at the annual meeting of the Midwest Political Science Association, Chicago, Illinois, April-May 1976), pp. 26-27.
39. Milsten, *Impact and Response*, pp. 41-43, 62-65; Iannaccone, "The Politics of Federal Aid to Education in Massachusetts," pp. 209, 211; Berke and Kirst, "Intergovernmental Relations," p. 391.
40. Frederic V. Malek, *Washington's Hidden Tragedy: The Failure to Make Government Work* (New York: Free Press, 1978), pp. 105-107.
41. See, for example, Milbrey W. McLaughlin, *Evaluation and Reform: The Elementary and Secondary Education Act of 1965/Title I* (Cambridge, Mass.: Ballinger Publishing Co., 1975), p. 19.
42. "$75 Million Aid Package for Nicaragua Approved by House," *Houston Post*, February 28, 1980, p. 8A.
43. Jones, *Clean Air*, pp. 304, 306.
44. Roberts and O'Farrell, "The Political Economy of Implementation," pp. 152, 156-158.
45. "Pollution Progress Report," *Congressional Quarterly Weekly Report*, June 7, 1975, p. 1175. See also Derthick, *Uncontrollable Spending*, p. 93.
46. Radin, *Implementation, Change, and the Federal Bureaucracy*, pp. 59, 109, 159, 168, 171-173, and 199. See also Iannaccone, "The Politics of Federal Aid to Education in Massachusetts," p. 209.
47. "House Approves $73 Billion for Labor, HEW," *Congressional Quarterly Weekly Report*, June 30, 1979, p. 1288; David S. Salkever and Thomas W. Bice, *Hospital Certificate-of-Need Controls: Impact on Investment Costs and Uses* (Washington, D.C.: American Enterprise Institute, 1979).
48. Handler, *Social Movements and the Legal System*, pp. 50-52.
49. U.S. Department of Justice, "LEAA News Release," Statement of LEAA Acting Administrator James M. H. Gregg before the Select Committee on Narcotics Abuse and Control, House of Representatives, Concerning LEAA Narcotics Program and Accountability, June 8, 1977.
50. Milsten, *Impact and Response*, p. 91. See also Kirst, "Federal Aid to Public Education: Who Governs?" p. 66.
51. Roberts and O'Farrell, "The Political Economy of Implementation," pp. 153, 156, 163-165.

52. Handler, *Social Movements and the Legal System*, pp. 86, 103-104.
53. Ibid., pp. 25, 81.
54. For another example, see Liroff, *A National Policy for the Environment*, pp. 64-70.
55. "Hospitals Hurting, Ask Congress for Help," *Congressional Quarterly Weekly Report*, March 22, 1980, p. 807.
56. See, for example, Milsten, *Impact and Response*, pp. 87-88.
57. Judith M. Feder, *Medicare: The Politics of Federal Hospital Insurance* (Lexington, Mass.: D. C. Heath & Co., 1977), pp. 12, 15-18, 20-21.
58. See, for example, Stoner, "Federal Auditors as Regulators," p. 211; Berke and Kirst, "Intergovernmental Relations," p. 378.
59. Handler, *Social Movements and the Legal System*, pp. 158-159.
60. Hughes and Hughes, *Equal Education*, p. 64; Murphy, "The Education Bureaucracies;" Radin, *Implementation, Change, and the Federal Bureaucracy*, pp. 62-63; Jerome T. Murphy, *State Education Agencies and Discretionary Funds* (Lexington, Mass.: D. C. Heath & Co., 1979), p. 24. See also Van Horn, "Implementing CETA," p. 26.
61. Radin, *Implementation, Change, and the Federal Bureaucracy*, pp. 14, 122; Hughes and Hughes, *Equal Education*, p. 66; Berke and Kirst, "Intergovernmental Relations," p. 378.
62. Berke and Kirst, "Intergovernmental Relations," pp. 379, 391.
63. Iannaccone, "The Politics of Federal Aid to Education in Masschusetts," p. 211.
64. Bullock and Rodgers, *Coercion to Compliance*, p. 20.
65. Helen Ingram, "The Political Rationality of Federal Air Pollution Legislation," in *Approaches to Controlling Air Pollution*, ed. Ann F. Friedlaender, p. 42.
66. See, for example, Bullock and Rodgers, *Coercion to Compliance*, pp. 20, 60.
67. For a discussion of the concern of bureaucratic units for organizational maintenance, see George C. Edwards III and Ira Sharkansky, *The Policy Predicament* (San Francisco: W. H. Freeman, 1978), pp. 121-126.
68. Eugene Bardach, *The Implementation Game: What Happens After a Bill Becomes a Law* (Cambridge, Mass.: MIT Press, 1977), pp. 72-73.
69. Andrews, *Environmental Policy*, pp. 153-154, 157-158. See also pp. 107, 109.
70. Ibid., pp. 158-160.
71. Jameson W. Doig, "Police Policy Behavior: Patterns of Divergence," *Policy Studies Journal* 7 (Special Issue 1978): 427-428.
72. Handler, *Social Movements and the Legal System*, pp. 24, 54, 174-175, 195-196, 201, 204-205.
73. Ibid., pp. 135-139.
74. For example, see Radin, *Implementation, Change, and the Federal Bureaucracy*, pp. 125-126.
75. Roberts and O'Farrell, "The Political Economy of Implementation," pp. 153, 166.
76. Ibid., p. 168.
77. Advisory Commission on Intergovernmental Relations, *The Intergovernmental Grant System: An Assessment and Proposed Policies*, Report A-57, *Community Development: The Working of a Federal-Local Block Grant* (Washington, D.C.: U.S. Government Printing Office, 1977), pp. 38-39.
78. Harold Wolman, *Politics of Federal Housing* (New York: Dodd, Mead & Co., 1971), pp. 26-28.

79. Nichols and Zeckhauser, "Government Comes to the Workplace," p. 54.
80. Handler, *Social Movements and the Legal System,* p. 180.
81. Bullock and Rodgers, *Coercion to Compliance,* pp. 26-27, 40, 44, 59, 64-66, 125.
82. Hughes and Hughes, *Equal Education,* pp. 63-66.
83. Michael W. Kirst, "The Politics of Federal Aid to Education in Texas," in Berke and Kirst, eds., *Federal Aid to Education,* p. 256.
84. Liroff, *A National Policy for the Environment,* pp. 66-67.
85. See, for example, Roberts and O'Farrell, "The Political Economy of Implementation," pp. 167-168; Milsten, *Impact and Response,* pp. 39, 41-42.
86. Feder, *Medicare,* pp. 2-3, 18-19, 35-42.
87. Ibid., pp. 17-19, 40-41.
88. Ibid., pp. 11, 40, 66-69, 135. Also, if hospitals were certified, the Social Security Administration could enforce nondiscriminatory policies, and it was administratively easier not to become too involved in evaluating hospitals. Ibid., p. 12.
89. Frederick A. Lazin, "The Failure of Federal Enforcement of Civil Rights Regulations in Public Housing, 1963-1971: The Co-optation of a Federal Agency by its Local Constituency," *Policy Sciences* 4 (September 1973).
90. Radin, *Implementation, Change, and the Federal Bureaucracy,* p. 112. For other examples of this technique, see Hughes and Hughes, *Equal Education,* p. 55.
91. General Accounting Office report cited in "Carter, Congress to Focus on Education," *Congressional Quarterly Weekly Report,* February 11, 1978, p. 255. For other examples of federal agencies accepting purely "paper compliance" see Van Horn, "Implementing CETA," pp. 27-28; Martha Derthick, *The Influence of Federal Grants* (Cambridge, Mass.: Harvard University Press, 1970), pp. 200, 210; Berke and Kirst, "Intergovernmental Relations," p. 396.
92. Hughes and Hughes, *Equal Education,* pp. 51-52; Berke and Kirst, "Intergovernmental Relations," p. 378.
93. Hughes and Hughes, *Equal Education,* pp. 77-80.
94. McLaughlin, *Evaluation and Reform,* pp. 19-20, 23, 24.
95. Hughes and Hughes, *Equal Education,* pp. 52-53, 65, 69, 75-80, 86; Kirst, "Federal Aid to Public Education," p. 66; Kirst, "The Politics of Federal Aid to Education in California," pp. 79-80; Scribner, "The Politics of Federal Aid to Education in Michigan," pp. 133, 147, 153-154; Iannaccone, "The Politics of Federal Aid to Education in Massachusetts," pp. 196, 210, 213-215; Kirst, "The Politics of Federal Aid to Education in Texas," pp. 237-238; Edith K. Mosher, "The Politics of Federal Aid to Education in Virginia," in Berke and Kirst, eds. *Federal Aid to Education,* p. 281; Frederick M. Wirt, "The Politics of Federal Aid to Education in New York," in Berke and Kirst, eds. *Federal Aid to Education,* pp. 328, 359; Berke and Kirst, "Intergovernmental Relations," p. 389; Stoner, "Federal Auditors as Regulators," p. 209. This is also true of state boards of education. See Kirst, "Federal Aid to Education," p. 68.
96. "New Child Health Program Awaits Floor Vote; Budget Backlash Feared," *Congressional Quarterly Weekly Report,* August 18, 1979, pp. 1715-1716.
97. Helen Ingram, "Policy Implementation Through Bargaining: The Case of Federal Grants-in-Aid," *Public Policy* 25 (Fall 1977): 499-526.

98. Donald C. Baumer, "Implementing Public Services Employment," in May and Wildavsky, eds., *The Policy Cycle,* pp. 177, 178, 191.

99. Milsten, *Impact and Response,* pp. 60, 86, 108.

100. See, for example, Gross, Giacquinta, and Bernstein, *Implementing Organizational Innovations,* pp. 135-139.

101. "Agency to Protect Federal Whistleblowers from Abuses Struggles with Money Woes," *Congressional Quarterly Weekly Report,* June 2, 1979, pp. 1057-1058.

102. "Study Claims Military Computers Obsolete," *The Eagle,* March 11, 1980, p. 5A.

103. Ibid.

4

Dispositions

In previous chapters we have seen that implementors must know what to do and have the capability of doing it if policy is to be implemented effectively. In this chapter we examine a third factor with important consequences for implementation: the dispositions of implementors. If implementors are well-disposed toward a particular policy, they are more likely to carry it out as the original decisionmakers intended. But when implementors' attitudes or perspectives differ from the decisionmakers', the process of implementing a policy becomes infinitely more complicated. Those who implement policies are in many ways independent of their nominal superiors who directly participate in the original policy decisions. As a result of various grant and revenue sharing programs and the nature of our judicial system, many national and state policies are ultimately implemented by officials or judges of another jurisdiction. This magnifies the independence of implementors, and independence provides them with opportunities to use their discretion, just as does the lack of clear and consistent communications that we analyzed in Chapter 2.

Because implementors generally have discretion, their attitudes toward policies may be obstacles to effective policy implementation. Richard Nixon was aware of this when he reversed his decision to launch a secret plan to deal with violent domestic dissenters. He knew that if he gave FBI Director J. Edgar Hoover a direct order to help implement the policy, Hoover would carry out the order in form. The president also knew, however, that the FBI director would see to it that he had cause to reverse himself. Thus, the lack of cooperation of a direct presidential appointee meant that the decision of the president mattered little.[1]

Why do many bureaucrats view policies from a different perspective than top decisionmakers? In this chapter we attempt to answer this question and examine the many ways in which the dispositions of implementors, including those in the private sector, affect implementation. We also consider the reasons why top officials are limited in their ability to replace existing personnel with staff more responsive to their desires. In discussing staffing problems, we examine executive appointments, civil service and judicial personnel systems, and methods of bypassing personnel. In the final section we investigate the question of altering implementors' dispositions through the use of incentives. We first show how incentives influence implementors' behavior, and then we examine the potential and limitations of manipulating rewards.

EFFECTS OF DISPOSITIONS

Many policies fall within a "zone of indifference." These policies will probably be implemented faithfully because implementors do not have strong feelings about them.[2] Other policies, however, will be in direct conflict with the policy views or personal or organizational interests of implementors. When people are asked to execute orders with which they do not agree, inevitable slippage occurs between policy decisions and performance. In such cases implementors will exercise their discretion, sometimes in subtle ways, to hinder implementation.

Sources of Parochialism

Although judges and private citizens also implement policies, officials in public bureaucracies are the most common implementors, and it is important that we understand some of the particular influences on their dispositions or attitudes. Government agencies have a tendency toward inbreeding. The selective recruitment of new staff helps to develop homogeneous attitudes. Those attracted to work for government agencies are likely to support the policies carried out by those agencies, whether they be in the fields of social welfare, agriculture, or national defense. Naturally, agencies prefer hiring like-minded persons. All this results in a relatively uniform environment in which policymaking takes place. More generally, bureaucrats serving in national, state, and local governments in the United States tend to have more liberal attitudes concerning most policy issues than the general public and often than their elected representatives.[3]

Aside from the initial recruitment of like-minded personnel, other aspects of organizational life foster parochial views among bureaucrats. All but a few high-level policymakers spend their careers within one agency or department.[4] Since people want to believe in what they do for a living, this long association strongly influences the attitudes of bureaucrats. For example, agency affiliation is a better predictor of most of the policy attitudes of upper level civil servants than is their personal background.[5] One result of this cliquishness is that intraorganizational communications pass mainly among persons who share similar frames of reference and who re-enforce bureaucratic parochialism by their continued association.

Related to longtime service in an agency is the narrow range of each agency's responsibilities. Officials in the Department of Education, for example, do not deal with the budget for the entire national government, but only with that part which pertains to their programs. It is up to others to recommend to the president and Congress what is best for national defense, health, or housing. With each bureaucratic unit focusing on its own programs, there are few people to view these programs from a wider perspective. For example, one author found that responsibility for developing the country's air transportation infrastructure is in the hands of bureaucrats whose predominant conception of the public good is a high quality of service for the small percentage of the public traveling by air. The perspective of these officials is narrow; the trade-offs involved in improved air service, such as higher costs and increased environmental damage, which are borne by the entire public, are ignored by them.[6]

The impact of self-recruitment and narrow service experience and responsibilities is buttressed by two other factors. Within each agency the distribution of rewards creates further pressure to view things from the perspective of the status quo. Personnel who do not support established organizational goals and approaches to meeting them are unlikely to be promoted to important positions.[7]

Influences from outside an agency also encourage parochial views among bureaucrats. When interest groups and congressional committees support an agency, they expect continued bureaucratic support in return. Since these outsiders generally favor the policies the bureaucracy has been carrying out all along (which the outsiders probably helped initiate), what they really want is "more of the same."

The influence of parochialism is strong enough that even some political appointees, who are in office for only short periods of time, adopt the narrow views of their bureaucratic units. The Nixon White House felt that even close associates of the president, such as Attorney General John Mitchell and Secretary of State William Rogers, were "captured" by the bureaucracy. Mitchell and Rogers were considered more responsive to their subordinates' views than to the president's.[8] The dependence of such officials on their subordinates for information and advice, the need to maintain organizational morale by supporting established viewpoints, and pressures from their agencies' clienteles combine to discourage high-ranking officials from maintaining broad views of the public interest.

As a result of these forces, bureaucrats will often be unfavorably disposed toward enthusiastic implementation of policies established by higher officials. Moreover, implementors will tend to see the health of their organizations as a high priority. Inevitably, there will be differences in policy viewpoints with top decisionmakers, differences in policy viewpoints between bureaucratic units, and efforts to serve narrow organizational interests. All of these factors affect implementation.

Dispositions Hindering Implementation

Implementors may oppose a policy, and their opposition can prevent a policy option from ever being tried. For some time there had been a policy debate over whether there should be a work requirement for those receiving welfare payments and able to work. During the Nixon administration, however, many top officials concluded that welfare administrators would not enforce a work requirement provision, even in the face of presidential exhortations and congressional demands. Thus, they had to turn to other alternatives, such as tax incentives, to encourage welfare recipients to work.[9]

Opposition to a policy may also defeat some of its immediate goals after it becomes law. The 1902 Reclamation Act limited the amount of land a farmer could own and irrigate with water from federal water projects. Farmers were also required to live on their land, and if they owned more than the allowable amount of land, they had to make a recordable contract promising to sell the excess within a specified time period. Interior Department officials opposed the law, however. They did not enforce the acreage limitation and recordable contract provisions, and they dropped (contrary to law) the residency requirement.

The field of education provides examples of the disinclination of implementors to carry out policies. Federal efforts to evaluate education programs fail unless local education officials are inclined to collect the requisite data. Often they are not.[10] One reason that many funds for Title I of the Elementary and Secondary Education Act of 1965 were not spent on disadvantaged children (as the law required) was that most of the administrators above the U.S. Office of Education desk officers responsible for monitoring compliance with Title I were not interested in enforcing the law. In addition, some state and local education agencies deliberately overlooked violations and covered them up.[11]

As we saw in Chapter 2, White House aides sometimes disregard ill-conceived presidential orders issued in anger. This refusal to transmit orders is often beneficial to both the president and the country. When those who directly implement policies ignore superiors' orders, the result can also be beneficial. For example, officials in the Internal Revenue Service refused to follow orders from the Nixon White House to conduct tax audits on the president's political opponents.[12] The country clearly benefited from this display of bureaucratic backbone.

Competing policy interests of implementors may hinder implementation efforts. During the 1973 Arab-Israeli Yom Kippur War, President Nixon ordered that supplies be sent to the Israelis. The order took four days to execute because of foot-dragging by the Pentagon, which feared alienating Arab countries and the Soviet Union. The Pentagon wanted to use civilian planes instead of Israeli planes at U.S. military bases to transport the supplies, but civilian planes were not readily available. Disagreement over which military planes to use ensued. Finally, the president had to call the secretary of defense and demand immediate action.[13]

Sometimes implementors selectively perceive instructions that they receive and thereby ignore instructions which are not congruent with their policy dispositions. In 1970 and 1971 the Army Corps of Engineers was not wholehearted in its attempt to implement the National Environmental Policy Act (NEPA). The Corps released environmental impact statements despite their nonconformity with its own guidelines and those of the Council on Environmental Quality. Few water resource projects were modified in response to environmental concerns, and the Corps did not request or use all the new professional help it needed to evaluate these concerns.

Similarly, the Soil Conservation Service (SCS) violated both the letter and the spirit of NEPA. The SCS did not broaden appreciably the range of environmental concerns it considered in evaluating the merits of water project proposals, and it avoided preparation of environmental impact statements whenever possible. It was not willing to alter either its priorities or its projects unless its staff and the local project sponsor wished to do so. The SCS interpreted NEPA as a narrow factional threat to its stream channelization projects and not to its soil conservation projects. Therefore, it stressed the complementary nature of environmental interests and soil conservation and glossed over inconsistencies between environmental interests and some of its water resource projects. (The Bureau of Sport Fisheries and Wildlife saw many adverse environmental effects of the projects of the SCS.) Both its and the Corps' environmental impact statements lacked detail, careful measurement of adverse environmental impacts of water projects, and objectively balanced discussions of the range of available alternatives. They consistently substituted undefended claims and judgments for factually supported conclusions.[14]

Judges also selectively perceive decisions of higher courts and engage in judicial foot-dragging in implementing them.[15] Values held by judges play an important role in their decisions, especially in cases where precedents and the law are ambiguous. In these cases judges have more discretion.[16] State judges or federal district court judges have often used their discretion to refuse to comply with Supreme Court decisions on controversial issues such as racial discrimination, or they have sought refuge in technicalities to avoid compliance.

Differences in organizational viewpoints may also impede the cooperation between agencies which is so often necessary in policy implementation. In the early 1970s the State Department and the Bureau of Narcotics and Dangerous Drugs (BNDD) did not work well together to control illicit drugs. The latter's emphasis on individual cases rather than on an overall strategy to help other countries control drugs upset State officials because they sometimes caused gunfights, embarrassment of corrupt foreign officials, and torture of American citizens peripherally involved in drug trafficking. Therefore, State resisted the expansion of the BNDD's foreign programs and tried to keep its agents under tight control. This, naturally, further frustrated BNDD agents.[17]

Officials in the BNDD and the Food and Drug Administration (FDA) also conflicted over drug control. They bickered over scheduling drugs such as new barbituates and amphetamines as controlled substances and setting production quotas for them. The FDA was suspicious of the BNDD's scientific capability to gauge the abuse potential of drugs and estimate legitimate medical uses for them. The BNDD, on the other hand, was suspicious of the FDA's commitment to controlling abusable drugs. As a result of these antagonisms, often new drugs were scheduled only after an epidemic of abuse had peaked, and quotas were set so loosely that neither production, inventories, nor prescriptions were restrained.[18]

The Oakland regional office of the Economic Development Administration (EDA) also illustrates how the different perspectives of bureaucratic units affect implementation. The Oakland program was not implemented successfully even though there was just one federal agency overseeing the policy and widespread agreement on the program's goals and the basic means of creating jobs through public works grants. The program was incompatible with some of the commitments of national and local agencies. The Department of Health, Education and Welfare, for example, saw EDA's attempts to train people for the airline industry as competing with its own skills centers for scarce funds. Other agencies with compatible goals lacked a sense of urgency about the project, preferred to see EDA function in nonurban areas, or had simultaneous commitments to other projects that demanded their time and attention. Thus, they also were not eager to aid in implementing the program. Finally, there were differences over which people and organizational units should run the program.[19]

There may also be differences in viewpoints within an agency between those with different program responsibilities. There was intra-agency conflict over the implementation of the National Environmental Policy Act (NEPA). Secretaries of transportation, for example, had a difficult time getting development-oriented agencies in the department, such as the Federal Highway Administration, to consider seriously the environmental consequences of their projects. One author found that the Highway Administration's environmental impact statements on urban highway projects were "arguments rather than findings, opinions rather than studies, and generalities rather than facts."[20] Standard phrases were used to dismiss potentially serious environmental damage. Highway planners just assumed that safer, more efficient highways had a positive effect on man's environment.

Similarly, intra-agency conflict in the Department of Housing and Urban Development (HUD) hampered implementation of NEPA. About 20 percent of the department was concerned with housing design, and it was these personnel who received responsibility for implementing the act. But those dealing with housing production dominated HUD, and therefore the department was slow to implement national environmental policies.[21]

Within most organizational units there is a dominant opinion about the organization's central mission. Although different groups within an organization have different primary functions, most organizations have some functions they clearly consider secondary. Generally, agencies allocate fewer resources and less time to those functions which they perceive as marginal. For example, top officials in the U.S. Department of Agriculture (USDA) did not provide resources or leadership for the enforcement of civil rights legislation regarding nondiscrimination in employment and the distribution of program benefits. Civil rights received low priority as attempts were made to circumvent enforcement, discourage staff initiatives to implement civil rights laws, and abolish the Office of Civil Rights. The position of director of the office was left vacant for 27 months.[22] Serving the needs of farmers is more important than enforcing civil rights laws in the eyes of most USDA officials.

Bureaucratic units usually seek responsibility for new programs which they feel will build upon and re-enforce the essential aspects of their policy missions. This may result in interorganizational bargaining and rivalries that may impede implementation. Some state education officials allocated federal funds appropriated under Title V of the Elementary and Secondary Education Act to the programs with the strongest advocates (or "squeaky wheels") rather than to programs selected after careful analysis and setting of priorities. Moreover, many new programs became permanent after once receiving funds because concern for the health of the organizations implementing each program led officials in those bureaucratic units to carry some programs beyond the point where their benefits exceeded their costs.[23] Similarly, the Massachusetts Department of Education's components have been accused of being empire builders, guarding their own federal programs and seldom working with people in another unit of the department. The main concern seems to be competition for funds rather than the most effective use of those funds.[24]

Bureaucratic units also resist vigorously the efforts of others to take away or share the resources deemed necessary to accomplish their missions. Feuding over responsibility for an activity has often hindered policy implementation. In the mid-1970s lack of cooperation between the Bureau of Customs and the Drug Enforcement Agency (DEA) hampered efforts to decrease the supply of narcotics and dangerous drugs entering the United States. The Customs Bureau was unfriendly to the DEA because it was angry at its loss of functions and personnel to the new agency. In return, the DEA tried to monopolize narcotics enforcement and exclude Customs, although the latter could have provided valuable assistance.[25]

Conflict within the Department of Health, Education and Welfare between the Office for Civil Rights and the Office of Equal Opportunity encumbered the department's attempts to implement Title VI of the 1964 Civil Rights Act. This title prohibited the use of federal funds in discriminatory programs. Each agency feared encroachment on its own programs, and this prevented the cooperation necessary for effective implementation.[26]

J. Edgar Hoover directed the Federal Bureau of Investigation with an iron fist from 1924 until 1972. According to Richard Nixon, Hoover

> ... had always been rigidly territorial when it came to the functions and prerogatives of the FBI. He totally distrusted the other intelligence agencies ... and, whenever possible, resisted attempts to work in concert with them.[27]

In 1970 the director cut off all liaison activities with the other intelligence agencies, such as the Central Intelligence Agency, the Defense Intelligence Agency, and the National Security Agency. This hindered President Nixon's efforts to control dissension at home. Hoover also dragged his feet on investigating Daniel Ellsberg, an antiwar activist who made available to the press copies of the "Pentagon Papers," a history of U.S. involvement in Vietnam based in part on classified information. Hoover resented the fact that other agencies were also investigating Ellsberg; he didn't want to share his territory with anyone.

Bureaucratic units try to achieve autonomy in carrying out their responsibilities. They think they know best how to perform their essential missions, and they do not want to be controlled by officials outside their organizations or to have to coordinate closely with other organizations. For example, the belief in local control of education is so strong in America that even state departments of education with good technical assistance capabilities often have limited impact on local school systems. Local school officials are generally too distrustful of outside interference to be very responsive to external direction.[28]

In 1969 Secretary of Health, Education and Welfare Robert Finch approved a plan to define more precisely guidelines and criteria for grants for community mental health centers and to delegate authority for awarding the grants to the top health official in each of HEW's 10 regional offices. Decisions were to be made by those closest to, and in the secretary's opinion, most able to evaluate, local needs, and the time required for communities to obtain grants was to be reduced greatly. Things did not work out this way, however. The National Institute of Mental Health (NIMH) strongly resisted the secretary's implementation directive. The director of NIMH felt his office should have discretion to make decisions on the grants, so he made a back-door appeal to a congressional subcommittee that appropriated funds for NIMH. The subcommittee was responsive to the director's wishes and wrote into the coming year's appropriations bill a requirement that all staffing grants had to receive a Washington-based advisory committee's approval. Although Finch transferred the NIMH director to a nonsupervisory role where he could not obstruct policy (he could not be fired), the new law blocked any chance of changing the program that year.[29]

The attitudes of private individuals may also affect significantly the process of implementing public policy. Private individuals who use or sell leaded gas can cause obvious setbacks to governmental antipollution efforts; it only takes two or three tanks of leaded fuel in a motor vehicle to ruin catalytic converters. Similarly, the disposition of private individuals toward racial integration in housing has a major influence on whether sellers and renters discriminate.

Sometimes the dispositions of the potential beneficiaries of a policy prevent them from exploiting available benefits. Efforts to establish and operate cooperative health associations for some rural Spanish-speaking communities in the U.S. failed, despite a great need for health care, largely because the members of the associations were not accustomed to the responsibility of participating in formal organizations. They did not like the impersonal nature of the cooperative organizations and found them too demanding in time and effort. Thus, they did not do their part to help the program succeed.[30]

STAFFING THE BUREAUCRACY

Implementors' dispositions pose serious obstacles to policy implementation. But if existing personnel do not implement policies the way top officials desire, why are they not replaced with people more responsive to leaders? In this section we attempt to answer this question by considering executive appointments, civil service systems, judicial personnel systems, and methods of bypassing existing personnel.

Appointments

A president and presidential designees have authority to appoint approximately 2,600 full-time officials in the executive branch. The president alone has authority to appoint about 650 persons. This total includes the White House staff, between 15 and 20 individuals in each of the cabinet-level departments, about 10 persons in each of the major independent agencies (such as the Veterans Administration and the National Aeronautical and Space Administration), the heads of some lesser agencies, and commissioners of the independent regulatory agencies (as their terms expire).[31] In the entire executive branch of the federal government, there are roughly five million employees. Far less than one percent are appointed by the president and his designees. This is an obvious constraint on the ability of any administration to alter personnel.

How are those persons who are appointed to the federal government selected? Are they carefully screened so that only the most competent individuals are appointed to political office? One former White House personnel adviser reports that most appointments at the beginning of a new administration (when most appointments are made) are the result of the BUGAT (bunch of guys around the table) approach rather than a more systematic and comprehensive talent search.[32]

After being elected, a president has less than three months to search for a new team to take over the government. Moreover, this must be done by the president-elect and aides who are exhausted from the long, arduous election campaign and have many other demands on their time, such as preparing a budget and a legislative program. Members of the cabinet and other appointees usually have little advance notice of their selection and are busy wrapping up their other responsibilities and doing their homework on the issues relevant to their new positions prior to their confirmation hearings. Thus, they, too, often resort to haphazard recruiting techniques when they make their appointments.[33]

Presidents are also constrained politically in their appointments. Usually they feel these appointments must show a balance of geography, ideology, ethnicity, sex, and other demographic characteristics salient at the time. Thousands of persons are urged upon an administration by themselves, members of Congress, or people in the president's party. (One Nixon aide put the number at 500 per week.) Few of these persons are qualified for available jobs, but due to political necessity, more than a few are appointed. Political favors may please political supporters, but they do not necessarily provide the basis for sound administration. Moreover, such appointments may result in incompatibilities with the president that lead to politically costly dismissals.[34]

The interest groups that appointments are designed to please keep a watchful eye throughout a president's tenure in office on who is appointed to what position. "Balance" is important not only at the beginning of a new administration, but remains a constraint on recruiting personnel. Thus, in the middle of a term White House aides may be ordered to find a Mexican-American woman to serve as U.S. Treasurer. A president also might desire to reward new groups. After the 1972 presidential election, Richard Nixon wanted his cabinet and subcabinet to represent more accurately his broadened electoral coalition. This led to a renewed emphasis on the demographic characteristics of appointees, delays in filling positions, and, most significantly, compromises in the quality of some appointees, such as many of those placed in top positions in the Labor Department to please the president's new "hard hat" constituency. It also led to a humorous incident in which Claude Brinegar was selected as secretary of transportation partly on the basis of his Irish Catholic background. The White House was in error, however. Brinegar was really a German Protestant.[35]

A different type of "political" constraint may arise if a strong member of an administration opposes a person the president desires to appoint. Usually the president can overcome this opposition within the ranks, but sometimes the price may be too high. In his second term President Nixon wanted to appoint John Connally secretary of state, but did not do so because of the opposition of his chief adviser on national security matters, Henry Kissinger. Instead, Kissinger was named to head the State Department.[36]

A surprising but nonetheless real limitation on personnel selection is that presidents often do not know qualified individuals for the positions they have to fill. Following his election in 1960, John F. Kennedy told an aide:

> For the last four years I spent so much time getting to know people who could help me get elected President that I didn't have any time to get to know people who could help me, after I was elected, to be a good President.[37]

Presidents often appoint persons they do not know to the highest positions in the federal government. While President Nixon was deeply involved in choosing the secretary of state, he had never even heard of his selections to head the Departments of Commerce and Transportation until his advisers recommended their names to him, and he never met them until they traveled to Camp David where he personally offered them their jobs.[38] Such actions are not unique to President Nixon; all recent presidents have made some cabinet selections with little personal knowledge of the candidates.

Early in their terms recent presidents have usually not imposed their preferences for subcabinet level officials upon those whom they appoint to head departments and agencies.[39] This has no doubt been partially due to the lack of organization in the personnel system. In addition, however, there has been a concern that since top officials will be held accountable for agencies' performances, they should be able to apoint subordinates whom they like and who will complement their own abilities and help them accomplish their jobs.[40] Naturally, top officials generally request this freedom. High officials also fight to name their subordinates because if they lose to the White House on personnel matters, their standing within their departments will drop.[41]

As presidential terms extend from weeks into months and years, the White House's perspective sometimes changes. Often frustrating problems in policy implementation lead the president and his staff to take a more direct interest in personnel matters below the levels of department and agency heads. For example, in mid-1978 the Carter administration began a review of subcabinet officials with the object of weeding out those who were incompetent or disloyal. Tim Kraft was promoted to the position of assistant for political affairs *and* personnel (indicating an appreciation for the linkage between the two). Kraft and his staff began taking more interest in appointees:

> We have told the personnel people in the departments that we want to be consulted on all appointments, whether they are presidential appointments or appointments to high GS [civil service] positions.[42]

Despite its frequent use, political clearance is often a crude process. Many policy views fit under a party label. Democrats range from very liberal to very conservative, and the range for Republicans is nearly as great. Moreover, political appointees are not necessarily responsive to the president. They may be motivated by materialistic or selfish aims, such as a fat cat donor in search of an ambassadorship or a young lawyer seeking experience in the Justice Department or a regulatory agency in hopes of cashing in on it later for a high-paying job in the private sector. Political appointees may also remain loyal to their home-state political organizations, interest group associations, or sponsors in Congress — rather than to the White House.[43]

Conversely, if political appointees are viewed as too close to the White House, they may be "shut out" in their departments and from their departments' client groups and thus be of limited usefulness to the president. No matter how loyal to the president appointees are, they need to know what to do and how to do it once they obtain their positions. People with these capabilities, as we have seen, are not easy to find. Moreover, too many political lieutenants in a department may separate the top executive from the bureaucracy and its services. They may also decrease the executive's opportunities to build personal support within the bureaucracy through communication, consultation, and access.[44]

U.S. attorneys present a special problem for policy implementation. While they litigate on behalf of the federal government and are political appointees, they cannot be dismissed by the U.S. attorney general. As direct presidential appointees, they have considerable independence and are a continuous source of frustration to Justice Department officials trying to coordinate litigation.[45]

The problems of staffing state and local governments are also substantial from the standpoint of affecting the dispositions of implementors. Governors often have few appointments open to them. Since heads of state-level departments such as education and agriculture are frequently elected independently of the governor and may be of a different party, a governor cannot even depend upon a cooperative cabinet.

Governors and other top state officials also face the same constraints the president faces in setting up comprehensive talent searches and in pleasing their electoral supporters. Moreover, they generally must rely upon state residents to fill their appointed positions, while the president can use the entire country as a talent pool. Mayors, city managers, county executives, school superintendents, and other local government executives face even greater problems in their search for talented people to fill positions. They draw from a more limited pool of individuals and often have few resources with which to screen applicants. Of course, these officials also must please their electoral coalitions. Thus, although some local government executives have a considerable number of appointments at their discretion, they are not necessarily able to use them to improve the chances of their policies being implemented as they desire.

Civil Service

Below appointed officials in the federal hierarchy rank most executive branch employees. Almost all civilian employees are covered by the protection of the civil service system. The system is designed to fill positions on the basis of merit and protect employees against removal for partisan political reasons. (The military and a few civilian agencies such as the FBI and the State Department have separate personnel systems designed to accomplish the same goals.)

Traditionally, there has been substantial distrust between "political" executives and the rest of the bureaucracy.[46] Distrust of the implementation efforts of the federal bureaucracy has been especially prominent in the administrations of Republican presidents. Nixon's White House chief of staff, H. R. Haldeman, complained that real policy decisions were made by civil servants who viewed a Republican administration as a "transient phenomenon."[47] At one point career officials in the Department of Health, Education and Welfare were chaperoned on visits to Capitol Hill to prevent them from displaying reservations about the administration's proposals. This practice ended when Senator Russell Long complained.[48]

Research on high-level bureaucrats during the Nixon presidency supports this view of a hostile executive branch. There were few Republicans in the senior civil service, especially in social welfare agencies such as Health, Education and Welfare and Housing and Urban Development, and the Democrats tended to provide considerably more support for liberal domestic policies than Republicans (or Republican presidents). Thus, the quip that "even paranoids may have real enemies" is particularly applicable to the Nixon administration.[49]

While it is possible for an incompetent or recalcitrant civil service employee to be dismissed, this rarely happens. In a 1978 press conference President Carter announced that "last year . . . only 226 employees lost their jobs for inefficiency."[50] More dramatically, press secretary Jody Powell later exclaimed, "It is damn near impossible to fire someone from this government for failure to do their job."[51] It simply takes more time, expertise, and political capital to fire a civil servant than most officials have or are willing to invest in such an effort.[52] Well aware of this situation, high federal officials must look to other means to remove unresponsive bureaucrats from positions in which they can obstruct implementation of the president's policies.

Both the frustration presidents often experience as a result of their dependence on the bureaucracy and the necessity of altering its make-up through indirect measures are captured in the following statement by President Nixon to his director of the Office of Management and Budget, George Schultz:

> You've got to get us some discipline, George. You've got to get it, and the only way you get it, is when a bureaucrat thumbs his nose, we're going to get him. . . . They've got to know, that if they do it, something's going to happen to them, where anything can hap -

pen. I know the Civil Service pressure. But you can do a lot there. There are many unpleasant places where Civil Service people can be sent. We just don't have any discipline in government. That's our trouble. . . . We got to get it in these departments. . . . So whatever you — well, maybe he is in the regional office. Fine. Demote him or send him to the Guam regional office. There's a way. Get him the hell out.[53]

Transferring unwanted personnel to less troublesome positions is one of the most common means of quieting obstructive bureaucrats. In President Carter's words, it is "easier to promote and transfer incompetent employees than to get rid of them."[54] Transferring unwanted personnel is much easier when the civil servants in question opt not to use the technicalities and protections of the civil service system or their allies in Congress and interest groups. Ironically, these are the types of persons most likely to be dedicated to the notion of a civil service and therefore the ones an executive would probably least desire to replace.[55]

Transferring personnel is not a panacea for the problems of implementors' dispositions because it doesn't solve problems; it just removes them. And some bureaucrats successfully resist transfer. In 1966 differences between Assistant Secretary of State Abba Schwartz and Passport Office Director Frances Knight were publicized. Knight opposed her superior's more liberal interpretation of the State Department's passport and visa policy. Unable to dismiss Knight, Schwartz attempted to transfer her within the department. But Knight rallied support to her defense in Congress. The controversy was resolved by a departmental reorganization designed to eliminate the position held by Schwartz himself.[56] Other techniques, such as early retirement, may also be used, but they are necessarily of limited utility.[57]

In response to President Carter's request, Congress established in 1978 a voluntary Senior Executive Service for top civil service executives. These officials will be easier to transfer and demote, but they will also be eligible for bonuses and substantial pay increases if their performance is outstanding. In September of 1979 the federal government announced that of the 5,619 top-ranking executives covered by civil service who were given the chance, at least 96 percent chose to leave the traditional civil service protection and join the new Senior Executive Service. Most of those who did not were nearing retirement.[58] While this policy directly affects only a small percentage of the civil service, those to whom it does apply are among the most powerful members of the career bureaucracy, and it may aid the president's efforts to improve the bureaucracy's implementation of federal policies.[59]

The Nixon administration abused the civil service system.[60] Political referral units in the departments were established, procedures to "get" enemies were considered, a manual for training political executives in the manipulation of the merit system was put out by the White House, and appointments to key civil service positions received political clearance from the White House. Although these abuses were more widespread and systematic than in previous administrations, this was a culmination of a trend toward politicizing the bureaucracy, a trend emphasizing operational control of the executive bureaucracy, not traditional patronage. Since Nixon had neither the charisma of Kennedy nor the innovative programs with new jobs of Johnson to engender loyalty to White House policies, he and his lieutenants relied more heavily on attempts to bring the executive branch under the comprehensive managerial control of the president.[61]

These efforts were not uniformly successful. One reason was resistance from political executives. Hugh Heclo concludes that in general the success of the Nixon White House's political referral and "must hire" directives varied inversely with the will of the executives receiving them to stand up for their prerogatives and protect their agencies' personnel procedures.[62]

An additional problem was the long period of time (often many months) required to have an outsider cleared by the Civil Service Commission for a career position, and the higher the position the longer the clearance time involved. The Civil Service Reform Act of 1978 delegated to agency heads the authority to examine and hire potential civil service employees. Whether this will significantly speed up the process remains to be seen.

The Nixon strategy was not a total failure. Comparing 1976 to 1970, two scholars found fewer Democrats and more Independents in both top career and politically appointed managerial positions, and the Independents were more likely to lean toward identifying with Republicans. Moreover, while all groups of top federal executives had favorable attitudes toward the Republican administration's domestic policies, those selected during the Republican White House years were, as a group, the most positive. If data were available for early 1969, these results might have been even more striking. Nevertheless, the number of vacancies the Nixon administration was able to fill was limited. After eight years of Republicans in the White House, nearly 70 percent of the existing top career and political executives had assumed their positions before the Nixon administration. (The figure for career executives alone was 85 percent.) Thus, filling vacancies is unlikely to be a sufficient strategy to alter the attitudes in the bureaucracy. The president must also influence those already holding their jobs.[63]

The president may possess other techniques of exercising influence over staffing the bureaucracy. Writing about the military, Arnold

Kanter argues that the president can indirectly elicit compliance with presidential policies by manipulating the services' perceptions of their organizational problems and opportunities. By changing the environment in which the services operate, bargaining advantages, i.e., high positions, can be reallocated within the services to those more sympathetic to the president's views. Kanter found that intraservice promotion opportunity ratios responded to changes in strategic military doctrine as operationalized in terms of budget allocations (the environmental factor which is manipulated). Following their organizational self-interests, the services promote officers to high positions who are more likely to reflect the president's views on national security policy.[64]

Such a strategy is limited by a number of factors. The president is limited in the range of alternative roles and missions the military services can fulfill, and there may be no group of officers whose professional perspectives are congruent with those of the White House. Actions such as uncompensated budget and personnel reductions may meet with unanimous resistance. Moreover, the promotion process is inevitably a slow one. Nevertheless, Kanter argues, by using formal authority to allocate budgetary resources in support of policy preferences, the president can move the service's definition of its tasks and responsibilities closer to his own.[65]

The extent of civil service coverage in state and local governments varies widely, and nobody seems to know for sure just who is and who is not covered. It is probably safe to say that most state employees and employees of school districts have the protection of a merit system of selection and can be fired for "cause" only. Policy differences with top officials usually do not constitute cause for removal. The freedom of executives to fill positions in the municipal bureaucracy with those who share their policy dispositions is also limited to some extent by merit systems. Aggressive unions representing public employees further limit the ability of executives to remove state and local employees whose dispositions impede the implementation of their policies.

Courts

The courts have unique staffing problems. While in theory the United States has a unified court system, federal courts have virtually no influence on the selection of judges to state and local courts and vice versa. All federal judges are appointed by the president and confirmed by the Senate, while state and local judges are either elected or appointed by state and local officials or special committees set up for judicial selection. Even within the federal system or a state system, higher court judges have little control over who occupies positions on lower courts. Since most federal judges have life terms and state and local judges usually can be removed only by the voters or by failing to gain reappointment at the end of their generally lengthy terms, higher court judges have virtually no means of removing unsatisfactory lower court judges. Once again we find that the courts are weak in their ability to control the implementation process.

Bypassing Personnel

One way to increase the chances that a policy will be implemented properly is to choose implementors favorably disposed toward that policy. In other words, bypass existing personnel who might object to a policy and utilize others. A simple example of this occurs when the president bypasses the State Department and relies upon a special envoy to carry out a diplomatic mission.

A new agency may be established — sometimes in the Executive Office of the President — to implement policy as top officials desire. President Johnson put the Office of Economic Opportunity in the Executive Office, and President Kennedy did the same for the Peace Corps and the U.S. Arms Control and Disarmament Agency. These actions dramatized the presidents' personal concern for these programs and focused national attention on them. Moreover, this technique gives the president direct control over the favored program, and White House backing helps insulate it from early erosion in bureaucratic warfare.[66]

New state and local agencies were set up for urban renewal and public housing policies, and governmental units were bypassed in setting up the Office of Economic Opportunity's community action programs and local job training centers under the Comprehensive Employment and Training Act. Federal officials then attempted to shape the values and conceptions of the personnel involved to be consistent with the intentions of federal policymakers.[67]

In the fall of 1969, the commissioner of education deliberately took pains to bypass the traditionalist Bureau of Elementary and Secondary Education to ensure the treatment of problems of Title I of the Elementary and Secondary Education Act at a higher level of consideration. He hoped to increase enforcement of Title I provisions through this means.[68]

Despite the attraction of bypassing existing personnel, top officials usually have no choice in assigning implementation to a given agency. In most instances existing departmental jurisdictions determine which agency will handle a given problem. Similarly, appellate courts have virtually no discretion concerning the lower courts to which they return their decisions for implementation. They must return them to the courts from which the cases initiated. Moreover, legislatures are not likely to support a proliferation of agencies to handle new policies. As we will see in the next chapter, new agencies only increase the fragmentation of government and may disturb the balance of power represented by committee jurisdictions in the legislature. New agencies are also likely to increase the cost of governing.

INCENTIVES

Changing the personnel in government bureaucracies is difficult, and it does not ensure that the implementation process will proceed smoothly. Another potential technique to deal with the problem of implementors' dispositions is to alter the dispositions of existing implementors through the manipulation of incentives. Since people generally act in their own interest, the manipulation of incentives by high-level policymakers may influence their actions. Increasing the benefits or costs of a particular behavior may make implementors more or less likely to choose it as a means of advancing their personal, organizational, or substantive policy interests. In this section we illustrate how incentives influence implementors' behavior, and we examine the advantages and difficulties of manipulating incentives to affect implementation.

Incentives and Implementors' Behavior

In Dolbeare and Hammond's study of communities' responses to the Supreme Court's school prayer decisions, they did not find that local school elites were hostile to the decisions. But they did not comply. Local officials, weighing their own preferences against the costs of compliance, concluded that above all conflict over compliance with the court decisions should be avoided. Understandably, they did not want to endanger such priority items as consolidation, building, taxation, and curriculum changes. Supporters of the Court's decisions were poorly organized, inactive, or fearful of being labeled dissidents. Hence there was little pressure on school officials from their communities to comply. School officials were neither rewarded nor punished for their actions. Since no one stood to gain by compliance, no one acted. "Officials at all levels," according to Dolbeare and Hammond, "operated under a personal cost-benefit equation, seeking only those goals which they valued most highly and sacrificing others."[69]

In the area of desegregation compliance, individuals also tried to increase their benefits and decrease their costs. Often public accommodations regulations were complied with simply because they were good for business. In other areas of integration, however, leaders responsible for implementation had to confront conflict, social ostracism, and strong opposition from opponents of the laws. This made implementation more difficult.[70]

Department of Justice officials and U.S. attorneys are often at loggerheads. Charged with the formulation of a coherent national policy, the department perceives the outlook of U.S. attorneys as too parochial. Justice Department officials accuse U.S. attorneys of resisting department directives by failing to prosecute cases at the right time or failing to prosecute the cases that will establish the best precedents. The core of the problem is that the U.S. attorneys lack specific responsibility for the formulation of national policy and therefore have few incentives to follow it. Moreover, attorneys in the two groups have different career ambitions. The U.S. attorneys are not careerists while those in the Justice Department often are. Thus, the former don't want to take cases that would make them look bad while the latter want control to improve their personal or departmental record.[71]

Studying the implementation of the National Environmental Policy Act (NEPA) in 1970 and 1971, one author found that projects of the Army Corps of Engineers were rarely cancelled, postponed, or significantly changed as a result of internal evaluations by the Corps or comments by other federal agencies. Instead, political pressures, specific threats, and controversy associated with certain projects brought about most of the changes. Similarly, few significant changes resulted directly from judicial decisions. Only when projects were threatened with delay or possible extinction, did the Corps of Engineers have the necessary incentive to apply NEPA procedures. Because the Corps was visible, it was vulnerable to political forces demanding the implementation of environmental policy and easily thwarted by the withdrawal of support by a governor or a member of Congress or by public opposition.[72]

The author of another study found that state employment services had pressured the U.S. Department of Labor to place less emphasis on serving the poor and others with special problems in finding jobs and revert to its old concerns of satisfying its clientele of employers by providing "attractive" people to fill openings. So the Office of Economic Opportunity (OEO) and its local community action agencies applied countervailing pressure on the Department of Labor to keep the emphasis on creating opportunities for the poor, locating employment offices in ghettos, and developing new kinds of programs. By threatening the employment services' organizational well-being, the OEO and its local agencies were able to increase the costs of not helping the poor.[73]

The previous examples illustrate not only that incentives affect implementation, but also that pressures external to the bureaucracy can and do provide incentives to implement policies in certain ways. The activities of Congress are particularly noteworthy in this regard. Congress continuously intervenes in policy implementation, usually in the form of individual members requesting special treatment for interested parties in their constituencies. Behind most of these requests are the unspoken but nevertheless very clear potential sanctions of cutting agency funding or authority if the requests are not met.[74]

Rewards in the Public Sector

Most of the pressures discussed above are beyond the control of top officials whose ability to exercise sanctions is severely limited. Rewards are the other side of the incentive coin, but they are even more difficult for executives to administer than penalties. In all levels of the executive and judicial branches of government, individual performance is difficult to reward with pay increases. In 1978 President Carter complained that "more than 99 percent of all federal employees got a so-called 'merit' rating."[75] Raises are almost always given "across-the-board," with everyone in the same category of employment receiving a similar percentage increase in salary regardless of differences in performance. The Civil Service Reform Act of 1978 provided for merit pay increases for many managers, supervisors, and top executives in the federal civil service, but the impact of this change remains to be seen.

Usually personal performance can only be rewarded by promotions, and they are necessarily infrequent. In many important public bureaucracies seniority — not performance — is the basis of promotions. Automatic promotions because of seniority are hardly an incentive. For judges there simply is no promotion system from within the judiciary. Most judges never move beyond the level they first attain.

Officials who oppose or who are indifferent to a policy are unlikely to employ incentives to further its implementation. Police officers are seldom rewarded for compliance with Supreme Court defendant rights decisions, nor are they often punished for noncompliance with them.[76] Similarly, there are few incentives for the Departments of Defense and Energy to comply with requirements for arms control impact statements. These departments receive their budgets from congressional committees with little interest in the statements.[77]

The effects of rewards may be mitigated by peer group pressure. Police officers will not want to be "deviant" and obey Supreme Court guidelines if their colleagues do not do so. Peer group pressure is especially strong for police because they depend upon their fellow officers due to the uncertainty and contradictions inherent in their roles. This may re-enforce views of potential conflict with outside authorities like the Supreme Court and also may cause officers to forego individual organizational advantages to conform to traditional behavior patterns.[78]

Rewarding an entire organizational unit for outstanding performance is almost impossible. Everyone cannot be promoted, nor can everyone receive special bonuses. What reward does a school system reap for integrating or a water resources agency for complying with environmental protection requirements? At best they avoid problems. They receive no extra benefits contingent upon their performance.[79]

Some efforts at employing rewards to encourage implementation are made, however. Subsidy programs are often legislatively packaged with more coercive programs. These "sweeteners" attempt to render the controversial programs more palatable. For example, in the Elementary and Secondary Education Act of 1965, Title V, which allocated funds to the state departments of education, was included in the bill in part to please state school officials who were upset by some of the other titles.[80] Similarly, Title III grants in the federal Water Resources Planning Act of 1965 were used as a "sweetener" for state governments in exchange for cooperation in implementing the more controversial Title II, which established regional river basin commissions.[81] The former Department of Health, Education and Welfare reshaped its regulation writing process and some of its regulations to facilitate agreement among federal, state, and local authorities who were competing over the implementation of health programs.[82]

Rewards in the Private Sector

As we have seen, private citizens and organizations have responsibility to implement many public policies. Positive economic incentives such as profits play a powerful role in influencing behavior in the private sector. Governments make some use of this type of incentive, such as offering tax reductions to a company for moving a plant to a community or to businesses or individuals who invest in the production of certain goods or services. More typically, however, governments rely upon negative sanctions, such as fines for noncompliance with the law.

A number of observers have suggested that governments make more use of positive incentives to foster private activity consistent with public goals.[83] They argue, for example, that governments ought to pay businesses not to train people for jobs but only if the trainees acquire skills. Or that rather than providing inexpensive capital to businesses in areas of high unemployment to create jobs, governments ought to pay part of the cost to businesses of minority workers actually hired. Another proposal would tax employers for industrial accidents rather than attempt to regulate working conditions comprehensively. Some suggest that instead of paying the private sector on a cost-plus basis or an open-ended basis, such as for tanks and Medicare, respectively, governments should contract in advance for what they will pay and what they will receive for that money.

To understand more fully the incentive approach, let us examine a policy area in which economic incentives have been most strongly advocated: environmental protection.[84] It is argued that we ought to provide tax reductions to industries that limit pollution, charge fees for the pollution that is discharged, or sell rights to pollute which can then be transferred between companies, rather than set standards and enforce them with negative sanctions. Here, as in other areas where policies are aimed at reducing the harmful side effects of private activities, private interests would have continuous incentives (to keep reducing their taxes, for example) and not stop improving the environment when a certain standard had been met. Private companies would also have an incentive to do as well as they could, even if they could not remove all the harmful side effects. Rather than failing to meet a given standard — the "all or nothing approach" — they would do the best they could and receive economic benefits accordingly.

Moreover, incentives would allow industry the flexibility to employ the most effective and efficient means to accomplish environmental goals. And since ends rather than means are specified, the costs of enforcing the law would be less. Information would have to be collected only on the results of environmental protection efforts and not on the ways in which the results were accomplished. In 1978 the Environmental Protection Agency began some limited experiments using economic incentives to regulate air pollution.

Carrying out such proposals successfully will be very difficult, however.[85] First, the problem of monitoring the discharge of pollutants remains under the market or fee system, contrary to the claims of some advocates. Indeed, it is even greater because compliance must be measured exactly in order to calculate the tax benefits to be distributed, the fees to be assessed, or the amount of pollution rights used. Under the present system an industry either pollutes or it does not. Thus, continuous and precise monitoring is less important. It is easier to use incentives when violations leave a trail of paper behind them; they can be discovered more easily.

A second problem with an incentive system is that we generally do not know the relationship between the incentives and the behavior we wish to encourage. If we set fees or taxes too high, we may force companies to spend enormous amounts of money to eliminate discharges, passing the costs on to consumers. That level of air or water quality may be more than that for which we are willing to pay, however. Or we may set the fees or taxes too low, thus making it worthwhile for industries to pay them and continue to pollute. If mistakes are made, they may be difficult to correct in our status quo-oriented system. Incentives will not be easily or rapidly adjustable.

A related type of problem with incentives arises in a policy such as performance contracting for education in which private companies are hired by school systems to teach students. The companies are paid on a sliding scale, depending upon the performance of the students on standardized tests at the end of the year. Such an approach was tried in several experiments but did not produce the intended results, i.e., better-educated students. One reason for this is undoubtedly our general lack of understanding of *how* to improve education.[86]

Yet another limitation on the use of market incentives to regulate polluters is that industries will remain as organized and as politically powerful as ever. Their ability to influence legislative decisions or to "capture" regulatory agencies will not be diminished by reliance upon one enforcement tool or another.

In sum, there is skepticism about the utility of incentives in at least some areas requiring private sector implementation of public policies. Until these concerns are satisfied, we shall probably continue to rely heavily upon the traditional approach of attempting to influence private sector behavior through establishing duties accompanied by penalties for failing to comply.

Goal Displacement

Incentives can lead to goal displacement. Bureaucrats who are provided incentives to implement policies may begin to pursue goals other than those intended by their superiors. Vague and diverse goals, poor measures of performance, and obscure implementation directives make it difficult to evaluate the success of many policies. When a criterion of success is developed for a policy, bureaucrats may attempt to beat the system by emphasizing most whatever is being measured by their supervisors, independent of whether or not their actions advance the policy's goals.

For example, if the criterion of success in a manpower training program is job placement, employees may try to place as many trainees in jobs as possible, regardless of their suitability or the wages, stability, and possibility of advancement of the jobs. If, on the other hand, implementation performance is evaluated on the basis of the potential for increasing the future earnings of trainees, program personnel may concentrate on the young, who have more earning years ahead of them, and on the most adept, who can be trained to achieve the highest levels of skill.[87] The criteria for successful performance ought to measure a combination of goals and be related to the difficulty of the implementation task, but this is not easy to do. Goal displacement is especially likely to occur when potential clients of a service agency are screened and some can be excluded from receiving the service the agency provides by personnel with broad discretion.

Even when decisionmakers seem to be sensitive to these problems, goal displacement may still take place. In an effort to make state employment services more responsive to the needs of the poor, executives in the Labor Department prescribed a new weekly form to be filled out by each local employment service. Instead of reporting how many people, irrespective of background, it had serviced the previous month, the local employment service was required under the new system to provide information only on job placement of the hard-core unemployed (those who had been out of work for 18 months and made under $3,000 a year). In other words, the Labor Department attempted to provide incentives to place the poor in jobs.[88]

Unfortunately, the incentive technique in this instance backfired. Overly enthusiastic local employees began using advance payments to entice drug addicts, prison convicts, and anyone else they could find into training programs. The program in the Cardozo section in Washington, D.C., was composed of more than 50 percent heroin addicts. The director of the program knew this but could not publicly admit it for fear of hurting his chances for funding in the next year, competing as he was with other local programs. Executives in the Labor Department knew what was going on also, but they were in competition for funds with the Department of Health, Education and Welfare over who could best serve the poor. Thus, they did not publicly try to bring about change. When White House Fellow Doris Kearns told President Johnson of the situation, he replied that if Congress knew of this, it would cut next year's funds. It was better to pass along the reports as they were and try to bring reform from within.[89]

One state attorney general complained that the Environmental Protection Agency (EPA) did not refer cases of noncompliance with pollution laws in his region to state attorneys general or U.S. attorneys for action, but issued administrative orders instead. In his opinion this procedure violated state implementation plans. The EPA issued administrative orders, he felt, because (1) it increased the involvement of the federal bureaucracy, and (2) each issued order counted as a "bean" under the agency's credit system. The regional agency got no credit if cases were referred to the state attorney general, but it did receive credit for every order issued to a noncomplying source, even if each of the orders merely extended the compliance schedule of the last one.[90]

An especially clear example of goal displacement due to the incentive system of an agency was exposed when it was found that federal drug control officials spent too much time arresting street pushers and compiling numbers of arrests and too little time searching for major dealers in illicit narcotics. The explanation for this misdirected activity was that the agents of the federal Drug Enforcement Agency perceived that career advancement was strongly related to the number of arrests they made. Therefore, they de-emphasized the more significant conspiracy cases which could immobilize major drug traffickers and syndicates, but which were also more time-consuming and had less chance of leading to arrests.[91]

Similarly, the Bureau of Narcotics and Dangerous Drugs' formal evaluation system of agents placed heavy emphasis on case productivity. Therefore, agents based in other countries tried to make cases rather than play staff roles in developing and training effective local police forces, or rather than serve as effective liaisons in making specific cases, they tried to operate on their own.[92]

The performance monitoring system within the Drug Enforcement Agency gave credit to a region only for a case that culminated with arrests in its own geographic area. If arrests occurred elsewhere, another regional office received credit. Funding arrangements usually required the region originating (but not culminating) a case to absorb the operational costs of the case. Thus, since one region could send a case and investigators into another region and pay all of the costs and yet receive none of the benefits, cases rarely moved between regions and interregional cooperation on specific cases was poor.[93] The effective implementation of federal drug policy was thwarted by this system.

Other ineffective incentives result from the reward structure for government personnel and the organization of government. Bureaucrats have little incentive to save government money; they are not rewarded for it. They may even have an incentive to perform poorly in implementation because this might indicate their task requires an increased bureaucracy, which in turn provides its members with a greater sense of importance and more opportunities for promotion.[94] Moreover, the rewards that do exist are usually for individual program performance and not for contributions to the overall performance of an agency although coordination between programs may be essential for meeting broad policy goals.[95]

CONCLUSION

Implementors have considerable discretion in implementing policies. Communications from superiors are often unclear or inconsistent, and most implementors enjoy substantial independence from their superiors. Some policies fall within the "zone of indifference" of administrators; others elicit strong feelings. These policies may conflict with implementors' substantive policy views or their personal or organizational interests. It is here that dispositions pose obstacles to implementation.

Several features of the bureaucracy limit the perspectives of government officials toward both substantive policy and the health of their organization. There is a tendency for persons who agree with the thrust of an agency's activities to be attracted to work for it and to be hired by it. People who are disposed toward government activities in general are prone to work in the public sector. Once in an agency, people tend to spend their entire careers there, carrying out responsibilities that are rather narrow in relation to those of the entire government. All of this helps to produce a relatively homogeneous environment for policymaking in which parochial views are easy to develop and maintain.

Added re-enforcement for parochialism comes from the manipulation of rewards within each agency. Promotions go to those who accept established organizational goals and approaches to meeting them. Interest groups and legislative committees sometimes work to maintain the status quo. People in other positions of authority also often desire services to continue as they have in the past. This further buttresses a narrow orientation among bureaucrats. The pressures from agency clienteles and other supporters, coupled with the need to maintain employee morale and to rely upon the expertise of career officials, often lead short-term political appointees to abandon a national perspective and to adopt the more parochial perspectives of their subordinates.

Because of these influences, bureaucrats may be less favorably inclined toward policies than those who made them. Implementors may react to policies not only from a parochial substantive viewpoint, but also from a standpoint of protecting their organization's health. These conditions lay the basis for slippage in implementation due to implementors' dispositions, slippage which emerges in many forms.

Dispositions may hinder implementation when implementors simply disagree with the substance of a policy and their disagreement leads them not to carry it out. In some instances top officials may refrain from establishing policies because they anticipate opposition. (Occasionally, such recalcitrance may be in the public interest as bureaucrats refuse to engage in improper activities.) Sometimes implementation is impeded by more complex situations, such as when implementors delay in implementing a policy of which they may approve in the abstract in order to increase the chances of achieving another, competing policy goal.

In addition, implementors may avoid the full impact of a policy by selectively perceiving its requirements, ignoring at least some of those which are at odds with their views. This allows them to appear to be in compliance with the law while avoiding its full consequences. Judges have often displayed such behavior as they seemingly miss the thrust of higher court decisions and apply them too narrowly or focus on procedural rather than substantive issues.

Different bureaucratic units are likely to have different views on policies. Intra- and interagency disagreements inhibit cooperation and hinder implementation. Within a single policy area, each relevant agency probably has different priorities, different commitments, and different methods of handling problems. Similar differences may arise between those with different program responsibilities within an agency. These differences are not conducive to creating the mutual trust and close working relationships that are frequently necessary for effective implementation.

Organizational interests as well as policy views affect implementation. Bureaucratic units will give priority in time and resources to implementing programs which they consider to be primary, and those policies which they consider secondary may be shortchanged. Organizations will also attempt to build upon and re-enforce their primary missions. This may lead to distortion in implementation as interorganizational bargaining over resources takes place. Sometimes decisions depend more on skills in bureaucratic infighting than on the criteria of effective and efficient use of resources.

Agencies also resist the efforts of others to take away, reduce, or share their primary functions and resources. Likewise, they oppose higher officials' efforts to share in their decisionmaking and to coordinate their activities with those of other agencies. These organizational interests may hinder implementation as organizations fail to cooperate with each other and waste resources in bureaucratic feuding.

The dispositions of individuals in the private sector may also be significant in policy implementation. A large portion of the population is involved in the implementation of one or more policies, and its implementation efforts are generally not very visible. Thus, the potential for slippage in implementation is substantial if citizens do not approve of a policy. The dispositions of private individuals toward certain types of service delivery systems may also impede implementation because it may prevent these persons from taking advantage of available benefits.

Dispositions of implementors present many obstacles to policy implementation, but top officials are limited in their ability to replace existing personnel with persons more responsive to their policies. Only a very small percentage of a typical bureaucratic unit is appointed by the chief executive of a government jurisdiction, and many of these appointments are made without a systematic and comprehensive talent search. There is usually little time to allocate to personnel decisions, and numerous political constraints limit the pool of persons from which appointees are drawn. These include demands for "balance," the necessity of pleasing constituencies, and a desire not to alienate persons already occupying public office. Personnel decisions are also limited by top officials' lack of knowledge of talented people and by the small talent pools available to state and local governments.

The president may try to control the appointments made by other appointees, such as cabinet members, but this is likely to be a crude process with substantial room for error. Moreover, appointees too close to the chief executive may be unable to work with career officials and their agency's clientele. A large number of political appointees may insulate the chief executive from the bureaucracy and diminish opportunities to build personal support. In state and local governments department heads may be elected independently of the governor or mayor, further limiting the chief executive's ability to influence appointments.

Most bureaucrats are covered by civil service protection and, for all practical purposes, are immune from removal. Independence from their nominal superiors provides bureaucrats considerable freedom in implementation, and the discretion this independence allows is not always used to advance the goals of high-level decisionmakers. Distrust between top executives and the rest of the bureaucracy is thereby created.

Transferring personnel to other positions within the civil service is one technique of dealing with recalcitrant implementors, but the inherent negativeness of such an approach and the ability of bureaucrats to fight transfers successfully limits its utility. President Carter's 1978 reorganization of the federal civil service system and his creation of a Senior Executive Service may provide the chief executive greater flexibility in using senior civil servants. The Nixon administration had some success in skirting civil service requirements and placing persons who had been politically cleared by the White House in high-level positions. Nevertheless, this procedure took time to work, met with resistance from department heads who wanted to choose their own subordinates, and was available for use in only a small percentage of all the top civil service positions. While other strategies for influencing the staffing of the bureaucracy are available, none of them seems to have had much impact.

Courts are especially limited in their choice of staff since judges have very little impact on the selection of other judges at any level. The judicial system is too decentralized for hierarchical control of personnel decisions. Moreover, there is usually no way for judges to influence significantly the removal of other judges.

If all else fails, executives can sometimes bypass existing personnel and utilize others, especially when new agencies are established to carry out functions in the public sector. Despite the potential of such a strategy, most new programs are tied to existing policies. Fears of increased costs and bureaucratic fragmentation and reluctance to alter legislative committee jurisdictions inhibit legislatures from establishing new agencies. Courts have virtually no discretion as to whom they will send their orders.

Since it is often impossible to change the personnel who implement policies, the question arises: Can the disposition of existing personnel be altered? Individuals and organizations respond to the costs and benefits of acting in certain ways. When pressures are applied to implementors — whether from superiors in an agency, other organizations, legislatures, or organized interests — they are inclined to act in the direction of the pressures. It is therefore an appealing idea to provide incentives to advance implementation.

However, most pressures are beyond the direct control of top officials whose ability to exercise sanctions is limited. Rewards are equally difficult to administer. Pay increases are primarily across-the-board, and promotions occur infrequently and are often based on seniority. In the federal system, merit pay increases exist in reality only for a few high-level civil servants. There is no system of promotion for judges. Entire organizations are never directly rewarded for outstanding performance.

The effects of rewards may be mitigated by two factors. First, those who actually have control over the distribution of what rewards do exist may oppose or be indifferent to the policies which are supposed to be implemented. Second, peer group pressure may limit further the impact of rewards as implementors respond to those with whom they work and upon whom they may have to depend to do their jobs.

Authorities sometimes offer "sweeteners" in the form of funds or lax regulations for lower level governments or tax breaks to those in the private sector to encourage behavior that will aid the implementation of certain policies. More typically, however, negative sanctions are relied upon.

Some observers advocate that governments make greater use of positive incentives to foster efficiency and compliance among implementors in the private sector. They suggest changes such as replacing regulations with tax incentives and open-ended or cost-plus contracts with performance-based contracts. Yet it is not clear that such proposals would decrease either the need to monitor implementation or the influence of organized interests on policymakers. There are also the problems of knowing where to set incentive levels and of implementors knowing how to achieve goals once incentives are established.

An important issue in the use of incentives is that of measuring performance. If this is done without sensitivity to the diverse goals of policies and the difficulty of the tasks being performed, goal displacement may occur. The development of criteria of success is very difficult because of vague and diverse goals, poor measures of output, and obscure implementation directives. Thus, the measures that are utilized sometimes encourage implementors to pursue goals other than those intended by their superiors.

NOTES

1. Richard M. Nixon, *RN: The Memoirs of Richard Nixon* (New York: Grosset & Dunlap, 1978), pp. 474-475.
2. Chester I. Barnard, *The Functions of the Executive* (Cambridge, Mass.: Harvard University Press, 1966), pp. 167-170.
3. See Joel D. Aberbach and Bert A. Rockman, "Clashing Beliefs Within the Executive Branch: The Nixon Administration Bureaucracy," *American Political Science Review* 70 (June 1976): 456-468; Kenneth J. Meier and Lloyd G. Nigro, "Representative Bureaucracy and Policy Preferences: A Study in the Attitudes of Federal Executives" (Paper delivered at the annual meeting of the American Political Science Association, San Francisco, California, September, 1975); Kenneth J. Meier, "Representative Bureaucracy: An Empirical Analysis," *American Political Science Review* 69 (June 1975): 540-541; Herbert Kaufman, *The Forest Ranger: A Study in Administrative Behavior* (Baltimore: Johns Hopkins University Press, 1960).
4. Hugh Heclo, *A Government of Strangers: Executive Politics in Washington* (Washington, D.C.: Brookings Institution, 1977), pp. 116-120.
5. Ibid., pp. 115-116; Eugene B. McGregor Jr., "Politics and Career Mobility of Bureaucrats," *American Political Science Review* 68 (March 1974): 22-24, 26; Meier and Nigro, "Representative Bureaucracy and Political Preferences."
6. Elliot J. Feldman, "Air Transportation Infrastructure as a Problem of Public Policy," *Policy Studies Journal* 6 (Autumn 1977): 22-23.
7. Herbert Kaufman, *The Forest Ranger*, pp. 182-183.
8. H. R. Haldeman, *The Ends of Power* (New York: Times Books, 1978), p. 171. For John Ehrlichman's views, see Richard P. Nathan, "The 'Administrative Presidency,'" *Public Interest* (Summer 1976): 44.
9. Daniel P. Moynihan, *The Politics of Guaranteed Income* (New York: Vintage Books, 1973), p. 220.
10. Milbrey W. McLaughlin, *Evaluation and Reform: The Elementary and Secondary Education Act of 1965/Title I* (Cambridge, Mass.: Ballinger Publishing Co., 1975), p. 119.
11. Floyd E. Stoner, "Federal Auditors as Regulators: The Case of Title I of ESEA," in *The Policy Cycle*, eds. Judith V. May and Aaron B. Wildavsky (Beverly Hills, Calif.: Sage Publications, 1978), p. 209.
12. Haldeman, *Ends of Power*, pp. 149-150.
13. Nixon, *RN*, pp. 922, 924, 926-927.
14. Richard N. L. Andrews, *Environmental Policy and Administrative Change* (Lexington, Mass.: Lexington Books, 1976), pp. 79-80, 99, 107, 109, 115,

129, 135, 144-145; Richard A. Liroff, *A National Policy for the Environment: NEPA and Its Aftermath* (Bloomington, Ind.: Indiana University Press, 1976), p. 117.

15. See Paul H. Sanders, "The Warren Court and the Lower Federal Courts: Problems of Implementation," in *Constitutional Law in the Political Process,* ed. John Schmidhauser (Chicago: Rand McNally, 1963); Walter F. Murphy, "Lower Court Checks on Supreme Court Power," *American Political Science Review* 53 (December 1959): 1017-1031; "Evasion of Supreme Court Mandates in Cases Remanded to State Courts Since 1941," *Harvard Law Review* 67 (1954): 1251-1259.

16. The literature on the role of values in decisionmaking is voluminous. For one prominent example, see Glendon Schubert, *The Judicial Mind Revisited: Psychometric Analysis of Supreme Court Ideology* (New York: Oxford University Press, 1974).

17. Mark H. Moore, "Reorganization Plan #2 Reviewed: Problems in Implementing a Strategy to Reduce the Supply of Drugs to Illicit Markets in the United States," *Public Policy* 26 (Spring 1978): 239.

18. Ibid., p. 244.

19. Jeffrey L. Pressman and Aaron B. Wildavsky, *Implementation* (Berkeley, Calif.: University of California Press, 1973), pp. 99-100.

20. Liroff, *A National Policy for the Environment,* p. 99, 126-127.

21. Ibid., pp. 128-129.

22. William C. Payne, "Implementing Federal Nondiscrimination Policies in the Department of Agriculture, 1964-1976," *Policy Studies Journal* 6 (Summer 1978): 509.

23. Jerome T. Murphy, *State Education Agencies and Discretionary Funds* (Lexington, Mass.: Lexington Books, 1974), pp. 16, 24, 120-122.

24. Lawrence Iannaccone, "The Politics of Federal Aid to Education in Massachusetts," in *Federal Aid to Education: Who Benefits: Who Governs?,* eds. Joel S. Berke and Michael W. Kirst (Lexington, Mass.: Lexington Books, 1972), pp. 209-210.

25. Domestic Council, Drug Abuse Task Force, *White Paper on Drug Abuse,* September 1975; Moore, "Reorganization Plan #2 Reviewed," p. 250.

26. Eugene Bardach, *The Implementation Game: What Happens After a Bill Becomes a Law* (Cambridge, Mass.: MIT Press, 1977), pp. 157-159. See also Mike M. Milsten, *Impact and Response* (New York: Teachers College Press, 1976, p. 74.

27. Nixon, *RN,* pp. 472-473, 513.

28. Lorraine M. McDonnell, "Implementation of Federal Education Policy: The Role of the States" (Paper delivered at the annual meeting of the American Political Science Association, Washington, D.C., August-September 1979), pp. 31-36. See also Martha Derthick, *Uncontrollable Spending for Social Service Grants* (Washington, D.C.: Brookings Institution, 1975), pp. 214-215.

29. Frederic V. Malek, *Washington's Hidden Tragedy: The Failure to Make Government Work* (New York: Free Press, 1978), p. 93.

30. Lyle Saunders, *Cultural Differences and Medical Care* (New York: Russell Sage, 1954), pp. 175-189.

31. Malek, *Washington's Hidden Tragedy,* p. 62.

32. Ibid., pp. 63-66.

33. Ibid., p. 85; Arnold Kanter, *Defense Politics: A Budgetary Perspective* (Chicago: University of Chicago Press, 1979), p. 98.

34. Malek, *Washington's Hidden Tragedy,* pp. 67-68.
35. Ibid., pp. 61, 78.
36. Ibid., p. 77.
37. Kenneth P. O'Donnell and David F. Powers, *Johnny, We Hardly Knew Ye: Memories of John Fitzgerald Kennedy* (New York: Pocket Books, 1972), p. 270.
38. Malek, *Washington's Hidden Tragedy,* p. 77.
39. William Safire, *Before the Fall: An Inside View of the Pre-Watergate White House* (New York: Doubleday & Co., 1975), p. 109; "Carter Sounds Retreat from 'Cabinet Government,'" *National Journal,* November 18, 1978, pp. 18, 21-22; George C. Edwards III, *Presidential Influence in Congress* (San Francisco: W. H. Freeman, 1980), pp. 157-159; "The TIP Talent Hunt — Carter's Original Amateur Hour?," *National Journal,* February 19, 1977, pp. 268, 270; Martin Tolchin, "Carter Takes Hands-Off Approach to Patronage, Irking Some in Party," *New York Times,* May 22, 1977, pp. 1, 17; Stephen J. Wayne, *The Legislative Presidency* (New York: Harper & Row, 1978), pp. 181, 184; Thomas E. Cronin, *The State of the Presidency* (Boston: Little, Brown & Co., 1975), p. 284.
40. See Tolchin, "Carter Takes Hands-Off Approach to Patronage," pp. 1, 17.
41. Heclo, *Government of Strangers,* pp. 97-98.
42. "Carter Sounds Retreat;" "Rafshoon and Co.," *Newsweek,* January 29, 1979, p. 23. See also Wayne, *Legislative Presidency,* p. 183.
43. Cronin, *State of the Presidency,* p. 284.
44. Heclo, *Government of Strangers,* pp. 97-98, 214, 223.
45. James Eisenstein, *Counsel for the United States: U.S. Attorneys in the Political and Legal Systems* (Baltimore: Johns Hopkins University Press, 1978), p. 61, passim.
46. Heclo, *Government of Strangers,* pp. 182-183.
47. Haldeman, *Ends of Power,* p. 149.
48. Nathan, "The 'Administrative Presidency,'" pp. 44-45.
49. Aberbach and Rockman, "Clashing Beliefs Within the Executive Branch," pp. 456-468.
50. Brooks Jackson, "Carter Aide Blasts Civil Service System as Being Inefficient," *New Orleans Times-Picayune,* April 23, 1978, Sec. 1, p. 26.
51. "Press Conference Text," *Congressional Quarterly Weekly Report,* March 11, 1978, p. 655.
52. Heclo, *Government of Strangers,* pp. 49, 217; Leonard Reed, "Firing a Federal Employee: The Impossible Dream," *The Washington Monthly* (July-August 1977): 15-25.
53. Quoted in Aberbach and Rockman, "Clashing Beliefs Within the Executive Branch," p. 457.
54. "Civil Service Reform," *Congressional Quarterly Weekly Report,* March 11, 1978, p. 660.
55. Heclo, *Government of Strangers,* pp. 140-141, 217.
56. Louis C. Gawthrop, *Bureaucratic Behavior in the Executive Branch: An Analysis of Organizational Change* (New York: Free Press, 1969), pp. 67-68. For a more optimistic view of transferring bureaucrats, see Malek, *Washington's Hidden Tragedy,* p. 103.
57. Heclo, *Government of Strangers,* p. 47.
58. "Reforms Belie Old Myth," *The Eagle,* July 27, 1979, p. 5A.
59. Heclo, *Government of Strangers,* Chapters 5-7.

60. For full documentation of these abuses, see U.S., Congress, House, Sub-committee on Manpower and Civil Service, Committee on Post Office and Civil Service, *Final Report on Violations and Abuses of Merit Principles in Federal Employment Together with Minority Views,* 94th Cong., 2d sess., 1976. Most of these abuses were ended by President Ford. See also Heclo, *Government of Strangers,* p. 55, fn. 22.
61. Heclo, *Government of Strangers,* pp. 73-75.
62. Ibid., pp. 135-136.
63. Richard L. Cole and David A. Caputo, "Presidential Control of the Senior Civil Service: Assessing the Strategies of the Nixon Years," *American Political Science Review* 73 (June 1979): 399-413.
64. Kanter, *Defense Politics,* Chapter 7.
65. Ibid.
66. Joseph A. Califano, Jr., *A Presidential Nation* (New York: W. W. Norton & Co., 1975), p. 36. For other examples of the placement of programs with implementation in mind, see James E. Anderson, *Public Policy-Making* (New York: Praeger Publishers, 1975), pp. 105-106.
67. Martha Derthick, *The Influence of Federal Grants* (Cambridge, Mass.: Harvard University Press, 1970), pp. 203-204.
68. John F. Hughes and Anne O. Hughes, *Equal Education* (Bloomington, Ind.: Indiana University Press, 1972), p. 56.
69. Kenneth M. Dolbeare and Phillip E. Hammond, *The School Prayer Decisions* (Chicago: University of Chicago Press, 1971), passim. For an example of private individuals using intimidation tactics to attempt to prevent elites from desegregating schools, see Charles S. Bullock III and Harrell R. Rodgers, Jr., *Coercion to Compliance* (Lexington, Mass.: Lexington Books, 1976), p. 23.
70. See Robert L. Crain, *The Politics of School Desegregation* (Garden City, N.Y.: Anchor, 1969); Harrell R. Rodgers, Jr. and Charles S. Bullock III, *Law and Social Change: Civil Rights Laws and Their Consequences* (New York: McGraw-Hill Book Co., 1972), pp. 189-192.
71. Eisenstein, *Counsel for the United States,* pp. 60, 62, 74.
72. Andrews, *Environmental Policy,* pp. 73-74, 126, 142.
73. Robert A. Levine, *The Poor Ye Need Not Always Have With You* (Cambridge, Mass.: MIT Press, 1970), pp. 232-233, 235. For other examples of cost-benefit calculations affecting personal and agency behavior, see Martin Shapiro, *The Supreme Court and Administrative Agencies* (New York: Free Press, 1968), Chapter 3; Neal Gross, Joseph B. Giacquinta, and Marilyn Bernstein, *Implementing Organizational Innovations* (New York: Basic Books, 1971), pp. 142-147.
74. See J. Theodore Anagnoson, "What Kind of Oversight? The Case of Federal Grant Agencies' Project Selection Strategies" (Paper delivered at the annual meeting of the American Political Science Association, Washington, D.C., August-September 1978).
75. "Press Conference Text," p. 655.
76. Stephen L. Wasby, "Police Training About Criminal Procedure: Infrequent and Inadequate," *Policy Studies Journal* 7 (Special Issue, 1978): 467.
77. Robert L. Butterworth, "The Arms Control Impact Statement: A Programmatic Assessment," *Policy Studies Journal* 8 (Autumn 1979): 82.
78. Wasby, "Police Training," pp. 466-467; Jameson W. Doig, "Police Policy and Police Behavior: Patterns of Divergence," *Policy Studies Journal* 7 (Special Issue, 1978): 440-441; Stephen L. Wasby, *Small Town Police and the Supreme Court: Hearing the Word* (Lexington, Mass.: Lexington Books,

1976), p. 54.

79. For a discussion of the limits of rewarding lower levels of government, see Martha Derthick, *New Towns In-Town* (Washington, D.C.: Urban Institute, 1972).
80. Murphy, *State Education Agencies*, p. 10.
81. Bardach, *The Implementation Game*, pp. 104-105.
82. Drew Altman and Harvey M. Sapolsky, "Writing the Regulations for Health," *Policy Sciences* 7 (December 1976): 429.
83. See Pressman and Wildavsky, *Implementation*, Chapter 7; Robert A. Levine, *Public Planning* (New York: Basic Books, 1972), pp. 173-174; Allen V. Kneese and Charles L. Schultze, *Pollution, Prices, and Public Policy* (Washington, D.C.: Brookings Institution, 1975); Albert H. Nichols and Richard Zeckhauser, "OSHA Comes to the Workplace: An Assessment of OSHA," *Public Interest* (Fall 1977): 64-67; Charles L. Schultze, *The Public Use of the Private Interest* (Washington, D.C.: Brookings Institution, 1977).
84. See Kneese and Schultze, *Pollution, Prices, and Public Policy*.
85. For useful discussions of these problems, see Alfred A. Marcus, "Converting Thought to Action.: The Use of Economic Incentives to Reduce Pollution" (Paper delivered at the annual meeting of the American Political Science Association, Washington, D.C., August-September, 1979); Marcus, "Recent Proposals to Improve Environmental Policy Making," *Harvard Environmental Law Review* 1 (1976): 632-644; Marc J. Roberts and Susan O'Farrell, "The Political Economy of Implementation: The Clean Air Act and Stationary Sources," in *Approaches to Controlling Air Pollution*, ed. Ann F. Friedlaender (Cambridge, Mass.: MIT Press, 1978), p. 173; Lettie McS. Wenner, "Pollution Control: Implementation Alternatives," *Policy Analysis* 4 (Winter 1978): 47-66.
86. See Edward M. Gramlich and Patricia P. Koshel, *Educational Performance Contracting* (Washington, D.C.: Brookings Institution, 1975).
87. Alice M. Rivlin, *Systematic Thinking for Social Action* (Washington, D.C.: Brookings Institution, 1971), p. 128. See also Donald C. Baumer, "Implementing Public Service Employment," in *The Policy Cycle*, eds. May and Wildavsky, p. 186; Lance Smith and Carl E. Van Horn, "The Role of Interest Groups and Subgovernments in Policy Formulation and Policy Implementation" (Paper delivered at the annual meeting of the Midwest Political Science Association, Chicago, Illinois, April 1980), pp. 26-27.
88. Doris Kearns, *Lyndon Johnson and the American Dream* (New York: Harper & Row, 1976), pp. 289-290.
89. Ibid.
90. Charles Coskin II, "Comment," in *Approaches to Controlling Air Pollution*, ed. Friedlaender, pp. 194-195.
91. "U.S. Drug Agency Strategy Faulted," *Wisconsin State Journal*, July 18, 1976, section 1, p. 7; Moore, "Reorganization Plan #2," p. 254. For other examples of goal displacement, see Kearns, *Lyndon Johnson*, p. 272; Robert L. Gallucci, *Neither Peace nor Honor* (Baltimore: Johns Hopkins University Press, 1975), pp. 86-177; Patrick J. McGarvey, *C.I.A.* (Baltimore: Penguin Books, 1973), p. 60; Carl E. Van Horn, "Implementing CETA: The Federal Role" (Paper delivered at the annual meeting of the Midwest Political Science Association, Chicago, Illinois, April-May 1976), pp. 27-29.
92. Moore, "Reorganization Plan #2," pp. 238-239.
93. Ibid, p. 252.
94. Bardach, *The Implementation Game*, pp. 70-71.
95. See Milsten, *Impact and Response*, p. 76.

5

Bureaucratic Structure

Policy implementors may know what to do and have sufficient desire and resources to do it, but they may still be hampered in implementation by the structures of the organizations in which they serve. Two prominent characteristics of bureaucracies are standard operating procedures (SOPs) and fragmentation. The former develop as internal responses to the limited time and resources of implementors and the desire for uniformity in the operation of complex and widely dispersed organizations; they often remain in force due to bureaucratic inertia. The latter results primarily from pressures outside bureaucratic units as legislative committees, interest groups, executive officials, state constitutions and city charters, and the nature of broad policies influence the organization of public bureaucracies. Of course, agencies also try to affect their own formal structures.

Despite the differences in origin of these organizational characteristics, SOPs and bureaucratic fragmentation both may hinder policy implementation. They often inhibit changes in policy, waste resources, generate undesired actions, impede coordination, confuse officials at lower level jurisdictions, result in policies working at cross-purposes, and cause some policies to fall between the cracks of organizational boundaries. In this chapter we will explore the consequences of SOPs and fragmentation for implementation as well as the reasons for their development.

STANDARD OPERATING PROCEDURES

Standard operating procedures (SOPs) are routines that enable public officials to make numerous everyday decisions. Whether we are discussing police on the beat making rapid decisions about whether a person is dangerous or a Social Security Administration caseworker deciding on the eligibility of a person for benefits, we find that SOPs

125

are commonly employed. The reason SOPs are widely used and the effects of SOPs on policy implementation are examined in this section.

Reasons for SOPs

SOPs save time, and time is valuable. If a caseworker had to invent a new rule for every potential client, few people would be helped. So detailed manuals are written to cover as many particular situations as officials can anticipate. SOPs also bring uniformity to complex organizations, and justice is better served if rules are applied uniformly. This is true for the implementation of welfare policies that distribute benefits to the needy, as well as for criminal law policies that distribute sanctions. Uniformity also makes personnel interchangeable. A soldier can be transferred to any spot in the world and still know how to carry out a function by referring to the proper manual.

Often SOPs are necessary because of a lack of resources. Officials usually lack the staff to research problems thoroughly, yet they must be able to make decisions rapidly. Thus, complex situations must be simplified. Instead of evaluating carefully each individual student's ability, busy teachers may rely upon cues, such as the student's manners, speech, dress, attitudes, parents, or behavior, as the basis of decisions about discipline or course selection.

A study of the implementation of a Massachusetts law is revealing in this regard. The law required school districts to identify, assess, and refer children with special education needs and develop plans for their education. The law created a great paperwork burden for school officials and greatly increased their workload. Prior to passage of the law, fewer children had to be evaluated and fewer people were involved in the evaluation process. After enactment, education plans had to be written in more detail, completed faster, and circulated to a wider audience. School personnel were short-handed and could not do everything the law required. The lack of resources created an inevitable tension between individualized education and mass processing.[1]

Massachusetts school officials were forced to cut corners. They did not assess all relevant students' educational needs, and they scheduled assessments in favor of children who were not likely to cost the school system extra money. Children who met the needs of school personnel seeking to practice their individual specialties also received particular attention. School officials decreased the time students were assigned to specialists, favored group over individual treatment, and used specialists-in-training rather than experienced instructors. They also short-circuited requirements for completing forms and for following procedures designed to protect the interests of parents. Thus, there was a constant need to routinize, to ration resources, and to define the task in ways that provided acceptable solutions to the demands of the new policy.[2]

Focusing on their specialized functions, bureaucrats often develop "tunnel vision" and slip imperceptibly into SOPs.[3] Moreover, "Once requirements and practices are instituted, they tend to remain in force long after the conditions that spawned them have disappeared,"[4] writes political scientist Herbert Kaufman. Routines are not regularly reexamined, and this has advantages for bureaucrats who, like most people, prefer stability to change and consensus to conflict. If SOPs are not seriously reviewed, existing arrangements will continue. Representatives of conflicting organizational interests that have been accommodated in current SOPs fear that renegotiating them might result in less satisfactory procedures. Organizations are also inhibited in changing their SOPs by the enormous "sunk costs" of time, effort, and money that have gone into developing these routines.[5]

Private individuals also use SOPs. For example, bank loan officers often use a person's race, ethnicity, or address as a primary criterion for making or refusing a loan. Although this procedure is discriminatory, it is used because it simplifies the decisionmaking process. To end such behavior, policies must overcome the attraction of these decisionmaking routines as well as state new implementation responsibilities.[6]

Problems with SOPs

While SOPs save time by enabling officials to avoid making individual judgments about specific situations, they may be inappropriate in many cases and may impede the implementation of many policies. Although designed to make implementing policies easier — at least in theory — SOPs can function as obstacles to action. Top officials have had many a plan thwarted by standard government practices. They certainly frustrated President Franklin D. Roosevelt:

> The Treasury is so large and far-flung and ingrained in its practices that I find it is almost impossible to get the action and results I want.... But the Treasury is not to be compared with the State Department. You should go through the experience of trying to get any changes in the thinking, policy, and action of the career diplomats and then you'd know what a real problem was. But the Treasury and the State Department put together are nothing as compared with the Na-a-vy.... To change anything in the Na-a-vy is like punching a feather bed. You punch it with your right and you punch it with your left until you are finally exhausted, and then you find the damn bed just as it was before you started punching.[7]

Standard operating procedures may hinder policy implementation by inhibiting change. Designed for typical situations, SOPs can be ineffective in unusual circumstances. They are particularly inadequate during a crisis when exceptions to the rules are often required. In 1962 the United States discovered the presence of Soviet missiles in Cuba and reacted by blockading the island. President John F. Kennedy was very concerned about the initial interception of Soviet ships, and he sent Secretary of Defense Robert McNamara to check with Chief of Naval Operations George Anderson on the procedures being followed. McNamara stressed to Anderson that the president did *not* want to follow the normal SOP whereby a ship risked being sunk if it refused to submit to being boarded and searched. Kennedy did not want to goad the USSR into retaliation. But Admiral Anderson was not co-operative. At one point in the discussion, he waved the *Manual of Naval Regulations* in the secretary's face and shouted, "It's all in here." To this McNamara replied, "I don't give a damn what John Paul Jones would have done. I want to know what you are going to do now."[8] The conversation ended with the admiral asking the secretary of defense to leave and let the navy run the blockade according to established procedures.

SOPs may also be inappropriate for more routine policies. The Bureau of Narcotics and Dangerous Drugs (BNDD) specialized in daring undercover operations. When it received responsibility for a program to control the diversion of drugs from manufacturers to wholesalers, it had difficulty adjusting its routines. To uncover such diversion, different types of personnel and investigatory procedures were required. Yet the new regulatory program never received adequate support from the agency, and its personnel were given lower status in terms of pay and authority than other BNDD employees. No special training programs were provided, no new personnel evaluation system was developed, and procedures for targeting and monitoring investigations were not well-defined.[9]

The BNDD is not alone in having inadequate SOPs for drug control. One of the State Department's principal functions is to maintain relations with foreign governments. Therefore, it is hard for it to pressure these governments toward specific goals. Rather than attempting to pressure governments, State prefers to rely upon an elaborate international system that "commits" countries to policies but provides neither means for effective monitoring of performance nor powerful sanctions to encourage it. Unfortunately, this routine approach has not proved very useful for mobilizing foreign governments to assist U.S. efforts to control narcotics.[10]

In the Social Security Administration (SSA), SOPs for administering social insurance programs are well-established. When Medicare officials acquired new responsibilities for health care cost containment, however, problems developed. They were accustomed to running a "payment" program — not a health program. Therefore, they had little interest in detailed involvement in health care decisions such as those involving planning and budgeting. Because of their familiarity with evaluating individual insurance claims for appropriate payment, the SSA focused on claims denial in response to unnecessary or uncovered health care. Only after the Senate Finance Committee criticized the SSA did it adopt an active role in cost containment, and even then it only considered a narrow range of options, none of which was inconsistent with the principle of social insurance.[11]

Because the new Environmental Protection Agency (EPA) had analytical strength in particular areas of environmental review, agencies whose projects impacted on these environmental matters were subjected to more scrutiny than those of other agencies. Thus, Atomic Energy Commission projects received criticism while the stream channelization projects of the Conservation Service (SCS) did not. The Bureau of Sport Fisheries and Wildlife (BSFW) in the Department of Interior had been critical of SCS projects, but the EPA inherited many of its personnel from Interior's Federal Water Pollution Control Administration. These officials had left principal responsibility for reviewing the environmental impact of SCS projects to the BSFW when they were in Interior, and they continued this routine after their transfer to the EPA.[12]

Some of the early opposition within the U.S. Navy to the Polaris missile program can be attributed to the difficulty naval officers had in adjusting to change. Many of their careers were jeopardized by this major weapons innovation. The Polaris program favored those with particular types of training (especially in submarines) over others. Officers unfamiliar with modern technologies found it difficult to appreciate the new missile's benefits. The Polaris also required a change in the naval tradition of one commander and crew for each vessel. To increase effectiveness, a two-crew concept was developed for each Polaris submarine. Long-established routines became obstacles to technological innovation, and careful planning and a substantial bureaucratic effort were required to overcome them.[13]

Another example of SOPs inhibiting change was in the U.S. Office of Education (USOE) where personnel traditionally saw their role as that of check writers. Few people in the USOE aggressively implemented evaluation requirements for the expenditure of federal funds for disadvantaged children. The guidelines that were formulated were not oriented toward reform. Instead they bolstered valued friendships with state officials and more or less maintained the status quo of federal-state relations. Federal officials decided at the outset to avoid evaluation issues that might frighten state and local administrators or cloud new "partner-client" relations. Uniform reporting standards were never set, measurement by standardized tests was not required, control groups were not established, and components of "effectiveness" were not suggested.[14] The old routines were maintained.

In a similar vein, the U.S. Office of Education was not very active in enforcing the guidelines and regulations governing federal aid to state and local education agencies because many of its employees had adopted the routine of passivity toward state and local programs. They felt it was inappropriate to tell another level of government what to do. Therefore, they oriented themselves as "professionals" and not "police."[15]

Despite federal funding for new programs to aid disadvantaged children, state and local distribution of education funds frequently remained unchanged.[16] Local administrators often adopted a "more of the same" approach, fitting children to programs instead of programs to children. Some disadvantaged students were placed in programs designed for average middle-class students. The new funds were often used for old programs while locally raised funds were used for whatever local officials wanted.[17] Thus, new programs on the federal level were often unable to alter the routines of state and local governments.

Similarly, state education agencies are slow to change. Although they may receive federal grants designed to encourage the hiring of new personnel with new roles, the development of new programs, and the adoption of alternatives to existing procedures, they use the funds for these purposes reluctantly. Changes that have occurred have been the result of outside pressure. Implementors have adapted the program to fit established organizational routines rather than change the SOPs to suit the new policy.[18]

A study of the introduction of adversarial counsel into youthful offender proceedings in two cities, in response to a U.S. Supreme Court mandate, found that the cities reacted quite differently, depending upon their routines. In one city the decision was implemented smoothly because its judicial system was oriented toward the resolution of conflict between youthful offenders and the state. This change in procedure did not pose a threat to the way the courts already functioned. Implementation was more difficult in the other city, however. Compliance with the Court mandate required radical changes in standard procedures because the relevant courts were organized as a cooperative rather than a conflictual system.[19]

As we have seen, the SOPs of an organization may make it unenthusiastic about accepting responsibility for new programs. Thus, the Justice Department was not eager to run law enforcement assistance programs because grant programs did not fit easily into its administrative structure. The Department of Health, Education and Welfare's administrative structure, on the other hand, was built around making grants, so it resisted assuming responsibility for nongrant programs.

The reluctance to accept new responsibilities may not only delay the implementation of new programs, but it also may forestall the implementation of part or all of a policy. Because the U.S. Public Health Service saw itself as an apolitical, highly professional, research-oriented organization that developed health standards to be enforced by state and local officials, it refused authority to regulate air quality in the late 1950s. The U.S. Public Health Service prided itself on its good relations with state and local health officials. Possessing its own enforcement powers, it argued, would decrease the initiative and authority of these officials and disrupt the close cooperation existing between the different levels of government.[20]

Delay is a frequent consequence of SOPs. The mayor of New York wanted to close a small garbage incinerator that was costing a lot of money and polluting the air. This incinerator provided heat for a garage. Before it could be closed, an alternative source of heat needed to be found. The Sanitation Bureau of Engineering had to draw up a contract to hire an outside engineer to design a new heating system. Then the contract had to be approved by the Engineering Division of the Bureau of the Budget. The sanitation engineers were busy. They did not view the design of a small heating system as a priority. Neither did the Bureau of the Budget. The incinerator remained standing for three years.[21]

Sometimes SOPs waste scarce resources. During World War II, armaments in England were in short supply. As the story goes, the British made use of some old artillery pieces and called in a time-motion expert to suggest ways to simplify the firing procedures. The specialist found that two of the five members of each gun crew ceased all activity a moment before firing and came to attention for a three-second interval until the gun discharged. Inquiring about this strange and time-consuming behavior, the efficiency expert discovered that the two crew members were adhering to an outmoded SOP designed to have men hold the horses while the gun fired![22]

Undesired Actions. Sometimes SOPs cause organizations to take actions superior officials do not desire, as the Cuban missile crisis dramatically illustrates. Despite President Kennedy's explicit order that the initial encounter with a Soviet ship not involve a Soviet submarine, the U.S. Navy, according to established procedure, used its "Hunter-Killer" antisubmarine warfare program to locate and float above Soviet submarines within 600 miles of the continental U.S. Also following standard "Hunter-Killer" procedures, the navy forced several Soviet submarines to surface. This drastic action was not ordered by the president or the secretary of defense. It "just happened" because it was the programmed response to such a situation. The highest U.S. officials, who ostensibly had authority over the navy, never imagined standard procedures would supplant their directives. SOPs become deeply embedded in an organization and are difficult to control — even in times of crisis.[23]

During the Cuban missile crisis, the Strategic Air Command also abided by SOPs. It sent B-47 bombers loaded with nuclear weapons to 40 civilian airports across the country, even though this activity was contrary to Secretary of Defense McNamara's "no cities doctrine," designed to discourage the Soviet Union from attacking U.S. population centers. Moreover, several of the airports to which the bombers were sent were in the southeastern region of the country and within range of the operational missiles in Cuba.[24]

Still other SOPs were operating during the crisis. A U.S. intelligence ship on a routine mission approached the Cuban coast, and a U-2 spy plane, on a routine yet potentially provocative mission, strayed over the Soviet Union. No one thought to order the ship not to sail or the plane not to fly. Either of these operations could have jeopardized the president's policy and escalated the crisis.[25]

According to former CIA official Patrick McGarvey, many intelligence collecting programs have imperceptible beginnings in the bureaucracy, but once they get started the programs gain a momentum of their own. Often it requires too much paperwork to stop them. For example, the ill-fated *Pueblo* mission was the result of a route chosen by a young navy lieutenant stationed in Japan. He based his recommendation on the concern of a navy lieutenant commander (a friend of his based in Hawaii) that the intelligence community was not paying enough attention to North Korea. The high-risk mission was given perfunctory approval by higher authorities, moving through all of official Washington in just three days. The lack of thought given to the request is not unusual because of the great mass of work facing most high-level decisionmakers and the limited time available in which to do it.[26] Thus, the routines of carrying out intelligence gathering do not necessarily alert policymakers to the implications of individual projects.

New Policies vs. Old Practices. New policies are the most likely to require a change in organizational behavior and are therefore the most likely to have their implementation hindered by SOPs. There is an old saying that the military is always prepared to fight the last war. The picture of American troops fighting in the early years in Vietnam as if they were on the plains of central Europe supports such a view. At times, the State Department, the Agency for International Development, and the United States Information Agency also behaved as if they were fighting a previous war.[27] The more a new policy requires change in an organization's SOPs, the less likely it will be implemented as its designers intended.[28] As we have seen, organizations usually find it difficult to change their ways.

If an organization is relatively young or if there has been a substantial turnover in its personnel, SOPs may be easier to change because they are less deeply embedded than in older, more stable organizations. If an organization has a long lead time to change its SOPs or if the new law is so clearly and narrowly written that the organization has little discretion, SOPs which are not conducive to implementing a new policy may also be easier to change.

Because of the difficulty SOPs sometimes place in the way of change, top policymakers may try to avoid giving an existing agency responsibility for a new program. As President Johnson once said, "The best way to kill a new idea is to put it in an old-line agency."[29] When the Small Business Administration was established in 1953, it was not put in the Department of Commerce (considered too oriented toward big business), and the Office of Economic Opportunity was not placed in the Department of Health, Education and Welfare in 1964. While creation of a new agency may facilitate policy implementation, such an approach is not always feasible because of the added costs of a new agency, political support for an old agency, or the need to coordinate related programs.

Advantages of SOPs

As we have seen, SOPs can and do hinder policy implementation in many ways. Nevertheless, they can sometimes aid organizations in adapting to change. The Army Corps of Engineers traditionally has been a construction-oriented organization with a strong commitment to resource development. Yet after passage of the National Environmental Policy Act (NEPA) in 1969, it underwent substantial reorganization to create the infrastructure necessary to incorporate environmental concerns into its decisionmaking. It hired new personnel, set new objectives of environmental awareness, and instituted more open planning of its projects. While environmental quality remains an auxiliary function of the Corps, it has made more change than most observers would have predicted.[30]

The Corps may have been more adaptable to change because it had within it "organizational slack." As one author explains, "Its large, diffuse program was composed of extended, well-defined, yet manipulable planning procedures, into which new components could be inserted."[31] It was easier and less disruptive to plug environmental concerns into its decisionmaking process than it was for agencies with smaller, less diverse, and more short-term planning programs to do so. Moreover, grant-awarding agencies such as the Department of Housing and Urban Development and the Federal Highway Administration are not as likely to have as much control as the Corps over planning and work flow.

FRAGMENTATION

The second aspect of bureaucratic structure that we will consider is fragmentation. Fragmentation is the dispersion of responsibility for a policy area among several organizational units.

The extent of government fragmentation is widespread. In the field of welfare, more than 100 federal human services programs are administered by 10 different departments and agencies.[32] The Department of Health and Human Services has responsibility for the Aid for Dependent Children program; the Department of Housing and Urban Development provides housing assistance for the poor; the Department of Agriculture runs the food stamp program; and the Department of Labor administers manpower training programs and provides assistance in obtaining employment.

Twelve agencies share responsibility for enforcing the Equal Credit Opportunity Act, which bars discrimination in lending on the basis of sex, marital status, race, color, age, national origin, or religion. They include the Federal Reserve Board, the Federal Deposit Insurance Corporation, the Comptroller of the Currency, the Federal Home Loan Bank Board, the Securities and Exchange Commission, the Federal Trade Commission, and the Small Business Administration.[33]

As we have seen, the power to do things in American government is broadly scattered both within and between branches and levels of government. In a May 1978 speech advocating reform of the civil service, President Carter stated:

> There are too many agencies, doing too many things, overlapping too often, coordinating too rarely, wasting too much money — and doing too little to solve real problems.[34]

The more actors and agencies involved with a particular policy and the more interdependent their decisions, the less the probability of successful implementation. In this section we will examine the causes of fragmentation in government and the consequences of fragmentation for policy implementation.

Why Fragmentation?

> Often we didn't know where to put a program — in which agency
> — and we didn't particularly care where it went; we just wanted
> to make sure it got enacted. That's one reason why the government
> is disorganized now.[35]

Thus Joseph Califano, President Lyndon B. Johnson's chief adviser on domestic issues from 1965 to 1969, explains a fragmented bureaucracy. Another way of explaining fragmentation is to consider the three actors in the national political system that support fragmentation for their own reasons: Congress, federal agencies, and interest groups.

Over the years Congress has created many separate agencies and favored categorical grants that assign specific authority and funds to particular agencies in order to oversee more closely and intervene more easily in the administration of policies. Dispersing responsibility for a policy area also disperses "turf" to congressional committees. In water resource policy, three committees in the House and three committees in the Senate have authority over the Army Corps of Engineers, the Soil Conservation Service, and the Bureau of Reclamation, respectively. None of these committees wants to relinquish its hold over these agencies. Thus, the agencies and programs that deal with a common problem remain divided among three departments.

Like congressional committees, agencies are possessive about their jurisdictions. Usually department or agency heads vigorously oppose executive branch reorganizations that encroach upon their sphere of influence.[36] For example, President Nixon issued a directive to CIA chief Richard Helms assigning him, as director of central intelligence, formal responsibility for an enhanced leadership role over all intelligence activities including preparation of a consolidated intelligence community budget and coordination of the intelligence activities of the Departments of State, Defense, and the Treasury; the National Security Agency; and the individual military services. There was strong resistance to this presidential directive, especially from the Defense Department. Helms knew he could not win the bureaucratic battle, so things continued as they had in the past despite the president's order.[37]

In his fiscal 1980 budget proposals, President Carter requested that funds for state drug abuse programs be divided into single, consolidated grants for mental health, drug, and alcohol abuse services. Congress refused to consent to this proposal, however. Professionals in the alcohol and drug abuse programs feared that their programs would be downgraded if they lost their separate legislative identities and were combined with mental health programs. They blocked the president's attempt to reduce program fragmentation.[38]

Interest groups are a third force supporting fragmentation. When Lyndon Johnson tried to move the Maritime Administration from the Department of Commerce to the Department of Transportation, he was successfully opposed by the AFL-CIO. Although it made sense administratively to house the Maritime Administration with other transportation-related agencies, labor leaders feared a bureaucratic reorganization would jeopardize their close relationship with the Maritime Administration. For a similar reason the AFL-CIO successfully opposed Johnson's attempt to merge the Departments of Labor and Commerce.[39] Groups also develop close working relationships with congressional committees and do not want to lose their special access in a reorganization of committee jurisdictions that might follow an executive branch reorganization.

Similar influences operate on a smaller scale at the state and local levels. Florida consolidated a number of social services into a comprehensive Health and Rehabilitative Services Department (HRS). When this reform failed to coordinate service delivery at the local level, the legislature created 11 service districts throughout the state, each of which was to be headed by a director who would coordinate the activities of state social service agencies in that district. Local agency heads, rather than reporting back to their agency heads in the state capital, would report to the local service director. Moreover, local state offices were to be located together for the convenience of clients.

Despite some initial success, this integrated approach to providing human services met with opposition from professional groups. The National Rehabilitation Association persuaded Congress that vocational and rehabilitation services should be provided "by a single state agency whose head would be responsible to no one." To comply with this requirement, Florida was forced to alter the structure of its rehabilitation programs. Although they remained within HRS, they had a separate budget, and lines of authority for them bypassed the district service director. In other words, the rehabilitation programs operated within a separate administrative structure in HRS.[40]

Often a combination of interest groups and legislative committees oppose reorganization. The new Department of Education is composed almost exclusively of education programs from the old Department of Health, Education and Welfare. Head Start, Indian education, the school lunch program, GI bill benefits, manpower training, and some vocational and rehabilitation education programs remained where they were because of opposition to their being moved. For example, the Senate Agriculture Committee opposed change out of fear of losing oversight responsibility for child nutrition programs, and the American

Food Service Association opposed change because it feared nutrition would not be a high priority with educators.[41]

One reason Carter's proposal for a new Department of Natural Resources failed to pass Congress was opposition from the timber industry. If the Forest Service were moved from the Department of Agriculture to the new department as called for in the president's plan, it would become more interested in environmental protection than in timber production, the industry argued. The House and Senate agriculture committees, fearful of losing jurisdiction over this and other programs, also strongly opposed the new department.[42]

State and local governments are often burdened with state constitutions or city charters that mandate a fragmented administrative structure. An extra burden is the fragmented federal administrative organization. Because state and local governments rely heavily upon federal grants, their administrative structures often mirror those of the federal government. While this may enhance their ability to deal with federal officials, it adds to fragmentation at the state and local levels. For example, state education agencies have tended to mirror the highly fragmented federal organizational structure for categorical programs in education, adding an obstacle to coherent education policy.[43] There seems to be little statewide planning for or coordination of federal education aid, but rather policies and guidelines for each separate program.[44]

The nature of public policy also is a factor in producing fragmentation. Broad policies, such as those dealing with environmental protection, are multidimensional and overlap with dimensions of other policies, such as agriculture, transportation, recreation, and energy. Thus, government agencies cannot be easily organized around just one policy area.

Consequences of Fragmentation

Fragmentation implies diffusion of responsibility, and this makes coordination of policies difficult. The resources and authority necessary to attack a problem comprehensively are often distributed among many bureaucratic units.

In the early 1970s organizations involved in drug control could produce many defendant-informants, but they lacked the capacity to follow up on the leads the informants provided. There was no national intelligence system to help agents evaluate the potential contributions of informants, and there was no central place where available information could be reported or stored, much less effectively analyzed and disseminated. Jurisdictional lines were not easily crossed, so informants were treated as exclusive property of their arresting officer and could not be readily used in another jurisdiction. There were even problems in moving an informant within the jurisdiction of a single agency (such as from Manhattan to Brooklyn). Similarly, each agency had a limited set of investigative tactics, skills, and support systems at its disposal. Rather than drawing upon the full range of resources available to the entire government, each agency made tactical choices in specific cases on the basis of its own information.[45]

Within the Drug Enforcement Administration, created in 1973 to lead federal efforts to control the supply of illicit drugs, coordination between enforcement agents and intelligence analysts was poor. The enforcement officials felt they could handle intelligence functions themselves, and since they dominated the agency, integrated intelligence functions would have received few resources, and intelligence analysts would have enjoyed little influence. For intelligence to be useful, however, it had to be coordinated with enforcement and used by agents. Organizationally, this was clearly a no-win situation.

The decision was made to set up a separate Office of Intelligence, but enforcement agents and intelligence personnel continued to feud. The new office, viewed by agents as competition rather than support, was largely ignored. It did not receive adequate resources and, on the whole, did not improve its intelligence capabilities. To make matters worse, key supervisory roles in the intelligence division were given to enforcement personnel who were weak in both general management skills and in intelligence expertise. Under these organizational circumstances, the cards were stacked against success.[46]

After passage of the 1966 Demonstration Cities and Metropolitan Development Act, the Department of Housing and Urban Development (HUD) requested the cooperation of other agencies. Implementing President Johnson's "Model Cities" program was a massive undertaking. The act gave grants to selected cities to restructure the entire environment of neighborhoods chosen for demonstration projects. Funds could be used for education, antipoverty, and other social programs, as well as for housing and physical improvements. HUD especially wanted priority given to grant applications growing out of Model Cities programs, flexibility in the administration of grant regulations, a substantial percentage of urban program money earmarked for local Model Cities projects, and the employment of newly-created community development agencies (CDAs) as a single channel for all federal aid affecting the model neighborhood. This was not to be.

Urban renewal officials within HUD itself were reluctant to cooperate with the CDAs by giving them a voice in planning renewal projects or reviewing authority over final plans. There were problems in coordinating other HUD programs as well. Worse than this, however, were the actions of other departments and agencies. There was a problem channeling Department of Health, Education and Welfare (HEW) funds through the CDAs. Most HEW funds were categorical aid grants allocated according to statutory formulas and state plans. In addition, many HEW bureau chiefs and regional officials were unsympathetic to HUD's requests. The Department of Labor did not cooperate much on manpower training programs, and the Office of Economic Opportunity was opposed to coordination because of its commitment to its own community action agencies. Despite persistent efforts, support from high White House aides, and friendly officials in other departments, HUD received little cooperation in implementing the Model Cities program. Later analysis of the program revealed that "virtually all categorical grant-in-aid programs continued to maintain their own application and planning requirements, their own review criteria and procedures, and their own sense of priorities."[47]

Similarly, when President Johnson wanted to establish "one-stop service centers" to provide easy access to federal social services in urban neighborhoods, bureaucratic bickering at the national and state levels prevented most of them from opening. The Department of Labor, the Office of Economic Opportunity, and the Department of Housing and Urban Development all wanted the service centers to bear their names to the exclusion of the others.[48]

Duplication in the provision of public services is another result of bureaucratic fragmentation. Although in some instances duplication is beneficial — reliance upon a single source of information is never ideal — it usually hinders implementation by wasting scarce resources that, as we saw in Chapter 3, can be put to better use in implementing policy.

In 1971 President Nixon complained:

> The Agriculture Department ... finds that its interest in agricultural labor is shared in the Labor Department, its regard for agricultural enterprise is shared by the Small Business Administration, and its concern for providing sufficient transportation for farm products is shared by the Department of Transportation. The Commerce, Labor and Agriculture Departments duplicate one another in collecting economic statistics, yet they use computers and statistical techniques which are often incompatible.... [T]he same locality may receive two or more grants for the same project.[49]

Seven years later President Carter echoed these views:

> There are ... at least 75 agencies and 164,000 Federal employees in police or investigative work. Many of them duplicate or overlap state and local law enforcement efforts unnecessarily....[50]

Fragmentation may result in two or more agencies working at cross-purposes. Quoting Richard Nixon again:

> One department's watershed project, for instance, threatens to slow the flow of water to another department's reclamation project downstream. One agency wants to develop an electric power project on a certain river while other agencies are working to keep the same area wild. Different departments follow different policies for timber production and conservation, for grazing, for fire prevention and for recreational activities on the federal lands they control, though the lands are often contiguous.[51]

Not only do such conflicts defeat the purposes of the programs involved, but they also force public officials to spend great amounts of time and energy negotiating with one another. Not only is this wasteful, but it also may result in compromises representing the lowest common denominators of officials' original positions. Unfortunately, "bold and original ideas are thus sacrificed for intragovernmental harmony."[52]

The fragmentation of program responsibilities is often so great that it confuses and even overwhelms those whom programs are supposed to serve. Speaking in 1978 about federal aid for community economic development, President Carter pointed out the existence of:

- over eleven different business assistance programs in more than ten agencies;
- 46 sewage-related programs in five different departments, two independent agencies, and eight regional commissions;
- at least 77 different housing programs in 15 different agencies;
- 60 transportation grant programs in the Department of Transportation and 25 other agencies;
- and 24 programs administered by ten agencies for employment and training.[53]

With such an array of programs, no wonder many state and local officials find federal assistance too complicated to master! The possibilities for aid may be great in number, but the expertise to match the relevant program with the appropriate qualifications and needs of a jurisdiction is often not available, especially in small communities.

Sometimes responsibility for a policy area is so fragmented that certain functions fall between the cracks. Some tasks do not fit neatly within an agency's formal authority. One author writes of serving in a Scandinavian embassy and hiring someone to read the local communist literature. From this a useful chart showing the hierarchy of the Communist Party was developed. The project was cut from the budget, however, because coverage of the communist movement was considered to be a CIA function, yet the CIA could not carry out this function because it was "overt," and the CIA was a clandestine organization.[54] Thus, the project fell between the divisions of organizational responsibility.

Diffused responsibility for policies typically results in agencies with narrow foci. This may impede the implementation of new policy requirements because, as we saw in the last chapter, agencies do not like to change their basic missions. If the range of programs in an agency is limited, it will be placed in the position of opposing change in order to preserve its essence. For example, it was easier for the Corps of Engineers, rather than the Soil Conservation Service (SCS), to react positively to the environmental concerns reflected in the National Environmental Policy Act. The Corps had a broader range of potential projects to administer than the SCS, and, therefore, it had more flexibility in adjusting its priorities.[55]

CONCLUSION

The structure of the organizations that implement policy have a significant influence on implementation. One of the most basic structural aspects of any organization is its standard operating procedures. These routines for handling common situations are pervasive in both public and private organizations. SOPs save implementors valuable time, allowing them to take shortcuts in dealing with most daily decisions. They also provide uniformity in the actions of officials in complex and widely dispersed organizations, which in turn can result in greater flexibility (persons can be transferred easily from one location to another) and greater equity in the application of rules.

The lack of resources necessary to implement policies properly helps account for the frequent use of SOPs. Implementors are rarely able to examine thoroughly and individually each situation with which they are faced. Instead they rely upon routines that simplify decisionmaking and match program responsibilities with available resources. Once routines are established, they tend to remain in force. Inhibited by the desire for stability and lack of conflict and by the high cost of developing SOPs, implementors find it to their advantage to maintain the status quo. It is unfortunate that SOPs are re-evaluated infrequently because sometimes they hinder implementation as much as they aid it.

Routines designed for typical situations in the past may inhibit change in policy because they are inappropriate for novel situations or new programs. While this drawback is especially clear during a crisis when nuances in policy may be particularly important, SOPs may be inappropriate for more routine policies as well. Most organizations have difficulty adjusting to change. Familiar routines are often applied to newer responsibilities, but they may greatly impede implementation by limiting the flexibility necessary to respond adequately to new situations; inhibiting the hiring of personnel with the proper skills; and discouraging the development of appropriate operational techniques. Sometimes organizations even shun new responsibilities because their leaders see them as inconsistent with established routines.

Following standard routines may be time-consuming and wasteful. Each component in the system that must clear programs or projects places its own priorities for action on them, priorities that are usually not the same as those most interested in the new policies. Waste of scarce resources essential for implementation may occur when routines designed for one purpose are maintained over time and applied in situations where they are not needed at all.

Not only do SOPs sometimes prevent appropriate actions, but they also may cause personnel to take actions senior officials do not want. Certain responses to situations are programmed into an organization's repertoire of behavior. These actions may take place, even though they jeopardize the policies of high officials. SOPs with low visibility can cause crises because policymakers are not aware of their implications.

SOPs are most likely to hamper the implementation of new policies that require new modes of operation or types of personnel to implement them. Moreover, the more a policy requires change in the routines of an organization, the greater the probability of SOPs hindering implementation. Bureaucracies in which SOPs are not deeply embedded — either because of the newness of the agency or the high rate of personnel turnover — may be more responsive to the need for new organizational routines. Similarly, long lead times and clearly prescribed behavior in laws may aid in overcoming inappropriate bureaucratic routines. In a few instances it is possible to bypass existing organizations and their SOPs and place new policies in new agencies which then can be programmed to implement them.

Despite the implementation problems SOPs can cause, at times they may be helpful. Organizations with flexible planning procedures and substantial control over flexible programs may be more adaptable to new responsibilities than bureaucracies without these characteristics.

A second feature of bureaucratic structure that significantly influences policy implementation is organizational fragmentation. Responsibility for a policy area is frequently dispersed among several organizations, often radically decentralizing the power to accomplish policy goals. Congress and other legislatures write many separate agencies into law in order to observe them more closely and specify their behavior. Having numerous agencies disperses "turf" and accompanying power to members of various committees. Existing agencies, as one would expect, fight to maintain their functions and oppose efforts to make them coordinate their policies with agencies running related programs. Fearful that the consolidation of agencies will diminish their special access to officials or alter substantially the priorities of existing programs, interest groups may also support fragmentation.

These influences on bureaucratic structure are buttressed by state constitutions and city charters, which mandate a fragmented administrative structure, and federal grant programs, which encourage state and local governments to mirror the fragmentation at the national level. The lack of attention many officials give to the consequences of new policies for the organizational structure of government and the multidimensional nature of many policies also contribute to fragmentation.

Hindering coordination is perhaps the worst consequence of bureaucratic fragmentation. The priorities of agencies differ, and bureaucrats do not like to coordinate their actions with their counterparts in other agencies. Yet the dispersal of the authority and resources to implement complex policies requires coordination to take place. The obstacles to effective policy implementation are exacerbated when the structure of government is fragmented. In general, the more coordination that is necessary to implement a policy, the less the chances of its succeeding.

Fragmentation, like SOPs, may waste scarce resources. The overlap and duplication that occur in the provision of public services, while sometimes beneficial by minimizing the danger of overreliance on one source of information, usually waste funds and manpower.

If one agency tries to drain a swamp while another tries to preserve it, the projects are unlikely to be a success. When there are many narrowly focused agencies functioning at once, there is always the possibility that some of them will be working at cross-purposes. Officials must spend many valuable hours negotiating with one another to overcome these no-win situations. Sometimes innovative ideas are lost in the quest for intragovernmental harmony.

Potential beneficiaries of government services may become confused by the bewildering array of available programs and be unable to isolate the ones most appropriate for their needs and for which they qualify. This is especially likely to be the case in jurisdictions without staff with expertise in federal grant programs.

The narrow foci of many agencies due to fragmentation has two other consequences detrimental to implementation. Sometimes responsibility for a policy area is so fragmented that no one ends up carrying out certain functions. With each agency having limited jurisdiction over an area, important tasks may fall between the cracks of organizational structure. Narrow foci of agencies may also inhibit change. If an agency has little flexibility in its missions, it will try to preserve its essence and may be more likely to resist new policies that require it to change.

NOTES

1. Richard Weatherly and Michael Lipsky, "Street-Level Bureaucrats and Institutional Innovation: Implementing Special Education Reform," *Harvard Educational Review* 47 (May 1977): 171-197.
2. Ibid., pp. 193-194.
3. Herbert Kaufman, *The Limits of Organizational Change* (University, Ala.: University of Alabama Press, 1971), p. 21.
4. Herbert Kaufman, *Red Tape: Its Origins, Uses, and Abuses* (Washington, D.C.: Brookings Institution, 1977), p. 13.
5. On this point see Anthony Downs, *Inside Bureaucracy* (Boston: Little, Brown & Co., 1967), p. 195.
6. Joel F. Handler, *Social Movements and the Legal System: A Theory of Law Reform and Social Change* (New York: Academic Press, 1978), pp. 86-87.
7. M. S. Eccles, *Beckoning Frontiers* (New York: Alfred A. Knopf, 1951), p. 336.
8. Graham T. Allison, *Essence of Decision: Explaining the Cuban Missile Crisis* (Boston: Little, Brown & Co., 1971), pp. 131-132.
9. Mark H. Moore, "Reorganization Plan #2 Reviewed: Problems in Implementing a Strategy to Reduce the Supply of Drugs to Illicit Markets in the United States," *Public Policy* 26 (Spring 1978): 244.
10. Ibid., p. 238.
11. Judith M. Feder, *Medicare: The Politics of Federal Hospital Insurance* (Lexington, Mass.: D. C. Heath & Co., 1977), pp. 40, 134-135, 149, 153-155.
12. Richard A. Liroff, *A National Policy for the Environment: NEPA and Its Aftermath* (Bloomington, Ind.: Indiana University Press, 1976), pp. 113-114.
13. Harvey M. Sapolsky, *The Polaris System Development: Bureaucratic and Programmatic Success in Government* (Cambridge, Mass.: Harvard University Press, 1972), especially pp. 34-35.
14. Milbrey W. McLaughlin, *Evaluation and Reform: The Elementary and Secondary Education Act of 1965/Title I* (Cambridge, Mass.: Ballinger Publishing Co., 1975), pp. 19, 21.
15. Jerome T. Murphy, *State Agencies and Discretionary Funds* (Lexington, Mass.: Lexington Books, 1974), p. 21; Jerome T. Murphy, "The Education Bureaucracies Implement Novel Policy: The Politics of Title I of ESEA, 1965-72," in *Policy and Politics in America: Six Case Studies*, ed. Allan P. Sindler (Boston: Little, Brown & Co., 1973), pp. 173-176.
16. In *Federal Aid to Education: Who Benefits? Who Governs?*, eds. Joel S. Berke and Michael W. Kirst (Lexington, Mass.: Lexington Books, 1972), see the following articles: Michael W. Kirst, "Federal Aid to Public Education: Who Governs?," pp. 64-66, "The Politics of Federal Aid to Education in California," p. 79; Jay D. Scribner, "The Politics of Federal Aid to

Education in Michigan," pp. 132-133; Lawrence Iannaccone, "The Politics of Federal Aid to Education in Massachusetts," pp. 195-196; Michael W. Kirst, "The Politics of Federal Aid to Education in Texas," pp. 236-237; Edith K. Mosher, "The Politics of Federal Aid to Education in Virginia," pp. 280-281; Frederick M. Wirt, "The Politics of Federal Aid to Education in New York," pp. 327-328; and Joel S. Berke and Michael W. Kirst, "Intergovernmental Relations: Conclusions and Recommendations," p. 390.

17. John F. Hughes and Anne O. Hughes, *Equal Education* (Bloomington, Ind.: Indiana University Press, 1972), pp. 97-106.

18. Murphy, *State Education Agencies,* pp. 7-8, 14-15, 119, 124-125, Chapters 3-6. For information on the failure of state education agencies to change their evaluation units, see Mike M. Milsten, *Impact and Response* (New York: Teachers College Press, 1976), p. 42. For more on SOPs and attempts at innovation, see Herbert H. Hyman, ed., *The Politics of Health Care* (New York: Praeger Publishers, 1973), p. 195 and Neal Gross, Joseph B. Giacquinta, and Marilyn Bernstein, *Implementing Organizational Innovations: A Sociological Analysis of Planned Educational Change* (New York: Basic Books, 1971), pp. 139-142.

19. William V. Stapleton and Lee F. Teitelbaum, *In Defense of Youth* (New York: Russell Sage Foundation, 1972). See also Michael Sosin, "Due Process Mandates and the Operation of Juvenile Courts," *Journal of Social Services Research* 1 (Summer 1978): 423-444.

20. Randall D. Ripley, "Congress and Clean Air: The Issue of Enforcement, 1963," in *Congress and Urban Problems,* ed. Frederic N. Cleaveland et al. (Washington, D.C.: Brookings Institution, 1969), p. 233.

21. Jerry Mechling, "Analysis and Implementation: Sanitation Policies in New York City," *Public Policy* 26 (Spring 1978): 270-271.

22. Elting E. Morison, *Men, Machines, and Modern Times* (Cambridge, Mass.: MIT Press, 1966), pp. 17-18.

23. Allison, *Essence of Decision,* p. 138.

24. Ibid., p. 139.

25. Ibid., p. 140.

26. Patrick J. McGarvey, *C.I.A.: The Myth and the Madness* (Baltimore: Penguin Books, 1972), pp. 100-111.

27. Morton H. Halperin, *Bureaucratic Politics and Foreign Policy* (Washington, D.C.: Brookings Institution, 1974), p. 243.

28. See Kaufman, *Limits of Organizational Change.*

29. Rowland Evans and Robert Novak, *Lyndon B. Johnson: The Exercise of Power* (New York: Signet, 1966), p. 430.

30. Daniel A. Mazmanian and Jeanne Nienaber, *Can Organizations Change?: Environmental Protection, Citizen Participation, and the Corps of Engineers* (Washington, D.C.: Brookings Institution, 1979).

31. Liroff, *A National Policy for the Environment,* pp. 138, 140.

32. "Carter Criticizes Federal Bureaucracy," *Congressional Quarterly Weekly Report,* June 3, 1978, p. 1421.

33. Handler, *Social Movements and the Legal System,* p. 86.

34. "Carter Criticizes Federal Bureaucracy," p. 1421.

35. "The Power Vacuum Outside the Oval Office," *National Journal,* February 24, 1979, p. 298.

36. Joseph A. Califano, Jr., *A Presidential Nation* (New York: W. W. Norton & Co., 1975), pp. 25, 31-33.

37. See, for example, William Colby, *Honorable Men: My Life in the CIA* (New York: Simon & Schuster, 1978), pp. 58-60, 67, 295-296, 330.

38. "Federal Drug Abuse Program Continued Through Fiscal 1981," *Congressional Quarterly Weekly Report,* January 12, 1980, p. 77.
39. Califano, *A Presidential Nation,* pp. 29, 139-140.
40. Neal R. Peirce, "A Florida Reorganization Effort Under Fire," *Minneapolis Tribune,* February 12, 1978, p. 13A.
41. "Carter's Reorganization Plans - Scrambling for Turf," *National Journal,* May 20, 1978, p. 791.
42. "The Reorganization Staff Is Big Loser in the Latest Shuffle," *National Journal,* March 10, 1979, p. 399; "The Best-Laid Reorganization Plans Sometimes Go Astray," *National Journal,* January 20, 1979, p. 90.
43. Lorraine M. McDonnell, "Implementation of Federal Education Policy: The Role of the States" (Paper delivered at the annual meeting of the American Political Science Association, Washington, D.C, August-September, 1979), pp. 19-20.
44. See Kirst, "Federal Aid to Education," p. 69; Kirst, "The Politics of Federal Aid to Education in California," p. 97; and Iannaccone, "The Politics of Federal Aid to Education in Massachusetts," pp. 215, 229.
45. Moore, "Reorganization Plan #2 Reviewed," pp. 241-242, 259-260.
46. Ibid., pp. 255-257.
47. Lawrence D. Brown and Bernard Frieden, "Guidelines and Goals in the Model Cities Program," *Policy Sciences* 7 (December 1976): 479-481.
48. Califano, *A Presidential Nation,* pp. 32-33.
49. Richard Nixon, "Government Reorganization — Message from the President," in *Perspectives on the Presidency: A Collection,* eds. Stanley Bach and George T. Sulzner (Lexington, Mass.: D. C. Heath & Co., 1974), pp. 252-261.
50. "Carter Criticizes Federal Bureaucracy," p. 1421.
51. Nixon, "Government Reorganization," p. 257.
52. Ibid., p. 252.
53. "Carter Criticizes Federal Bureaucracy," p. 1421.
54. Colby, *Honorable Men,* pp. 101-102.
55. Richard N. L. Andrews, *Environmental Policy and Administrative Change* (Lexington, Mass.: Lexington Books, 1976), pp. 143, 148, 156-157.

6

Problems and Prospects

Policymaking does not end once a bill is passed, an executive order or an administrative regulation is issued, or a judicial decision is handed down. As we have seen, the implementation of these decisions may have a great impact on policy results. In implementing policy as well as in its formulation, accommodations must be made to political interests, scarcity of resources, and the nature of bureaucracies and our political system.

This final chapter begins with an explicit examination of what has been implicit throughout the last four chapters: communications, resources, dispositions, and bureaucratic structure influence implementation indirectly as well as directly, through their interaction with each other. Second, we consider the types of public policies most likely to face implementation problems. Finally, we focus upon the question of improving implementation. The most basic technique for identifying and correcting implementation problems is follow-up. But many policymakers never monitor their decisions and orders to make sure that they have been implemented properly. The chapter concludes with a brief look at the possibilities of overcoming this and other barriers to effective implementation.

INTERACTIONS BETWEEN FACTORS

To this point we have focused upon the direct influence of the factors of communication, resources, dispositions, and bureaucratic structure on policy implementation. Aside from directly affecting implementation, however, they also indirectly affect it through their impact on each other. In other words, communications affect resources, dispositions, and bureaucratic structures, which in turn influence implementation. Figure 6.1 on the next page depicts these interactions.

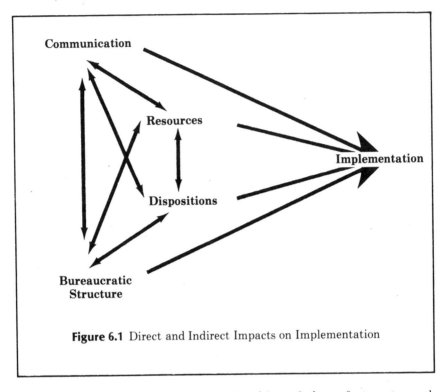

Figure 6.1 Direct and Indirect Impacts on Implementation

A brief review of some of the relationships of these factors to each other will clarify their role in implementation.

Directives that are not accurately transmitted, clear, or consistent provide implementors with discretion in responding to them. This discretion may be exercised directly or through formulating instructions for lower level officials. Once discretion is provided by lapses in communications, it allows dispositions to come into play. They strongly influence how implementors will exercise their discretion. Similarly, discretion provided by loose communications allows implementors to continue using their established routines. On the other hand, communications that are too detailed may lower the morale and independence of implementors, leading to goal displacement and the waste of valuable resources such as staff skills, creativity, and adaptability. Thus, the impact of communications on implementation is not only direct, but is also felt through its linkages with resources, dispositions, and bureaucratic structures.

Resources also indirectly influence implementation. They interact with communications in several ways. Insufficient staff can hinder the transmission of policy directives, as in the case of the courts. Top officials' lack of information is often the cause of the ambiguity in their implementation orders. Implementors' perceptions of implementation communications may be hindered by lack of time to pay full attention to them. SOPs are in part a reaction to limited resources.

Resources may affect the role of dispositions in implementation as well. If resources are plentiful, individuals and organizations involved in implementation will have less need to compete among themselves to maintain their personal and organizational interests. Moreover, the more resources that are available to an agency, the easier it will be for it to shift its priorities in response to new policy demands in the environment. Conversely, the limited staff and authority that are typically available diminishes the possibility that officials on one level can effectively control those on lower levels — whether through monitoring behavior, providing incentives, or exercising sanctions. Thus, there may be more opportunities for implementation to reflect the dispositions of officials of lower level jurisdictions.

The dispositions of implementors influence both how they interpret the policy communications they receive and whether and how they elaborate them and send them further down the chain of command. Dispositions also affect the willingness of officials to exercise their authority on behalf of the implementation of a policy. When a program assigned to an agency conflicts with the agency's core mission(s), its implementation is likely to be distorted. Agency personnel may allocate low priority and limited resources to the policy. Conversely, implementors of some programs may be disposed to expend more resources than are appropriate in the name of self-preservation. Dispositions of implementors may encourage the adoption and maintenance of SOPs that are convenient for implementors but counterproductive for implementation. Dispositions are also a primary cause of bureaucratic fragmentation as organizational units fight for resources and autonomy, often wasting resources in the process.

The fragmented bureaucratic structure of government increases the probability of communication failures. The more people who must receive implementation instructions, the greater the chances of message distortion. Fragmentation clearly limits the ability of top officials to coordinate all the relevant resources available to a jurisdiction. Moreover, the inefficiency inherent in fragmentation and in some SOPs wastes scarce resources.

Fragmentation affects dispositions in several ways. The establishment of numerous agencies with narrow responsibilities encourages the development of parochial attitudes among bureaucrats. This in turn leads to bureaucratic infighting and lack of cooperation. In addition, the multiple points of access for private interests provided by fragmentation increase the opportunities for these interests to pressure implementors to act on the basis of their personal dispositions rather than the orders of their superiors.

POLICIES APT TO FACE IMPLEMENTATION PROBLEMS

Are general types of policies likely to face implementation problems? Having examined and explained the direct and indirect impacts on policy implementation of four critical factors, we are now in a position to address this question.

The typologies of policies commonly employed by political scientists do not serve us very well in examining implementation. Policies as diverse as federal grants for education, environmental protection laws, and federal welfare programs obviously are substantively different. Moreover, they represent distributive, regulatory, and redistributive policies, respectively — the three types of policies in Theodore Lowi's famous classification.[1] Yet all these policies figure in each of the four preceding chapters; all of them experience substantial problems in implementation. Therefore, to reach broad generalizations about implementation it is necessary to categorize policies on the basis of other characteristics. We shall focus on policies that are new, decentralized, controversial, complex, crisis-related, and/or established by the judiciary.

New Policies

New policies are especially difficult to implement successfully. Well-developed channels of communication have not been established, and often goals are vague and directives inconsistent. When officials have to gear up a program from scratch, they do not always know what to order implementors to do. As officials learn their jobs and have a chance to experiment and get reactions from both implementors and interested parties in the legislature and in the private sector, communications may improve.

New programs are also among the most likely to face shortages of resources. Information on how to run a novel program to accomplish new goals may well be lacking. Similarly, there may be no staff waiting to implement the program, and hiring the requisite number of trained personnel may be difficult or impossible. Often existing agencies receive new program responsibilities without commensurate increases in staff.

If an agency is assigned responsibility to implement a new program, another problem may arise. If a new program is perceived by agency personnel as inconsistent with their current primary mission(s), they may give it low priority and allocate limited resources to its implementation. In addition, new programs may require actions inconsistent with existing routines. Yet the new policy may be altered by implementors to fit the old, inappropriate SOPs.

New programs are also the most likely to be hindered if directives are overly specific. When policies are new it is especially important that implementors be creative and have the flexibility to adapt them to unanticipated circumstances. If implementors' behavior is programmed too tightly, goal displacement, rigidity, or circumvention of regulations may occur.

Decentralized Policies

Policies that require highly decentralized implementation efforts often face implementation problems. Decentralized implementation means that ultimately many people are involved in carrying it out. The policies that fall into this category are diverse: law enforcement, civil rights, consumer protection, federal education grants, environmental protection, and others. To know how to implement decentralized policies, each person must receive instructions. Transmission channels are often primitive, however, especially to persons at lower levels of government or in the private sector. Moreover, the more organizational layers through which communications must pass, and the more persons who must elaborate, them, the greater the chances of distortion. When the ultimate implementors of a policy are far removed from those who are formulating instructions, the chances of implementors misunderstanding those directives are great. Sometimes the misunderstanding is accidental, and sometimes it is the result of implementors' selective perception.

Resources are especially critical in decentralized implementation. The more implementors involved, the more people whose behavior must be monitored. Yet information on the performance of implementors is often lacking, as are the personnel to gather and evaluate it. Not only does decentralized implementation imply large numbers of implementors, but possibly the involvement of two or more agencies, branches of government, or levels of government. The nature of the American political system ensures that responsibility for many policy areas will be shared. Consequently, the problems of coordinating disparate organizations, resistance to change, confusion, programs working at cross-purposes, waste, and functions falling between organizational boundaries result. Yet the authority and management skills necessary to overcome fragmentation are frequently lacking in government.

Controversial Policies

Also apt to face implementation problems are particularly controversial policies. Passage of a controversial policy often requires vague clauses that cover the compromises and multiple goals of the coalition that supported it. Ambiguity in the law also serves to avoid alienating groups in the public. It allows legislatures to avoid accountability for policies by letting the executive branch or a regulatory commission take the blame when the law is applied in specific situations. Moreover, controversial policies often have many intensely interested parties attempting to influence their implementation, a situation that produces inconsistent policy directives.

Ambiguous policy directives provide implementors in both the public and private sectors with discretion. Discretion allows implementors to act on the basis of their dispositions. Implementors may be especially likely to disagree with a controversial policy and therefore ignore some of its requirements or at least selectively perceive them. In addition, the competing policy interests and organizational and personal interests of implementors may result in opposition to the implementation of a controversial policy. Such resistance flourishes in an environment where top officials lack the authority and personnel to monitor implementation.

Complex Policies

Complex policies share many of the properties of controversial policies. Complex policies usually have multiple goals, and because they are complicated, top policymakers will often not know how to provide specifics. Vague laws result, which provides implementors with discretion. As we know, discretion will not necessarily be exercised to further the goals, however vague, of the original decisionmakers. Complex policies often involve highly technical matters, and implementation may suffer from a lack of properly skilled personnel.

Crisis Policies

Crises, especially those involving other countries, cause special burdens in policy implementation. It may be impossible to communicate with adversaries, especially if a new regime has recently come to power. In a crisis there may be no time to establish new channels of communication. Diplomatic messages sent between hostile countries are often unclear, and it is difficult to clarify them, at least in a short time frame. Resources may also be a problem, both in their absence (as in the case of a large, highly mobile military unit) or in equipment failure (as in the case of malfunctioning helicopters in the Iranian desert). Crisis situations often call for fast, flexible action, and the restriction of unwanted actions. Yet established bureaucratic routines are not easy to change, especially overnight.

Judicial Policies

Judicial decisions seem particularly prone to slippage in implementation. The formal channels for transmitting court decisions are virtually nonexistent, and informal channels are highly unreliable. Appellate court decisions end in vague statements to lower courts to follow the principles enunciated by the higher court, and judges cannot initiate new cases to clarify their decisions. Decisions may also appear to be inconsistent as judges overrule past decisions without overtly appearing to do so.

Insufficient resources in the judicial branch are similarly troublesome for implementation. The courts lack personnel to monitor compliance with their decisions. While the implementation of clear-cut decisions by highly visible individuals or institutions may be relatively easy to identify, such situations are atypical. Lacking authority to initiate actions themselves, judges must rely on others to bring cases regarding noncompliance to them. Yet the beneficiaries of many important judicial decisions lack the money and expertise to do this. Even in cases where judges have authority, they are reluctant to exercise it. Sanctions are rarely applied, and courts are hesitant to take on responsibilities requiring extensive administrative duties, partly because they lack the personnel and expertise to perform them well. Moreover, decisions based on statutory interpretation can be overturned by relevant legislative bodies, and any policy that is voided by a court may be replaced by a similar one.

Judges have little influence on the selection of other judges for their own or lower courts. Nor do judges on appellate courts have much in the way of rewards or sanctions available to them to provide incentives for lower court judges to heed their decisions. Once on the bench, judges are usually independent — even of those who put them there. When this independence of judges is coupled with the ambiguity and inconsistency that often exists in the law, we can see that judges are in a position to exercise discretion in their adherence to the decisions of lawmakers. Naturally, judges have even less influence on the selection of implementors outside the judiciary, and they have no rewards to offer them as incentives for faithful implementation.

Combinations of Characteristics

These are the types of policies most likely to face implementation problems. The categories of policies are not mutually exclusive, however. Policies may combine several of these characteristics. Those that do will probably be the most difficult to implement. Thus, a new, complex, controversial, and highly decentralized policy such as comprehensive national health insurance is likely to face substantial problems in implementation, especially in its early years.

PROSPECTS FOR IMPROVING IMPLEMENTATION

In this book we have identified and analyzed many problems of policy implementation. Although it is beyond the scope of our efforts to propose solutions to these problems, we can gain further insight into their persistence by examining the prospects for improvement. Before we look at overcoming specific obstacles to implementation, let us consider first a general technique for improvement: follow-up.

Follow-up

Because of all the hindrances to effective policy implementation, it seems reasonable to suggest that implementation would be improved if policymakers followed up on their decisions and orders to see that they have been properly implemented. The following example illustrates the importance of follow-up.

In 1970 President Nixon ordered the CIA to destroy its stockpile of biological weapons. CIA Director Richard Helms relayed the president's order to the deputy director for plans (the head of the covert action division), and he in turn relayed it to a subordinate. Five years later two lethal toxins were discovered in a secret cache. A middle-level official had disobeyed the president's order, later retired, and his successor had assumed the storage of the toxins had official approval. When called before Congress, Helms testified that he had undertaken no follow-up check on his own order, and when asked who told him the toxins were destroyed, he replied, "I read it in the newspapers." Indeed, if the official who discovered the toxins had not received a directive from the new CIA director, William Colby, to be on the constant lookout for illegal action, he might not have checked on the legality of the toxins, and they would still be sitting there.[2]

The importance of follow-up was made apparent to Nixon at many other points in his administration. Once he ordered the demolition of two old Department of Defense buildings on the Mall near the White House, but it took more than a year to get them down. White House aide William Safire explains:

> Because the President of the United States took a continuing interest, because at least two of his aides were made to feel that its success was a crucial test of their ability, and because the President kept prodding, prodding, issuing orders, refusing to be "reasonable," a few miserable buildings were finally knocked down and their occupants reassigned.

After the demolition the president called together his aides. With "pride, relief, and wonderment," he told them, "We have finally gotten something done."[3]

In his memoirs Nixon complains of the three weeks it took to implement his order to resume reconnaissance flights over North Korea in 1969 and the military's cancellation of similar flights in the Mediterranean without informing him. Thus, he warns, a president must constantly check up on his orders.[4] Nevertheless, most recent presidents, including Nixon himself, have not followed this advice. They and their staffs have been too busy with crisis management, electoral politics, or getting legislation passed to delve into the details involved in monitoring policy implementation. Follow-up on the whole has been haphazard.[5]

Executive Follow-up. Follow-up is more easily said than done. An aide to President Franklin D. Roosevelt wrote:

> Half of a President's suggestions, which theoretically carry the weight of orders, can be safely forgotten by a Cabinet member. And if the President asks about a suggestion a second time, he can be told that it is being investigated. If he asks a third time a wise Cabinet officer will give him at least part of what he suggests. But only occasionally, except about the most important matters, do Presidents ever get around to asking three times.[6]

One technique used by many executives to increase their capacity to follow up on their decisions is to enlarge the size of their personal staffs. This strategy can create additional burdens for top officials, however. Because executives can personally deal effectively with only a few people, they are forced to relay implementation orders and receive feedback through additional layers of their own staffs. This, in turn, increases both the possibility of communication distortion and the burden of administration — which the staff is supposed to lighten. The more authority is delegated to persons at the top of a hierarchy, the more possibilities there are for inadequate coordination, interoffice rivalries, communication gaps, and other typical administrative problems. Moreover, according to former White House aide Joseph Califano, a large number of aides with limited access to a top official such as the president increases the chance of their carrying out orders given in anger.[7] Those with limited access will be less likely to know the executive well enough or have enough confidence to hold back on implementing their supervisor's instructions.

A large staff for an executive has another drawback. Only a few people can credibly speak for an official. If too many people begin giving orders in the president's name, for example, they will undermine the credibility of all those claiming to speak for him. This credibility is important for aides trying to help the president implement policies. As one Carter aide explained:

> If you are perceived by people in a given agency as being close to the president because you have an office in the West Wing, your phone calls will be returned more rapidly and your requests for information or action will be taken more seriously.[8]

Johnson aide Harry McPherson has pointed out that presidential assistants carry the contingent authority of the president, authority which is essential to accomplish anything at all since under the law presidential assistants have no authority of their own.[9] But presidential authority is undermined if numerous people attempt to exercise it.

Excessively vigorous staff involvement in implementation decisions may cause other problems. For example, some observers of recent presidential administrations have concluded that as larger numbers of bright, ambitious, energetic assistants probe into the activities of departments and agencies, they will bring more issues for decision to the president, issues that were formerly decided at lower levels in the bureaucracy. Bureaucrats will begin to pass the buck upwards, and more and more decisions must then be made by the White House. This can easily make the Executive Office of the President top-heavy and slow. Involvement in the minutiae of government also may divert resources (including time) from the central objectives and major problems of a president's administration. In addition, if White House aides become intimately involved in the management of government programs, they may lose the objectivity necessary to evaluate new ideas regarding "their" programs.[10]

Overcentralization of decisionmaking at the highest levels may have other negative consequences. It may discourage capable people from serving in government posts where their authority is frequently undercut. It may lower morale and engender resentment and hostility in the bureaucracy. This may impede future cooperation; decrease respect for lower officials among their subordinates; reduce the time bureaucratic officials have for internal management because they must fight to maintain access to and support of the chief executive; and weaken the capability of agencies to streamline or revitalize their management.[11] Similarly, too much monitoring of subordinates' behavior may elicit hostility or excessive caution and lack of imagination in administering policy.[12]

At the beginning of his second term of office in 1973, President Nixon introduced throughout the executive branch a system of follow-up called management by objectives. It was a loose system designed to circulate information about the goals of bureaucratic units, define responsibility for achieving those goals, and assess progress toward meeting them. Conversely, it did not impose objectives on the bureaucracy, carry out performance audits, apply sanctions, offer rewards, make decisions, control actions, or provide plans for achieving results.[13]

Although its aims were modest enough, management by objectives did little to improve implementation in the executive branch. It was often difficult to obtain meaningful objectives from agencies. "Ending crime," for example, was too utopian and too broad to be useful. Sometimes agencies were vague about their objectives to avoid alienating congressional committees and interest groups. Another problem was that many of the objectives were to develop a plan or pass legislation and therefore were not closely related to implementation. It was hard to quantify the objectives of policies such as research or diplomacy, and agencies chose "safe" objectives to state and monitor, not objectives they would have a difficult time achieving. In short, agencies seriously adopted management by objectives when it was in their interests to do so — not because the president desired it. Neither the White House nor the Office of Management and Budget, which had overall responsibility for the new system, was much interested in the information produced by management by objectives, and President Nixon did not devote much time to program management.[14] Not surprisingly, a few years after it began management by objectives was all but forgotten.

A different factor inhibiting follow-up is secrecy. Secretly executed policies, such as those implemented by the CIA, require few reports to Congress or to superiors in the executive branch. Consequently, officials' actions are not routinely monitored. Since members of Congress risk criticism for violating national security if they make public any secret information, they are reluctant to do so and have incentives to forego their responsibility for oversight and follow-up of certain secret policies.[15] When President Johnson's fear of leaks regarding decisions on the war in Vietnam led him to restrict his direct communications to a few top officials (the Tuesday lunch group), he did without a prearranged agenda or minutes of the meetings which would have recorded decisions and made possible follow-up on them.[16]

An organization's personnel may be aware of implementation problems but fail to report them. There are several reasons for this. An obvious one, which we noted earlier, is that subordinates may fear that reporting implementation failures will reflect poorly on their own performance and also possibly anger their superiors. Employees may also have a natural loyalty to their organization or to others in the organization who might be hurt by their negative reports. Police officers, for example, are generally reluctant to provide information on the misbehavior of their fellow officers.[17] Finally, the informal norms against reporting negative information may be very strong. Thus, employees may withhold information from their superiors to escape social ostracism in their peer groups.

Some employees ignore problems they don't want to see. They don't like to think that a policy that they helped administer is not working. Or they may feel that their superiors will not pay attention to their reports anyway, so why bother? Indeed, superiors may reenforce such views by failing to act on evidence of implementation failure. Sometimes prosecutors do not try to dismiss or refuse to prosecute cases based on illegal searches, and police officials do not usually penalize subordinates for engaging in illegal searches.

Organizations may fail to report problems in policy implementation for political reasons, such as the fear of losing public or legislative support for their programs. One study found that the Massachusetts Department of Education failed to develop adequate evaluation and review procedures due in part to its desire to avoid the conflict and potential program cuts that might accompany unfavorable evaluations.[18] Also, within some organizations rivalries between headquarters and field personnel make the latter reluctant to expose themselves to negative reactions to their implementation efforts.

When information indicating poor implementation is made available to top officials, in many instances they fail to use it. One reason for this is that often information coming from the field is circumstantial, inconsistent, ambiguous, unrepresentative — in sum, unreliable. In addition, information arrives in fragments at different places, without integrated patterns of timing, content, or form. Top officials may not be in a position to see the whole as the sum of a program's numerous parts. Moreover, it is difficult for government officials to cull useful follow-up information from the tremendous volume of information they receive, particularly given the many pressing demands competing for their time and attention, such as those for substantive policy changes. Thus, it takes dedicated, sensitive leaders to both assemble and interpret correctly information on the actions of implementors.[19]

Sometimes officials prefer not to know the truth about implementation efforts. In the midwestern cities Dolbeare and Hammond studied, state and local officials (and relevant interest groups) really did not check on prayers and Bible reading in the public schools. Their neglect was often deliberate. These officials preferred to view follow-up as someone else's responsibility.[20]

Selective perception can also play a role here. The authors of a study on civil rights enforcement found that despite the availability of quantitative measures of school integration objectives and success, officials at the Health, Education and Welfare and Justice Departments, although genuinely interested in implementing the law, did not correctly perceive the most successful techniques for desegregating school systems. They felt that whatever technique they used was the most effective. Thus, even when the evidence is clear, it can be distorted at the top. Those responsible for implementation cannot necessarily be depended upon to evaluate their performance objectively.[21]

There are also technical problems in follow-up. Tracing the uses to which public funds have been allocated is not always easy. This is especially true in a school system that receives funds from federal and state grants, bonds, and property taxes. Trying to determine just where any one category of funds is spent can be very difficult.[22]

Another problem is that of monitoring behavior, which, as we have seen, is difficult to accomplish with insufficient resources. Police behavior, for example, is especially difficult to monitor because implementation is highly decentralized. It is easier to monitor the provision of a service — such as counseling or job training — than the provision of a product with market value — such as food stamps or methadone. While a service can be directed specifically at an individual, goods with market value may be sold by recipients and end up in other hands than those for whom they are intended. Goods are harder to control than services and provide an inviting target for theft. Given the decentralized and illegal nature of such transactions, they are almost impossible to monitor.

While there are limitations on performing follow-up properly, this does not mean follow-up cannot work. And we have seen substantial evidence that it needs to be done. One study found that the Nixon administration's efforts to monitor and evaluate the actions of welfare caseworkers, especially to review them for errors that allowed ineligible persons to receive funds under the Aid for Dependent Children program, had a significant influence on reducing the number of persons receiving welfare. (Unfortunately, it appears that this approach also resulted in many eligible persons not receiving welfare payments.)[23]

Judicial Follow-up. Judges face a unique problem in following up their decisions: they must wait for others to bring cases to them before they can act to correct a problem. If courts spot slippage or outright disobedience in implementation, they cannot move on their own to correct these problems. Moreover, those who should bring suit often lack the resources to do so. Sometimes this is because they are poor and ignorant of the law. At other times middle-class groups such as environmentalists possess some resources and are fairly knowledgeable about the law, but still lack the time, money, and technical proficiency to monitor a project. The construction and maintenance of the Trans-Alaskan Pipeline, for example, involved innumerable low visibility and highly technical decisions. To sue successfully, environmental groups needed facts. Some facts, such as those concerning the consistency of stream crossings with environmental stipulations, are not easy to obtain. Thus, while statutes like the National Environmental Policy Act allow social reform groups to challenge in court alleged failures of public or private organizations to follow statutory duties, there is no guarantee that they will actually be able to do so.[24]

Legislative Oversight. Congress has oversight responsibility for federal programs, yet the attention it pays to their implementation is intermittent. When members of Congress do examine bureaucratic performance, they tend to focus on broad policy questions, waste and dishonesty, abuses of discretionary authority, or specific decisions involving their constituents and supporters rather than on a systematic study of implementation per se.[25] One reason for disinterest in implementation is the lack of incentives to spend time on it. Most of the constituents of members of Congress neither know nor care much about policy implementation. Thus, the members tend to concentrate on activities that have more potential for electoral rewards.

The busy schedules of members of Congress also discourage attention to policy implementation. Members lack the time to dissect the complex activities involved in implementation. Moreover, they are reluctant to devote what little available time they do have to a lengthy investigation that may only reveal that a program is being implemented properly.[26]

The increasing dispersal of power to subcommittees is another factor that undermines congressional oversight of implementation. As subcommittee jurisdictions become narrower, each subcommittee becomes more dependent upon the agency or agencies over which it has jurisdiction. Attempts to discipline and control agencies are infrequent because subcommittees rely upon close cooperation with them in order to function effectively. Similarly, subcommittee members may become dependent upon the interest groups active in the narrow policy area over which they have jurisdiction. Members of Congress do not want to upset their potential contributors and supporters, who usually oppose substantial changes in agency behavior. The dispersion of power has also resulted in subcommittees with overlapping jurisdictions, as we saw in Chapter 5. Thus, if one subcommittee is pressing an agency to change its behavior or provide information, the agency and its interest group supporters can turn to other subcommittees for protection.[27]

The fragmented structure of Congress also means that committees will not necessarily have oversight jurisdiction over the agencies that are implementing laws the committee initiated. The committees that have jurisdiction may not be interested in these policies at all. For example, congressional concern with the implementation of the National Environmental Policy Act was minimal, according to the findings of one study. In this environment, agency administrators, who owed primary allegiance to the committees that authorized their programs and appropriated their funds — not to the committees directly involved in the passage of NEPA — did not overly concern themselves with implementing the law's provisions.[28]

Although Congress has developed oversight techniques — such as the legislative veto of agency actions, requirements for formal reports from agencies, and periodic reauthorization of agency programs — it has not used these techniques to improve the implementation of policies. Instead, they have been used by legislative committees, which authorize policies, to strengthen their hands against the appropriations committees, which fund programs and whose oversight jurisdiction overlaps with theirs. The latter, in return, have refined the techniques of informal or at least nonstatutory communications and understandings with agencies to combat the encroachments of the authorizing committees. Both types of committees have used these oversight tools to defend "their" agencies and programs against the president's attempts to exert more centralized control over the executive branch. Not only is this orientation counterproductive from the standpoint of improving implementation, but it also allows agencies to maintain their independence by playing authorization and appropriations committees off against each other.[29]

Most state legislatures are in a very weak position to exercise systematic influence over the implementation of policies. They lack the staff and other resources to monitor agency behavior, and they are usually in session only a few months each year. When these limitations are added to the fact that their incentives to engage in oversight of implementation are just as weak as those of members of Congress, we can understand why the impact of state legislatures on improving implementation is generally minimal.

Potential of Other Remedies

Are there other possibilities for improving implementation? The first step in evaluating proposed remedies is to understand what the obstacles to implementation are and why they exist. Then we must try to alter the situations that produce these factors. Although we have discussed attempts to overcome obstacles to effective policy implementation in previous chapters, our primary purpose has been to explain why implementation occurs as it does. With this background we can better understand why there are no easy panaceas for implementation failures and just how much we can expect proposed remedies to accomplish.

The roots of most implementation problems are embedded deeply in the fabric of American government and politics. Top officials are very busy and lack the expertise to elaborate laws. Decisionmakers must bargain and compromise in order to obtain agreement on policies. Interest groups have free access to policymakers, and policymakers, fearful of alienating groups in the public, seek to avoid accountability for many decisions. And judges often do not clarify their decisions because they cannot initiate actions and may hesitate to overrule precedents. In light of the above, it is not surprising that communications are often vague or inconsistent.

Similarly, there are numerous reasons why these communications are transmitted poorly. Implementors must expand communications as they descend through the bureaucracy; implementors often disagree with policy decisions; implementors selectively perceive and search for the "true" intention of policy directives; and implementors must rely upon indirect or underdeveloped channels of communication to the bureaucracy, the private sector, the judiciary, and other countries. Therefore, as long as American government and politics are structured anything like they are now, communications are likely to pose obstacles to public policy implementation. Moreover, policymakers are becoming even busier, American society and thus its laws are becoming more complex, and pressures on public officials are increasing and becoming more heterogeneous. This does not bode well for the communications of the future.

The picture for resources is no brighter. As long as we fear big government, especially its policing functions; as long as we prefer low taxes; as long as we are reluctant to spend public funds on government itself; and as long as governments attempt to accomplish new goals, for which expertise is often lacking, then many policies will lack the staff, information, authority, or facilities to implement them effectively. Since we live in an age of increasing scarcity of resources, high inflation, and decreasing support for government programs, there is good reason to expect that these attitudes will support continuation of the present situation in which too few resources are allocated to policy implementation.

In addition, public officials underutilize the resources that they do have. There are many reasons for this. Officials are reluctant to exercise their authority to cut off funds for fear of inducing the intervention of politically powerful officeholders or the criticism of the press. There is also the danger of penalizing innocent third parties or those whom a policy is designed to aid, or signaling higher authorities that budgets are excessive. Other sanctions are often too strong or too weak to be credible. Moreover, officials prefer not to exercise their authority over officials of lower level jurisdictions because of a professional ethos, friendships, the need to maintain goodwill, or previous experience at that level. Procurement regulations are overly complex, and citizens oppose the location of some government facilities near them. Given the persistence of such behavior, public officials will continue to have difficulty fully utilizing the resources at their disposal.

Our federal system, bureaucratic personnel systems such as civil service, the insulation of each tier of the judiciary, and reliance on the private sector to implement many policies provide implementors with a great deal of independence from their nominal superiors. When this is coupled with the frequent lack of clear and consistent communications, implementors enjoy considerable discretion in implementing policy. Bureaucratic inbreeding due to selective recruitment and self-recruitment into agencies, long careers within one agency, narrowness of agency responsibilities, the distribution of rewards within agencies, and the pressures toward continuity from outside interests serve to channel this discretion in directions that may be contrary to those desired by top decisionmakers.

The ability of high-level officials to influence the exercise of bureaucrats' discretion is limited by the lack of rewards available to them to induce desired behavior, the political appointments available to them, the time and knowledge which they can apply to these decisions, and the flexibility they have in choosing persons to fill appointed positions. Influence over those in other branches or levels of government or in the private sector is even less. No substantial alteration of any of these fundamental characteristics of American government appears on the horizon. Barring an unprecedented change in human nature, implementors' dispositions will continue to play a role in policy implementation.

Finally, there is not much prospect for change in government structures. As long as implementors lack the time and the resources to implement policies fully; as long as officials desire flexibility in the use of personnel; as long as we value uniformity in the application of regulations; and as long as policymakers prefer not to interrupt existing arrangements and open up previous bargains and compromises, SOPs will play a major role in policy implementation. If anything, the growing complexity of the world and the increasing scarcity of resources in the United States will strengthen the role of bureaucratic routines in implementation.

Government fragmentation serves important functions for powerful political forces. The proliferation of programs and agencies increases the ability of legislators to affect the implementation of programs, and it distributes "turf" and accompanying influence to committees. Similarly, agencies, at least partly due to parochialism, want program responsibility and do not want to consolidate or coordinate their activities with other organizations. Interest groups enjoying special access to bureaucratic units with narrow jurisdictions fight changes in existing structures. In addition, provisions in many state constitutions and local government charters and the broad nature of many policies ensure that government will be fragmented. Unless legislators, agencies, and interest groups no longer desire to have special influence over policy implementation, and unless there is change in the fundamental laws of state and local governments and the substance of public policy, fragmentation is likely to remain a basic characteristic of American government. Any such change is unlikely.

A FINAL WORD

The scenario for the future need not be pessimistic. If policymakers increase their understanding of why policy implementation works as it does, they may be able to work at the margins and anticipate and pre-empt some of the problems of implementation discussed in the previous chapters. Whether this happens is problematical. But if top executives remain more concerned with shaping legislation to pass in the legislature than with the implementation of the law after it is passed, if they persist in emphasizing public relations rather than policy, and if "crisis" situations continue to dominate their time, little progress is likely to be made in improving policy implementation.[30] Moreover, until the public provides incentives for officials to devote more attention to policy implementation and to develop better administrative skills, these priorities probably will not change. Given both the low visibility of most policy implementation activities and the lack of interest of most Americans in government and politics, the prospects for a change in incentives are not very favorable.

Failures in the public sector should not lead us necessarily to conclude that we should opt for greater reliance upon the private sector to accomplish the goals of public policies. Sometimes the private sector may be more efficient and creative than government agencies in providing services. Yet we have seen throughout this book that there are serious problems in trying to communicate with persons or organizations in the private sector, that they often lack sufficient resources to implement policies, and that they may be antagonistic toward the goals of policies. Moreover, private sector organizations are not organized around implementing public policies and are burdened with many of the same internal problems of SOPs and parochialism that face public agencies. Turning government over to the private sector will not solve the problems of implementation.

Because public policies face problems in implementation, should we cut back on public policies? Not necessarily. What we should do is have more realistic expectations. What benefits are likely to occur when policies are established? Are the benefits of programs worth their costs? Greater attention to these questions should help reduce the alienation many people feel toward the public sector, alienation based partially upon unreasonably high expectations of government performance.

An antigovernment orientation is self-defeating. We are always going to have public policies, and antagonism toward them will not improve their implementation. Indeed, hostility or at least coolness toward the public sector is one reason why implementors often lack sufficient resources to perform their tasks effectively. Effective public policies deserve high priority. It is worth working to educate both policymakers and the public about implementation. It is time to lay the groundwork for improvement.

NOTES

1. Theodore Lowi, "American Business, Public Policy, Case Studies, and Political Theory," *World Politics* 16 (July 1964): 677-715.
2. William Colby, *Honorable Men: My Life in the CIA* (New York: Simon & Schuster, 1978), pp. 440-441; "Intelligence Failures, CIA Misdeeds Studied," *Congressional Quarterly Weekly Report,* September 20, 1975, p. 2025.
3. William Safire, *Before the Fall: An Inside View of the Pre-Watergate White House* (New York: Doubleday & Co., 1975), pp. 250-260. For an example of the success of follow-up at the state level, see Eugene Bardach, *The Implementation Game: What Happens After a Bill Becomes a Law* (Cambridge, Mass.: MIT Press, 1977), pp. 17-26.
4. Richard M. Nixon, *RN: The Memoirs of Richard Nixon* (New York: Grosset & Dunlap, 1978), p. 385.
5. See, for example, Stephen J. Wayne, *The Legislative Presidency* (New York: Harper & Row, 1978), pp. 182-188; Doris Kearns, *Lyndon Johnson and the American Dream* (New York: Harper & Row, 1976), pp. 294-295; Frederic V. Malek, *Washington's Hidden Tragedy: The Failure to Make Government Work* (New York: Free Press, 1978), p. 145; Thomas E. Cronin, "Presidents as Chief Executives," in *The Presidency Reappraised,* eds. Rexford G. Tugwell and Thomas E. Cronin (New York: Praeger Publishers, 1974), pp. 237-238.
6. Jonathan Daniels, *Frontiers on the Potomac* (New York: Macmillan Co., 1946), pp. 31-32.
7. Joseph A. Califano, Jr., *A Presidential Nation* (New York: W. W. Norton & Co., 1975), p. 46.
8. Stephen J. Wayne, "Working in the White House: Psychological Dimensions of the Job" (Paper delivered at the annual meeting of the Southern Political Science Association, New Orleans, Louisiana, November, 1977), pp. 16-17.

9. Harry McPherson, *A Political Education* (Boston: Little, Brown & Co., 1972), pp. 284-285.

10. See Califano, *A Presidential Nation*, p. 49; Harold Seidman, *Politics, Position, and Power: The Dynamics of Federal Organization*, 2d ed. (New York: Oxford University Press, 1975), pp. 90-91; Robert Wood, "When Government Works," *Public Interest* (Winter 1970); Richard P. Nathan, *The Plot that Failed: Nixon and the Administrative Presidency* (New York: John Wiley & Sons, 1975), pp. 51-54; Thomas E. Cronin, *The State of the Presidency* (Boston: Little, Brown & Co., 1975), p. 158.

11. Malek, *Washington's Hidden Tragedy*, pp. 230-231; Seidman, *Politics, Position, and Power*, pp. 90-91; and Cronin, *The State of the Presidency*, p. 158.

12. See Herbert Kaufman, *Administrative Feedback* (Washington, D.C.: Brookings Institution, 1973), pp. 70-71.

13. Richard Rose, *Managing Presidential Objectives* (New York: Free Press, 1976).

14. Ibid.; Malek, *Washington's Hidden Tragedy*, pp. 24, 154-159. For a different view of the success of management by objectives, see pp. 160-163.

15. See Leon V. Sigal, "Official Secrecy and Informal Communication in Congressional-Bureaucratic Relations," *Political Science Quarterly* 90 (Spring 1975).

16. Chester Cooper, *The Lost Crusade* (New York: Dodd, Mead & Co., 1970), p. 414.

17. Jameson W. Doig, "Police Policy and Police Behavior: Patterns of Divergence," *Policy Studies Journal* 7 (Special Issue, 1978): 440.

18. Kearns, *Lyndon Johnson*, p. 290; Lawrence Iannaccone, "The Politics of Federal Aid to Education in Massachusetts," p. 195 and Frederick M. Wirt, "The Politics of Federal Aid to Education in New York," pp. 170-171, 368, in *Federal Aid to Education: Who Benefits? Who Governs?*, eds. Joel S. Berke and Michael W. Kirst (Lexington Mass.: Lexington Books, 1972).

19. For the best discussion of this problem, see Kaufman, *Administrative Feedback*.

20. Kenneth M. Dolbeare and Phillip E. Hammond, *The School Prayer Decisions* (Chicago: University of Chicago Press, 1971), pp. 44-45, 51-52, 64, 80, 148.

21. Harrell R. Rodgers, Jr. and Charles S. Bullock, III, *Coercion to Compliance* (Lexington, Mass.: Lexington Books, 1976), pp. 89-93.

22. Joel S. Berke and Michael W. Kirst, "Intergovernmental Relations: Conclusions and Recommendations," in *Federal Aid to Education*, eds. Berke and Kirst, p. 379.

23. Ronald Randall, "Presidential Power versus Bureaucratic Intransigence: The Influence of the Nixon Administration on Welfare Policy," *American Political Science Review* 73 (September 1979): 795-810.

24. Joel F. Handler, *Social Movements and the Legal System: A Theory of Law Reform and Social Change* (New York: Academic Press, 1978), pp. 55, 192-193.

25. See, for example, Morris S. Ogul, *Congress Oversees the Bureaucracy: Studies in Legislative Supervision* (Pittsburgh: University of Pittsburgh Press, 1976); Lawrence C. Dodd and Richard C. Schott, *Congress and the Administrative State* (New York: John Wiley & Sons, 1979), p. 170; and Randall B. Ripley and Grace A. Franklin, *Congress, the Bureaucracy,*

and *Public Policy,* rev. ed. (Homewood, Ill.: Dorsey Press, 1980), pp. 222-225.

26. Walter J. Oleszek, *Congressional Procedures and the Policy Process* (Washington, D.C.: Congressional Quarterly Press, 1978), pp. 211-212.
27. Dodd and Schott, *Congress and the Administrative State,* pp. 173-184.
28. Richard A. Liroff, *A National Policy for the Environment: NEPA and Its Aftermath* (Bloomington, Ind.: Indiana University Press, 1976), pp. 124, 139.
29. Dodd and Schott, *Congress and the Administrative State,* pp. 228-248.
30. For example, see Kearns, *Lyndon Johnson,* pp. 218, 292-294.

Suggested Readings

Aberbach, Joel D., and Rockman, Bert A. "Clashing Beliefs Within the Executive Branch: The Nixon Administration Bureaucracy." *American Political Science Review* 70 (June 1976).

Allison, Graham. *Essence of Decision.* Boston: Little, Brown & Co., 1971.

Andrews, Richard N. L. *Environmental Policy and Administrative Change.* Lexington, Mass.: Lexington Books, 1976.

Bardach, Eugene. *The Implementation Game: What Happens After a Bill Becomes a Law.* Cambridge, Mass.: MIT Press, 1977.

Berke, Joel S., and Kirst, Michael W., eds. *Federal Aid to Education: Who Benefits? Who Governs?* Lexington, Mass.: Lexington Books, 1972.

Brown, Lawrence D., and Frieden, Bernard. "Guidelines and Goals in the Model Cities Program." *Policy Sciences* 7 (December 1976).

Bullock, Charles S., III, and Rodgers, Harrell R., Jr. *Coercion to Compliance.* Lexington, Mass.: Lexington Books, 1976.

————. *Law and Social Change: Civil Rights Laws and Their Consequences.* New York: McGraw-Hill Book Co., 1972.

Chambers, Raymond L. "The Executive Power: A Preliminary Study of the Concept and Efficacy of Presidential Directives." *Presidential Studies Quarterly* 7 (Winter 1977).

Cole, Richard L., and Caputo, David A. "Presidential Control of the Senior Civil Service: Assessing the Strategies of the Nixon Years." *American Political Science Review* 73 (June 1979).

Derthick, Martha. *Uncontrollable Spending for Social Services Grants.* Washington, D.C.: Brookings Institution, 1975.

Dolbeare, Kenneth M., and Hammond, Phillip E. *The School Prayer Decisions.* Chicago: University of Chicago Press, 1971.

Doig, Jameson W. "Police Policy and Police Behavior: Patterns of Divergence." *Policy Studies Journal* 7 (Special Issue, 1978).

Feder, Judith M. *Medicare: The Politics of Federal Hospital Insurance.* Lexington, Mass.: D.C. Heath & Co., 1977.

Friedlaender, Ann F., ed. *Approaches to Controlling Air Pollution.* Cambridge, Mass.: MIT Press, 1978.

Gross, Neal; Giacquinta, Joseph B.; and Bernstein, Marilyn. *Implementing Organizational Innovations: A Sociological Analysis of Planned Educational Change.* New York: Basic Books, 1971.

Handler, Joel F. *Social Movements and the Legal System: A Theory of Law and Social Change.* New York: Academic Press, 1978.

Heclo, Hugh. *A Government of Strangers: Executive Politics in Washington.* Washington, D.C.: Brookings Institution, 1977.

Hughes, John F., and Hughes, Anne O. *Equal Education.* Bloomington, Ind.: Indiana University Press, 1972.

Jones, Charles O. *Clean Air.* Pittsburgh: University of Pittsburgh Press, 1975.

Kaufman, Herbert. *Administrative Feedback.* Washington, D.C.: Brookings Institution, 1973.

————. *The Forest Ranger: A Study in Administrative Behavior.* Baltimore: Johns Hopkins University Press, 1960.

Kneese, Allen V., and Schultze, Charles L. *Pollution, Prices, and Public Policy.* Washington, D.C.: Brookings Institution, 1975.

Lazin, Frederick A. "The Failure of Federal Enforcement of Civil Rights Regulations in Public Housing, 1963-1971: The Co-optation of a Federal Agency by Its Local Constituency." *Policy Sciences* 4 (September 1973).

Liroff, Richard A. *A National Policy for the Environment: NEPA and Its Aftermath.* Bloomington, Ind: Indiana University Press, 1976.

Malek, Frederic V. *Washington's Hidden Tragedy: The Failure to Make Government Work.* New York: Free Press, 1978.

Mazmanian, Daniel, and Nienaber, Jeanne. *Can Organizatons Change?: Environmental Protection, Citizen Participation, and the Corps of Engineers.* Washington, D.C.: Brookings Institution, 1979.

McLaughlin, Milbrey W. *Evaluation and Reform: The Elementary and Secondary Education Act of 1965/Title I.* Cambridge, Mass.: Ballinger Publishing Co., 1975.

Mechling, Jerry. "Analysis and Implementation: Sanitation Policies in New York City." *Public Policy* 26 (Spring 1978).

Milner, Neal A. *The Court and Local Law Enforcement: The Impact of Miranda.* Beverly Hills, Calif.: Sage Publications, 1971.

Milsten, Mike M. *Impact and Response.* New York: Teachers College Press, 1976.

Moore, Mark H. "Reorganization Plan #2 Reviewed: Problems in Implementing a Strategy to Reduce the Supply of Drugs to Illicit Markets in the United States." *Public Policy* 26 (Spring 1978).

Murphy, Jerome T. *State Agencies and Discretionary Funds.* Lexington, Mass.: Lexington Books, 1974.

Nathan, Richard P. *The Plot that Failed: Nixon and the Administrative Presidency.* New York: John Wiley & Sons, 1975.

Nichols, Albert H., and Zeckhauser, Richard. "OSHA Comes to the Workplace: An Assessment of OSHA." *Public Interest* (Fall 1977).

Patton, Michael Q. *Utilization-Focused Evaluation.* Beverly Hills, Calif.: Sage Publications, 1978.

Pressman, Jeffrey L., and Wildavsky, Aaron B. *Implementation.* Berkeley, Calif.: University of California Press, 1973.

Radin, Beryl A. *Implementation, Change, and the Federal Bureaucracy.* New York: Teachers College Press, 1977.

Rose, Richard. *Managing Presidential Objectives.* New York: Free Press, 1976.

Sabatier, Paul, and Mazmanian, Daniel. "The Implementation of Public Policy: A Framework of Analysis." *Policy Studies Journal* 8 (Special Issue No. 2, 1980).

Sapolsky, Harvey M. *The Polaris System Development: Bureaucratic and Programmatic Success in Government.* Cambridge, Mass.: Harvard University Press, 1972.

Stoner, Floyd E. "Federal Auditors as Regulators: The Case of Title I of ESEA." In *The Policy Cycle,* edited by Judith V. May and Aaron B. Wildavsky. Beverly Hills, Calif.: Sage Publications, 1978.

Van Meter, Donald S., and Van Horn, Carl E. "The Policy Implementation Process: A Conceptual Framework." *Administration and Society* 6 (February 1975).

Wasby, Stephen L. *The Impact of the United States Supreme Court: Some Perspectives.* Homewood, Ill.: Dorsey Press, 1970.

_____. *Small Town Police and the Supreme Court: Hearing the Word.* Lexington, Mass.: Lexington Books, 1976.

Weatherly, Richard, and Lipsky, Michael. "Street-Level Bureaucrats and Institutional Innovation: Implementing Special Education Reform." *Harvard Educational Review* 47 (May 1977).

Williams, Walter, and Elmore, Richard F., eds. *Social Program Implementation.* New York: Academic Press, 1976.

Index

X, Y, Z